the **diabetes**
cookbook

the **diabetes** cookbook

Editorial Consultant **Amy Campbell, MS, RD, LDN, CDE**

LONDON, NEW YORK, MELBOURNE, MUNICH, AND DELHI

Photography William Shaw

Project editor Robert Sharman
Designer Katherine Raj
Senior creative art editor Caroline de Souza
Managing editor Dawn Henderson
Managing art editors Christine Keilty, Marianne Markham
Category publisher Mary-Clare Jerram
Art director Peter Luff
US editorial Rebecca Warren, Liza Kaplan, Nancy Ellwood
Production editor Ben Marcus
Production controller Poppy Newdick
Creative technical support Sonia Charbonnier

DK INDIA
Designer Devika Dwarkadas
Senior editor Saloni Talwar
Production manager Pankaj Sharma
Design manager Romi Chakraborty

Important Every effort has been made to ensure that the information contained in this book is complete and accurate. However, neither the publisher nor the authors are engaged in rendering professional advice or services to the individual reader. Professional medical advice should be obtained on personal health matters. Neither the publisher nor the authors accept any legal responsibility for any personal injury or other damage or loss arising from the use or misuse of the information and advice in this book.

First American Edition, 2010
This edition published in 2013
Published in the United States by
DK Publishing
375 Hudson Street
New York, New York 10014

13 14 15 16 17   10 9 8 7 6 5 4 3 2 1

001-176801-Jun/13

A catalog record for this book is available from the Library of Congress.

ISBN 978-1-4654-0854-9

DK books are available at special discounts when purchased in bulk for sales promotions, premiums, fund-raising, or educational use. For details, contact: DK Publishing Special Markets, 375 Hudson Street, New York, New York 10014 or SpecialSales@dk.com.

Printed and bound in China by South China Printing Co. Ltd

Discover more at **www.dk.com**

CONTENTS

EATING WELL WITH TYPE 2 DIABETES

Food plays a crucial role in determining our health, vitality, and well-being. Various foods we eat are broken down into glucose, which passes into the bloodstream. Our blood glucose level should not become too high or too low, so to regulate it, the pancreas produces insulin. If you have Type 2 diabetes, you'll know that your pancreas isn't producing enough insulin, or the insulin isn't doing its job properly. (If you have Type 1 diabetes, your body isn't making any insulin at all.)

It is important for everyone to eat healthily, but when you have Type 2 diabetes, diet is even more relevant. Choosing the right foods will help you to manage your condition and reduce the risk of other health problems associated with diabetes. In one study, people with Type 2 diabetes were able to reduce their blood glucose levels by an average of 25 percent just by following a simple diet plan similar to

Carrot and Ginger Soup (page 74)

Summer Pudding (page 314)

the one we recommend. Although people often talk about healthy and unhealthy foods, there is no such thing as a good or a bad food: it is the balance of foods that you eat throughout the day that is important.

HOW THIS BOOK CAN HELP

The recipes in this book are designed to help you achieve a healthy, balanced diet that includes wholegrains, low-GI carbohydrates, lean protein, dietary fiber, low-fat dairy products, and plenty of vegetables and fruit. They are also lower in sodium, fat and sugar. All this equals a great diet, whether you have Type 2 diabetes or not.

Where the book goes further is in providing "Guidelines per serving" for each recipe (see right), which show you whether the dish is relatively high (3 dots), medium (2 dots) or low (1 dot) in GI, calories, saturated fat, and sodium—the four key dietary areas to watch when you have Type 2 diabetes. For information on how to use these charts to balance your diet and ensure that you are eating appropriately, see page 53.

GUIDELINES PER SERVING

GI

CALORIES

SATURATED FAT

SODIUM

Chorizo, Chickpea, and Mango Salad (page 146)

Fruit and Seed Soda Bread (page 340)

YOUR FOUR HEALTH GOALS

MANAGE YOUR WEIGHT

1 To give yourself the best chance of controlling Type 2 diabetes, and avoiding some of the many health risks it can expose you to, it is important that you are a healthy weight. People who are overweight can improve their diabetes control, lower their blood pressure, and reduce levels of fats in the blood, including cholesterol, by losing weight. The two key factors in controlling your weight are a healthy diet and regular exercise. This book will help you adapt to a healthier diet, and also allows you to monitor your calorie intake, so you can see how much energy you need to be using up through exercise. For more information on healthy weight loss, see pages 34–37.

BALANCE YOUR BLOOD GLUCOSE LEVELS

2 Keeping blood glucose levels within a healthy range is a vital part of managing diabetes. If you have too much glucose in the blood for long periods of time, it can damage the vessels that supply blood to vital organs such as the heart, kidneys, eyes, and nerves. The type and amount of carbohydrate you eat are the main dietary factors that determine blood glucose levels. Slow-release carbohydrates keep blood glucose on an even keel; carbohydrates that are digested rapidly cause unwelcome surges in blood glucose levels. See pages 16–17 for more about carbohydrates, and pages 18–19 for information on the glycemic index.

If you've been diagnosed with diabetes, make these four health goals your priority. They will help you to manage your condition and live life to the fullest.

LOOK AFTER YOUR HEART

3 People with diabetes are five times more likely to suffer from heart disease or a stroke, so it is vital to eat the right foods to keep your heart healthy. One of the most important steps you can take is to reduce your intake of saturated fat. Saturated fat causes the body to produce cholesterol, and in the same way that hard water can clog water pipes and appliances with limescale, cholesterol clogs the blood vessels and causes them to narrow, restricting the flow of blood to the heart and brain. See pages 20–21 for more information on fats. Other important routes to heart health are to give up smoking, take regular exercise, and prevent high blood pressure.

CONTROL YOUR BLOOD PRESSURE

4 High blood pressure increases the risk of heart disease, stroke, and kidney problems. A diet high in sodium is a major factor in the development of high blood pressure (see pages 22–23 for ways to reduce your sodium intake)– but sodium isn't the whole story. The DASH study (Dietary Approaches to Stop Hypertension) carried out in America found that people who had a moderate sodium intake, but who increased their intake of potassium, calcium, and magnesium by eating plenty of fruit, vegetables, and low-fat dairy products, showed more significant reductions in blood pressure that those who simply restricted sodium. Ask your doctor to check your blood pressure regularly.

FIVE-POINT EATING PLAN

Choosing the right diet is a vital part of managing diabetes. A healthy diet will help you to control your blood glucose levels, cholesterol, blood pressure, and weight. It will also help to improve your energy levels, digestion, and immunity. The good news is that eating well when you have diabetes doesn't have to be boring or hard work, and you don't have to miss out on the foods you enjoy. There are five areas of your diet where you can boost your health and well-being by making a few changes. Learn more about these by turning to the relevant pages.

EAT MORE FRUIT AND VEGETABLES

1 Fruit and vegetables are the cornerstone of a healthy diabetes eating plan. They provide vitamins, minerals, and phytochemicals which, among other benefits, will help to keep your heart and eyes healthy; potassium, which helps to lower blood pressure; and dietary fiber, which encourages the digestive system to function smoothly (see pages 12–13).

CHOOSE THE RIGHT CARBOHYDRATES

2 Carbohydrates are converted into glucose, which causes the level of blood glucose to rise. The level to which it rises and the length of time it remains high depend on the type and amount of carbohydrates that you eat. Certain carbohydrates are digested more slowly than others, keeping blood glucose levels even and sustaining energy levels. Understanding the effect of carbohydrates on blood glucose levels is the key to living with diabetes (see pages 16–17).

SWAP BAD FATS FOR GOOD

3 Reduce your intake of "bad fats"– saturated fats and trans fats–which increase the risk of heart disease and stroke. Eat more "good fats", such as unsaturated oils, which have a protective effect (see pages 20-21).

REPLACE SALT WITH GOOD FLAVORINGS

4 A diet high in sodium is believed to be a major factor in the development of high blood pressure– something that people with diabetes are at greater risk of. Experts suggest that reducing our intake of sodium to no more than 2.4g a day can reduce the risk of stroke or heart attack by a quarter. Instead of relying on salt to make food tasty, use other ways to add flavor (see pages 22-23).

LOWER YOUR SUGAR INTAKE

5 Sugar provides what nutritionists call "empty calories"– calories that provide nothing in the way of protein, fiber, vitamins, or minerals and so offer no health benefit. Eating large amounts of sugar will cause your blood glucose levels to rise and in the longer term can lead to weight gain. You do not need to avoid sugar completely, but cut back on it as much as possible and try other ways to sweeten food (see pages 24-25).

1

EAT MORE FRUIT AND VEGETABLES

A HEALTHY REGIME

One of the easiest ways to improve your diet is to eat more vegetables. Ideally, at mealtimes, around half of your plate should be filled with vegetables. However, don't just think of them as an accompaniment: regard them as an ingredient that you can incorporate into your favorite recipes.

As well as being low in calories and a good source of fiber, vegetables are an excellent source of antioxidant vitamins, minerals, and phytochemicals, and can help reduce the risk of many of the health problems associated with diabetes.

Fruit is also a great source of vitamins and minerals, and may lower the risk of heart disease, certain cancers, and digestive problems. However, fruit also contains natural sugars that can affect your blood glucose level, so take care not to eat too much all at once. Dried fruit in particular is a very concentrated source of these sugars, while fruit juice releases its sugar into the bloodstream very quickly, so it is preferable to eat whole fresh fruit.

THE FIVE-A-DAY TARGET

Healthy eating guidelines recommend that we should all eat at least five portions of vegetables and fruit a day. A portion is approximately 3oz (85g). For a quick visual guide, clench your fist—that's about the size of a portion. Five is the minimum number of portions you should be eating each day; the more you can cram into your diet, the healthier you'll be. Aim to eat a variety of vegetables and fruit.

Q&A

ARE SOME FRUITS AND VEGETABLES HEALTHIER THAN OTHERS?

Reports show that pesticide levels in most foods are well within acceptable limits. However, those in favor of organic farming say that it's impossible to predict the effect that a mixture of different pesticides, eaten over a long period of time, will have on our health.

Research has proved that eating plenty of fruit and vegetables offers genuine and important health benefits, and that these benefits far outweigh any risk that may be associated with pesticide residues.

10 EASY WAYS TO EAT MORE FRUIT AND VEGETABLES

1 **Add a handful of vegetables.** Mix chopped vegetables such as carrots or peppers into spaghetti bolognese, shepherd's pie, or lasagna.

2 **Give salad a fruit boost.** Add apple, pineapple, or pear to a green salad; a few raisins, pomegranate seeds, or dried apricots to rice, pasta, or couscous.

3 **Serve roast pumpkin instead of roast potatoes.** Roast chunks of pumpkin, drizzled with a little oil, at 400°F (200°C) for 30–40 minutes.

4 **Breakfast wisely.** Spread mashed banana on toast instead of jam. Add a few chopped apricots or a handful of fresh berries to cereal.

5 **Serve meat or fish with a spicy salsa.** Mix finely chopped red onion, chile, and tomato with avocado; or try onion, chile, mango, and cucumber.

6 **Give pizzas an extra topping.** Pile pizzas high with vegetables such as spinach, peppers, artichokes, and mushrooms.

7 **Serve healthy snacks at parties.** Instead of chips, offer pieces of raw carrot, pepper, celery, or cauliflower with a yogurt dip or salsa.

8 **Keep a bowl of fruit on your desk at work.** It means you've always got a healthy snack close at hand, and will help you to resist candy and cookies.

9 **Swap your lunchtime sandwich for a bowl of vegetable soup.** Increase your nutrient intake further by adding some beans and pulses to it.

10 **Choose healthy snacks.** Keep a plastic container or plastic bag filled with washed and prepared vegetables in the refrigerator.

EAT A RAINBOW

Fruit and vegetables of different colors contain different vitamins, minerals, and phytochemicals. These all help to keep you healthy in various ways, so try to eat at least one serving of fruit or vegetables from each of the color bands every day.

RED	ORANGE	YELLOW	GREEN	BLUE/INDIGO/VIOLET
Strawberries, raspberries, apples, watermelon, red peppers, tomatoes	Carrots, pumpkins, oranges, mangoes, papaya, apricots	Bananas, melons, pineapples, grapefruit	Broccoli, spinach, peas, kiwi fruit, kale, spring cabbage, celery, green beans, cauliflower	Eggplant, blueberries, blackberries, prunes, red cabbage, plums, red onions, beets

Satisfying hunger

USE LOW-CALORIE FOODS TO FEEL FULL FOR LONGER

When you are trying to lose weight by cutting down the amount of food you consume, it can be a problem making sure that you don't feel hungry. The feeling of fullness, or being sated, that you get after eating depends on what you've eaten. At a technical level, there is a system for ranking foods based on their ability to satisfy hunger—this is called the satiety index (see Useful Websites on page 352). On a simpler level, one of the most important factors is just the volume of food you consume. Think about it—if you snack on cheese, you will need to limit yourself to a tiny portion because of the amount of calories it contains. You are likely to find this less satisfying than if you choose fruit and vegetables, because their lower calorie count means you can crunch your way through a much larger amount.

The examples here compare quantities of different foods that contain the same number of calories. As you will see, if you choose the healthy fruit and vegetable options on the right, you will be able to enjoy a far greater volume of food, keeping you satisfied until your next meal.

MAKE BETTER CHOICES: WITH DRINKS

If you are having nibbles with drinks, you can serve up a much more impressive amount of food if you go for vegetable crudités with a healthy dip.

2oz (50g) CHEESE

5½oz (150g) TZATZIKI, 3½oz (100g) CARROT, 3½oz (100g) PEPPER, 2½oz (75g) ASPARAGUS

MAKE BETTER CHOICES: SALAD

When you are making a salad, you might consider adding a few chopped peanuts. If you would prefer a greater quantity though, you would be well advised to leave these out and opt for cherry tomatoes instead.

½oz (15g) PEANUTS

1lb (450g) CHERRY TOMATOES

MAKE BETTER CHOICES: BREAKFAST

At breakfast, you might find a glass of apple juice refreshing, but will it fill you up as much as two whole apples?

9fl oz (250ml) APPLE JUICE

2 APPLES (3½oz/100g EACH)

MAKE BETTER CHOICES: SNACKS

A small amount of dried fruit makes a good snack, but opt for fresh and you can enjoy a lot more food for the same number of calories.

1oz (30g) RAISINS

5oz (140g) GRAPES

CHOOSE THE RIGHT CARBOHYDRATES

WHAT ARE CARBOHYDRATES?

Carbohydrates are an essential source of energy in our diet. This group of foods can be divided into two main types: starchy carbohydrates and sugars. Starchy carbohydrates include bread, potatoes, pasta, rice, noodles, and cereals. Sugars include sucrose (table sugar), lactose (the sugar found in dairy foods), and fructose (the sugar found in fruit).

Starchy carbohydrates can be divided into two groups – refined carbohydrates such as white bread, white rice, and products made with white flour; and unrefined, wholegrain carbohydrates, such as wholemeal bread and brown rice.

CARBOHYDRATES AT WORK

Refined carbohydrates release their energy quickly and can cause a surge in blood glucose levels. Unrefined, wholegrain carbohydrates release their energy slowly, and this keeps blood glucose levels even. People with diabetes should eat a diet that is high in slow-release carbohydrates which are good sources of energy and nutrients. Some carbohydrates are also better than others at making you feel full for longer after eating.

The glycemic index (GI) is a way of measuring the effect of a food on blood glucose levels. Low-GI carbohydrates are converted into glucose slowly and so release glucose into the bloodstream gradually. They produce less of a spike in blood glucose levels, which is better for your health. See pages 18–19 for more about the glycemic index.

Q&A

ARE CARBOHYDRATES FATTENING ?

Although carbohydrates such as bread and potatoes have a reputation for being fattening, they are low in fat and relatively low in calories. It's only when they are eaten with lots of fat—pasta with a rich, creamy sauce, fried potatoes, chips, or bread spread thickly with butter—that they become highly calorific.

Carbohydrates are an important part of a well-balanced diet. Aim for a third of the food you eat every day to consist of carbohydrates, and eat at least one food from this group at every meal.

The illustration below shows how your blood glucose level might fluctuate over the course of a day depending on your choice of slow or quick release carbohydrates. The steadier effect of the slow release carbohydrates is better for your health and energy levels.

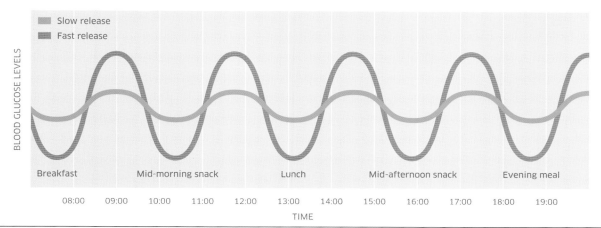

WHY WHOLEGRAINS ARE THE SMART CHOICE

Most of the carbohydrates we eat should be starchy carbohydrates, fruit and vegetables, and some dairy products. For people targeting a healthy diet, wholegrain products are by far the best starchy carbohydrates. When grains are refined, they lose fiber, vitamins, and minerals. If you eat refined carbohydrates, you are missing the opportunity to consume more of these important nutrients.

Wholegrains can be milled into flour to make foods such as bread and pasta. The fiber in wholegrain foods slows the conversion of starch into glucose, and this helps to balance blood glucose levels. Fiber keeps the digestive system healthy, and a further benefit of choosing wholegrains is that they may also lower the risk of heart disease and cancer.

GI and GL

WHAT IS THE GLYCEMIC INDEX?

The glycemic index (GI) is a system that ranks carbohydrates according to how quickly they are converted to glucose in the body, and the extent to which they raise your blood glucose level after you've eaten them. Foods with a high GI (70 or above) are broken down very quickly, resulting in a rapid rise in blood glucose—which people with diabetes need to avoid. Low-GI foods (55 and below) are absorbed more slowly into the bloodstream, causing a steadier, more controlled, rise in your blood glucose level.

CALCULATING GLYCEMIC LOAD

Glycemic load (GL) is based on similar information to GI but also takes into account the overall quantity of carbohydrate in a food. Multiply the GI by the amount of carbohydrate in a portion, and you get the GL. Although GI is more commonly used, in certain cases GL can be a better predictor of how a food will affect blood glucose levels. For example, carrots and chocolate both have a GI of 49—but you don't need to be a nutrition expert to know that carrots are better for you. In this case, the foods' respective GLs confirm that carrots are the healthier choice.

WHAT ARE THE HEALTH BENEFITS OF A LOW-GI DIET?

Low-GI diets were originally developed to help people with diabetes achieve better control of their blood glucose levels, but they have also been shown to help to reduce the risk of heart disease and because they can help control appetite and delay hunger, they can help with weight management.

⋩ **Cherries** have a low GI and are rich in vitamin C and fiber.

Q&A

HOW DOES PROCESSING FOOD AFFECT ITS GI?

All types of processing affect the GI of a food, because they make it easier for the digestive system to break down carbohydrates. Processed food therefore has a higher GI than unprocessed food. For example, canned tomatoes have a higher GI than raw tomatoes, and mashed potato has a higher GI than whole new potatoes eaten with their skin.

SIX EASY WAYS TO REDUCE THE GI AND GL OF YOUR DIET

1 **DON'T OVERCOOK PASTA** Eat pasta *al dente*—it has a lower GI than soft pasta, because it takes digestive enzymes longer to break down the carbs.

2 **REDUCE THE IMPACT OF HIGH-GI FOOD** If you eat a high-GI food such as a baked potato, combine it with a low-GI food such as beans.

3 **CHOOSE RICE CAREFULLY** Basmati rice has a GI of 57, compared with long-grain white rice (GI of 72), and jasmine rice (GI of 89).

4 **USE VINAIGRETTE INSTEAD OF CREAMY SALAD DRESSING** It's lower in fat, and the vinegar's acidity slows digestion and lowers the GI of the meal.

5 **WATCH YOUR PORTION SIZES** The larger the portion of a carbohydrate, the more it will increase your blood glucose, regardless of its GI.

6 **OPT FOR MINIMALLY PROCESSED FOOD** The less a food is processed, the lower its GI. Think about the food that you buy, and the way that you cook it.

SWAP BAD FATS FOR GOOD FATS

KNOW YOUR FATS

Nutritionists distinguish between two main types of fats: saturated fats and unsaturated fats. Unsaturated fats can be monounsaturated or polyunsaturated; polyunsaturated fats can be subdivided further into omega-3 and omega-6 fats. There is also a further group: trans fats.

The types of fat you eat can affect your health, so fats are often referred to as "bad fats" and "good fats". A diet high in saturated and trans fats—bad fats—will encourage the body to produce cholesterol, which can clog blood vessels and arteries and increase the risk of heart disease and stroke. Polyunsaturated and monounsaturated fats are considered to be good fats. Monounsaturated fats help to reduce cholesterol. Omega-3 fats protect the heart by making the blood less likely to clot, by lowering blood pressure, and by encouraging the muscles lining the artery walls to relax, improving blood flow to the heart. It's important to have a balance of omega-3 and omega-6 fats in the diet. Most of us eat too much omega-6 fat and not enough omega-3 fat.

You should remember that, despite the health benefits of unsaturated fats, all types of fat contain twice as many calories as protein or carbohydrate, so eat fats—even good fats—in moderation.

GOOD FATS

MONOUNSATURATED FATS These are found mainly in olive oil, canola oil, nuts, and avocados.

Q&A

DOES MARGARINE CONTAIN LESS FAT THAT BUTTER?

Both margarine and butter contain the same amount of fat, and the same number of calories—around 37 calories per teaspoon. They differ, however, in the type of fat they contain. Butter is classified as a saturated fat; margarine is available in monounsaturated or polyunsaturated versions.

Low-fat and reduced-fat spreads contain less fat and fewer calories than margarine.

POLYUNSATURATED FATS Omega-6 fats are found in vegetable oils and margarines such as sunflower, safflower, corn, and soybean oil. Omega-3 fats are found mainly in oil-rich fish such as salmon, fresh tuna, sardines, and mackerel. Plant sources include linseed (flaxseed) and its oil, canola oil, soybean oil, and walnuts.

BAD FATS

SATURATED FATS Found in full-fat dairy products (cheese, yogurt, milk, cream), lard, ghee, fatty cuts of meat and meat products such as sausages and burgers, pastry, cakes, cookies, coconut oil, and palm oil.

TRANS FATS These occur naturally in small amounts in meat and dairy products, but they are also produced during hydrogenation, a process that food manufactures use to convert vegetable oils into semi-solid fats. Although, chemically, trans fats are unsaturated, in the body they behave like saturated fat. In fact, some research suggests they are more unhealthy than saturated fat.

« Make the most of good fats by including them in a tasty salad dressing. Choose from a variety of oils such as olive, avocado, or pumpkin seed.

« Walnut oil is a light oil and a good source of omega-3 fat.

« Eat avocados for their good fats.

4 REPLACE SALT WITH GOOD FLAVORINGS

WHY CUT DOWN ON SALT?

If you have diabetes, you are already more likely than most people to suffer from heart disease or a stroke. To reduce this risk it is important that you control your blood pressure, and one of the key ways to do this is to minimize the amount of salt you eat. Salt is composed of sodium and chloride; sodium is the component that damages health. Most of the sodium in our diet comes from salt, but some comes from additives such as flavor enhancers and preservatives.

Small amounts of sodium occur naturally in many foods, including meat, fish, vegetables, and even fruit. Although cutting back on the salt we add during cooking and at the table will reduce our intake, around 75 percent of the sodium we consume comes from processed foods. Check whether products are high in sodium by reading the labels before you buy. If they list overall salt content, you can easily calculate the sodium—simply divide the figure by 2.5.

LESS SALT DOESN'T MEAN LESS FLAVOR

It is recommended that you consume no more than 2.4g of sodium—6g of salt—per day. Many people eat more than this. The more salt you eat, the less sensitive to it your taste buds become. However, you can retrain yourself to enjoy foods with less salt. If you gradually reduce the amount you add to meals, your taste buds will adapt, the salt receptors on the tongue becoming more sensitive again. This usually takes 2–3 weeks. Experiment with other flavorings instead of salt, using the ideas opposite as a starting point.

Q&A
IS NATURAL SEA SALT BETTER THAN ROCK SALT?

Although sea salt contains traces of minerals such as magnesium, calcium, and potassium—which you don't find in ordinary (rock) salt–it doesn't contain enough of these to make a significant contribution to your diet.

Many chefs prefer to use sea salt because they believe it has a better flavor than rock salt, but in terms of dietary salt content and health, there really isn't any difference.

EGGS

If you don't eat oil-rich fish, choose eggs that advertise themselves as especially rich in omega-3 fats. Eggs are also a good source of iron.

BREAKFAST CEREALS

Choose wholegrain breakfast cereals without added sugar, with at least 3g fiber per serving. Alternatively, make muesli from oats, seeds, nuts, and dried fruit.

DAIRY PRODUCTS

You can obtain a good supply of protein and calcium from dairy products; go for low-fat versions if possible.

RICE

Choose basmati or brown rice, which has a lower GI than long-grain white rice and is a good source of B-vitamins.

OIL-RICH FISH

Oil-rich fish such as mackerel, salmon, and fresh tuna provide omega-3 fats, which help heart health. Eat at least one portion a week; choose a different type of fish for another meal during the week.

POULTRY AND LEAN MEAT

Choose chicken and lean meat rather than fatty cuts of meat. Keep portions modest–3½–5oz (100–140g) is more than enough for one person.

CANNED BEANS

Beans are high in fiber and have a low GI. Look for the ones canned without salt or sugar; if canned in brine, rinse thoroughly before using.

BREAD

Buy wholegrain bread. It is more nutritious than white and has a lower GI.

EATING FOOD ON THE RUN

Sometimes you can't avoid buying lunch or a snack while you are away from home. Look at the nutrition information on the food labels before you buy, to make sure that you pick products that are as healthy as possible.

HOW TO READ FOOD LABELS

The Nutrition Facts panel on a food package will tell you how many calories, total fat, saturated fat, carbohydrate, fiber, and sodium a food contains, per serving, and how that contributes to the total amount you can or should eat in a day. You can use this information to make sure that your diet is balanced. However, your calorie and nutrient goals may be different, based on your own individual needs. A dietitian can help determine what the right amount of these nutrients is for you.

PERCENT DAILY VALUES	WOMEN	MEN
Calories	2,000	2,500
Total fat	<65g	<80g
Saturated fat	<20g	<25g
Total Carbohydrate	300g	375g
Dietary Fiber	25g	30g
Sodium	<2400mg (2.4g)	<2400mg (2.4g)

Foods that are low fat have 3g or less per serving; foods low in saturated fat have 1g or less per serving. A low-sodium food has 140mg or less per serving. Per serving, a good source of fiber has 2.5-4.9g; an excellent source has more than 5g.

USDA DIETARY GUIDELINES

Keep total fat intake to 20-35% of calories.
Limit saturated fats to less than 10% of your calories.
Limit trans fats to 1% of calories.
Limit cholesterol to 300mg per day, less if you have diabetes.

LUNCH

OPTION 1 — WHOLE GRAIN SANDWICH

If opting for a sandwich, choose one made with whole grain, oatmeal, or rye bread with a lean protein filling such as chicken, fish, shellfish, or hummus; add salad or vegetables

OPTION 3 — BROWN RICE SALAD »

If you want a change from sandwiches, try a salad made with brown rice, pasta, barley, or quinoa.

OPTION 1

THREE DRIED APRICOTS »

A small, healthy snack in the middle of the morning and afternoon helps to keep your blood glucose level stable and hunger pangs at bay. Dried fruit can be high in carbohydrate, however, so keep portions small.

« SOUP

Soup is a healthy and filling option, but it can be high in sodium and fat, so check the label. Choose soups made with beans or lentils and avoid those containing cream or coconut milk—these are high in calories and fat.

OPTION 2

« BANANA

Make sure that snacks do more than satisfy hunger. They should also provide nutrients such as vitamins and minerals, and fiber. Bananas are a great source of potassium, which helps to control blood glucose.

OPTION 3

LOW-FAT YOGURT »

A small container of low-fat yogurt provides protein and calcium, making it a great, hunger-busting snack. It will also help to keep your bones healthy.

« BEAN SALAD

Aim to have at least one serving of fruit and one serving of vegetables at lunch. A mixed bean or lentil salad will count toward your five-a-day target and is a good low-GI option.

OPTION 4

« CRISPBREAD

For a fiber-rich snack, reach for a couple of crispbread or rice cakes; team with hummus, salsa, or low-fat soft cheese.

10 TIPS FOR DINING OUT

	TIP	WHY?
1	**AVOID BUFFET-STYLE SELF-SERVICE RESTAURANTS**	Studies show that the greater the choice of food on offer, the more calories we're likely to eat. If you are faced with a buffet, don't try a little of everything—limit yourself to three or four dishes.
2	**BEFORE YOU ORDER, LOOK AROUND TO SEE WHAT OTHER PEOPLE'S MEALS LOOK LIKE**	If you're in a restaurant that serves up huge portions of food, it might be best to limit temptation by taking steps to make sure that you aren't faced with a mountainous plate. For example, you could think about ordering two starters or side dishes to constitute the main course.
3	**ASK FOR WATER AS SOON AS YOU SIT DOWN**	Ask the waiter to bring a pitcher of water. Drink a large glassful before you start eating, and it will take the edge off your appetite. Drinking water will also help you avoid drinking large quantities of alcohol.
4	**ASK QUESTIONS ABOUT THE MENU BEFORE ORDERING**	It's not always easy to tell how healthy or fattening a dish will be, so ask the waiter how it is prepared if you have any doubts. Don't be afraid to request vegetables served without butter, or fish or meat without a rich sauce—make sure you specify when giving your order.
5	**BE THE FIRST TO ORDER**	We may enter a restaurant full of good intentions to select the healthy options on the menu, but we're often swayed by other people's less than healthy choices. To help you stick to your resolution to eat healthily, order your meal first.

Dining out needn't be an ordeal when you are sticking to a healthy eating strategy. Follow these tips to stay on the straight and narrow while enjoying your food.

	TIP	WHY?
6	START YOUR MEAL WITH SOUP OR A SALAD	Soup helps to fill your stomach so you won't eat as much for the main course. One study found that when people had soup as a first course, they ate 20 percent fewer calories for the overall meal. In summer, begin with a salad (with fat-free dressing), which works in the same way.
7	GET AN EXTRA SIDE ORDER OF VEGETABLES	Most restaurant food is short on vegetables. To make sure that your meal includes a healthy dose of vitamins and minerals, order a portion of vegetables on the side, or add a salad.
8	DON'T LOAD UP ON BREAD BEFORE YOUR MEAL ARRIVES	If bread arrives and you know you won't be able to resist, ask the waiter to take it away. If you want to nibble on something while you're waiting for your order, ask for olives.
9	DON'T ALLOW THE WAITER TO TOP UP YOUR WINE GLASS BEFORE IT IS EMPTY	Alcohol is high in calories so you should keep track of how much you are drinking. If your glass is constantly being refilled, it becomes difficult to do this.
10	YOU DON'T HAVE TO MISS OUT ON DESSERT	Desserts don't have to be a no-go area: just choose wisely. Stick to fruit-based desserts, or sorbet, or share a dessert with your dining partner. Don't add extra fat and calories by drenching the dessert in whipped cream.

MAKEOVER RECIPES

	TIP	WHY?
1	**ADD A CAN OF BEANS OR LENTILS**	Beans and lentils are full of fiber and have a low GI. Add them to salads, soups, stews, and casseroles. For recipes that specify ground meat, halve the normal quantity of meat and add an equal amount of canned lentils.
2	**SNEAK IN EXTRA VEGETABLES WHENEVER POSSIBLE**	Bulk out meat dishes such as chili con carne or spaghetti bolognese by adding vegetables such as corn, diced carrots, or frozen peas. This allows you to use less meat; it also increases your veg intake. Add chopped spring onions, steamed spinach, cabbage, or puréed carrot to mashed potato.
3	**WHEN BAKING, REPLACE SOME OF THE FAT WITH PRUNE PURÉE**	Use prune purée to replace up to 50 percent of the butter or oil in baked goods such as cookies, muffins, and cakes. To make the purée, put 8oz (225g) of ready-to-eat pitted prunes and 6 tablespoons of hot water in a food processor or blender and process to make a smooth purée.
4	**USE WHOLEMEAL FLOUR FOR BAKING INSTEAD OF ORDINARY FLOUR**	If haven't used wholemeal flour before, start by substituting it for half the white flour in a recipe. As you get used to cooking with wholemeal flour, you can gradually increase the proportion. Wholemeal flour is a little drier than white flour, so you will need to add more liquid than usual.
5	**USE A SPRAY OIL FOR DISHES THAT REQUIRE LIGHT FRYING**	Oil expands once it gets hot, so when you are softening onions or vegetables, you don't need to add as much as you might think. A spray coats the pan with a film of oil, giving you a saving on fat and calorie content.

Don't abandon your favorite recipes: with a few additions and straightforward changes, it's easy to adapt them to your new goals.

	TIP	WHY?
6	USE SWEET POTATOES IN PLACE OF WHITE POTATOES	Sweet potatoes have a lower GI than white potatoes and are an excellent source of betacarotene. You can use them in exactly the same way that you would use white potatoes. Try them baked in their skins or peel, boil, and mash with a little butter and a touch of cinnamon.
7	USE FILO PASTRY RATHER THAN FLAKY PASTRY	Filo pastry has just 3.6g fat per 100g compared with 28g fat for shortcrust pastry, and 36g for flaky pastry. If you're making your own filo pastry, use vegetable oil rather than melted butter to brush the sheets of pastry.
8	ADD A SQUEEZE OF LEMON JUICE	Lemon helps to reduce the need for salt. It also helps to slow the breaking down of starch into sugar, and so will lower the GI of a meal. Vinegar and other acidic foods have the same effect.
9	USE CANOLA OIL FOR COOKING	Olive oil is a good source of monounsaturated fats, but it can be expensive. Canola oil offers many of the same benefits at a fraction of the price. It has a mild flavor and can used for sautéing, baking, or salad dressings.
10	MAKE CREAM LIGHTER	Reduce the fat content in recipes that call for double cream by using half the stated quantity of cream mixed with an equal amount of Greek yogurt. Choose a reduced-fat version to lower the calorie content still further.

WEIGHT MANAGEMENT

Being overweight makes it more difficult to manage diabetes, and puts you at greater risk of developing some of the complications associated with diabetes, such as heart disease. So if you are overweight you should make weight loss your number one priority. To ascertain whether you are overweight, the body mass index (BMI) chart below provides a quick reference. If you have a lot of weight to lose, the prospect of trying to get down to your ideal weight can seem rather daunting; however, even losing 5–10 percent of your weight will bring significant health benefits.

BODY MASS INDEX (BMI)

ARE YOU A HEALTHY WEIGHT?

The body mass index (BMI) is a ratio of weight to height. Locate yourself on the graph below, where your height and weight cross, to find out whether or not you are a healthy weight. Alternatively, calculate your BMI by dividing your weight in kilograms by the square of your height in meters.

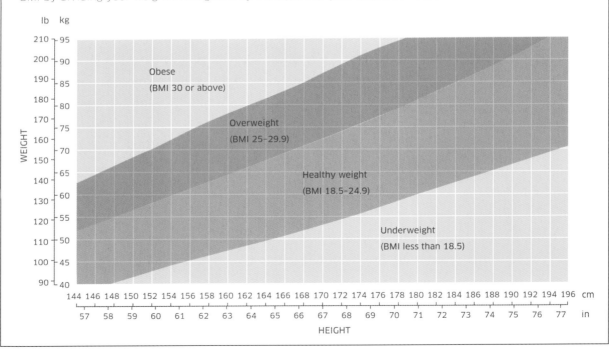

YOUR WAIST MEASUREMENT

Your BMI is only part of the story when it comes to assessing and managing your weight. Fat stored around the middle increases the risk of developing heart disease, high blood pressure, and diabetes. You can check the distribution of fat on your body by measuring your waist. Find the bottom of your ribs and the top of your hips. Measure your circumference midway between these two points (for many people, this will be the belly button). Make sure that the tape is parallel to the floor and taut, but not pressing into the skin. Breathe out normally and take the measurement at the end of this breath.

The guidelines of the World Health Organization advise that men should not have a waist measurement exceeding 37in (94cm). Above this, the risk of heart disease, high blood pressure, and diabetes is increased. A measurement of over 40in (102cm) puts a man at high risk of these conditions. For women, the thresholds are lower: a waist measurement of 32in (80cm) or above warns of increased risk, and a measurement of 35in (88cm) or above sounds the alarm for high risk.

There is slight variance between ethnic groups, the most significant being that Asian men are advised to target a slightly smaller waist, as a measurement of 36in (90cm) or above can bring increased health risks.

THE ENERGY BALANCE EQUATION

Your weight is determined by a simple equation. To maintain weight, you need to use up the same amount of energy (calories) you take in from food and drink. If you consume more calories than your body uses, the surplus is stored as fat. Eating even a small amount in excess of our needs will result in a slow but steady weight gain—if we eat just 100 calories a day more than we need (the equivalent of two small chocolate chip cookies), it will result in a weight gain of 10lb in a year.

To lose weight, you need to tip the balance the other way, so that you use more calories than you consume; in this situation, the body will draw on fat reserves to provide the energy it needs. You can lose weight by restricting the number of calories you eat, or by increasing the number of calories you use—being more active. Without doubt, the best way is a combination of diet and exercise.

10 STEPS TO WEIGHT LOSS

	TIP	WHY?
1	**SET REALISTIC GOALS**	If you set unrealistic goals for losing weight, you're more likely to become disheartened and quit. Aim for a slow, but steady weight loss of 1–2lb (0.5–1kg) a week and you're more likely to keep the weight off.
2	**PLAN AHEAD AND BE ORGANIZED**	If you plan a week's menu in advance, it means that you don't have to make decisions about what to eat at the end of the day, when you're tired and vulnerable to making poor choices. You'll also save money, because ingredients are carefully planned and nothing will be wasted.
3	**SPRING-CLEAN YOUR REFRIGERATOR AND PANTRY**	Get rid of anything that will tempt you into unhealthy food choices. Make sure that you've got plenty of healthy snacks such as crispbread, low-fat yogurts, fruit, and vegetables.
4	**LOOK AT FOOD LABELS**	Processed food often contains hidden fat and sugar, so check the calorie count on the packaging. It's also worth comparing brands, because they can vary considerably. Remember that foods labeled as low-fat, reduced fat, or reduced sugar are not necessarily low in calories.
5	**START THE DAY WITH A HEALTHY BREAKFAST**	Skipping breakfast in an attempt to cut calories is a false economy: by kick-starting the metabolism, breakfast ensures your body uses up more calories during the morning than it would otherwise. If you skip breakfast you are also far more likely to be reaching for the snacks by mid-morning.

Making small changes to the way you shop, cook, eat, and think about food can be the key to losing weight and, more importantly, keeping that weight off.

	TIP	WHY?
6	TAKE A PACKED LUNCH TO WORK	If you usually buy lunch from a sandwich shop or other fast-food outlet, make it at home instead and take it to work. You can control what you put into your lunchbox, and won't be tempted by unhealthy choices in elsewhere. You can use the time regained from shopping by going for a brisk walk.
7	SIT DOWN TO EAT	If you have a tendency to pick at food, make a rule that you can only eat when sitting down at the dining room or kitchen table. This will help you to restrict the bulk of your eating to mealtimes and cut out unconscious nibbling.
8	SLOW DOWN AND FOCUS	If you eat too quickly, you miss the signals that the stomach sends to the brain to say that it's full. Chew food thoroughly and put down your knife and fork between mouthfuls. Distractions such as the television can also cause you to miss these signals, so switch it off at mealtimes.
9	GET THAT MINTY-FRESH TASTE	As soon as you have finished eating, brush your teeth, rinse your mouth with mouthwash, or chew some sugar-free gum. The minty taste in your mouth will signal that the meal is at an end and stop you picking at leftovers.
10	HARNESS THE POWER OF POSITIVE THINKING	A recent study found that people who believed they could lose weight and keep it off were more likely to succeed. Try to visualize a new, slimmer and healthier version of yourself and keep that image in your mind.

KEEPING A FOOD DIARY

We eat for all sorts of reasons, and often it has nothing to do with being hungry. We use food to celebrate, to relieve boredom, or to make us feel better when we're unhappy or lonely. Certain people, places, moods, and situations can also prompt us to eat. Keeping a food diary will help you to identify the external triggers that cause you to eat when you're not really hungry. This will help you to manage your weight, and to substitute healthier choices when snacking.

HOW TO DO IT

Buy a notebook and divide the pages into columns, as shown on the opposite page (or you could take photocopies if you prefer). Start noting down each snack you eat and what time it was when you ate it. Record where you were, how hungry you were, who you were with, and how you felt after eating. At the end of a week, review your diary and make a list of all the triggers that prompted you to eat when you were not really hungry. Once you've identified these, you can start to work out strategies that will help you to avoid or change the way you behave when faced with these triggers.

If, for instance, you find that when you get home after work you're so hungry that you end up eating a family-sized pack of cheesy snacks while preparing the evening meal, have a healthy snack such as banana or a yogurt before you leave the office, so you won't be so hungry when you get home. If your food diary reveals that you use food as a way of making yourself feel better when you're unhappy or depressed, make a list of activities—unrelated to food—that will help lift your spirits when you're feeling low. Rather than reaching for a chocolate bar, watch an engrossing film, have a manicure, or take a long, leisurely bath. Old habits are hard to break, and changing ingrained behavior patterns is not something you can achieve overnight, so allow yourself plenty of time to adjust to a new regime.

SAMPLE DAILY FOOD DIARY				DAY:	
TIME	WHERE I WAS	HOW HUNGRY	WHO I WAS WITH	WHAT I ATE	HOW I FELT AFTERWARD

MEAL PLANNERS

The following pages provide an array of daily eating plans, centered around the recipes in this book, that guarantee a healthy, balanced diet and a controlled amount of calories per day. Whether you follow the 1400, 1600, 1800, 2000, or 2500 calories per day planner depends on a number of factors—whether you are male or female, how tall you are, and whether your target is to lose weight or to maintain your healthy weight. For advice on which planner might suit you, consult your doctor or nutritionist.

As well as controlling your calorie intake, these planners are based on the following principles:

Aim to eat roughly 25 percent of your total daily calories at breakfast, 30 percent at lunch, 35 percent at your evening meal, and 10 percent in snacks (one mid-morning, and one mid-afternoon).

Ensure you have at least one serving of vegetables or fruit at each of your main meals.

To provide enough calcium to keep your bones healthy, aim to have at least 2 servings of dairy a day (1 serving = 7fl oz milk, 1oz cheese, or a small container of low-fat yogurt).

Aim to eat oily fish at least twice a week, such as mackerel, salmon, or sardines.

1400 CALORIES A DAY

	BREAKFAST	MID-MORNING SNACK	LUNCH		MID-AFTERNOON SNACK	EVENING MEAL
DAY PLAN 1	1½oz bran flakes or other whole grain/fiber-rich cereal • ½oz raisins • 1 tsp sunflower seeds • 5fl oz skim milk	orange		Grilled halloumi and roast tomato salad *p.150* • 2oz whole wheat roll • 1 kiwi fruit	7fl oz skim milk	Mushroom and cilantro rice *p.169* • 4½oz grilled cod • slice of melon
DAY PLAN 2	1½oz bran flakes or other whole grain/fiber-rich cereal • 1 small banana • 5fl oz skim milk	apple	Falafel *p.101* • mixed green salad with fat-free dressing • small container low-fat yogurt • pear		reduced-fat whole grain cookie	Butternut squash and zucchini pasta *p.162* • Sugar-free peach sorbet *p.320* • 1¾oz blueberries
DAY PLAN 3	2 Apple and oat pancakes *p.58* • 3 tbsp low-fat yogurt • fruit	1 rye cracker spread with ¾oz low-fat soft cheese		Carrot and ginger soup *p.75* • 2oz whole wheat roll • small banana	7fl oz skim milk	Tuna with black-eyed pea and avocado salsa *p.204* • Sugar-free peach sorbet *p.320*
DAY PLAN 4	1 boiled egg • 2 small slices of whole wheat toast thinly spread with margarine	orange	Mulligatawny *p.91* • small container low-fat yogurt		2 rye crackers topped with salsa	Lamb with eggplant purée *p.258* • sugar snap peas • 7oz new potatoes • fruit salad
DAY PLAN 5	1 slice of Fruit and seed soda bread *p.340* topped with mashed banana	pear	Yellow split peas with peppers and pea shoots *p.96* • fruit salad		1 rye cracker with 1oz low-fat soft cheese	Butternut squash and spinach curry *p.184* • 5⅓oz cooked brown rice • 2 tbsp plain low-fat natural yogurt • 3oz raspberries
DAY PLAN 6	1 slice Seven-grain bread *p.336* with thin scrape of margarine and low-sugar jam	7fl oz skim milk	Mushroom, leek, and red pepper filo pie *p.181* • green salad with fat-free dressing • small container low-fat yogurt • 2 plums		1½oz dried apricots	Spaghetti with tomatoes and goat cheese *p.161* • slice of fresh pineapple
DAY PLAN 7	Rainbow muesli *p.56* • 7fl oz skim milk	apple		Shredded pork and spring onion wrap *p.98* • large orange	reduced-fat graham cracker	Vegetable curry *p.177* • 1 Chapatti *p.338* • small container low-fat yogurt • peach

Suitable for some women as part of a weight-loss plan. Mix and match the daily menus for a balanced diet.

	BREAKFAST	MID-MORNING SNACK	LUNCH	MID-AFTERNOON SNACK	EVENING MEAL
DAY PLAN 8	1 slice of Fruit and seed soda bread p.340 topped with mashed banana	7fl oz skim milk	Aduki bean and vegetable soup p.82 • 2 small plums	2 sticks celery filled with 1¾oz low-fat soft cheese	Mushroom and chile pilaf p.170 • 4½oz roast chicken • fruit salad
DAY PLAN 9	1½oz bran flakes or other whole grain/fiber-rich cereal • ½oz raisins • 1 tsp sunflower seeds • 5fl oz skim milk	orange	Tortilla p.114 • mixed salad with fat-free dressing • 1 small mango	1 rye cracker spread with low-fat soft cheese	Spicy udon noodles with tuna p.120 • Roasted figs with citrus crème fraîche p.330
DAY PLAN 10	1 slice Seven-grain bread p.336 thinly spread with margarine and low-sugar jam	apple	Quinoa tabbouleh p.127 • small container low-fat yogurt • 1¾oz blueberries	7fl oz skim milk	Mushroom lasagna p.164 • mixed salad with fat-free dressing • Lemon cheesecake p.331 • fresh raspberries
DAY PLAN 11	Rainbow muesli p.56 • 7fl oz skim milk	1½oz dried apricots	Oven baked red pepper and tomato frittata p.113 • mixed salad with fat-free dressing • apple	reduced-fat whole grain cookie	Pasta with green beans and artichokes p.163 • small container low-fat yogurt • peach
DAY PLAN 12	1 poached egg • 2 small slices of whole wheat toast thinly spread with margarine	7fl oz skim milk	Sweet potatoes with a smoky tomato filling p.107 • small container low-fat yogurt • 3oz strawberries	2 sticks celery filled with 1¾oz low-fat soft cheese	Butternut squash and zucchini pasta p.162 • Sugar-free peach sorbet p.320 • 1¾oz blueberries
DAY PLAN 13	5½oz non-fat Greek yogurt • 1½oz oatmeal • 1¾oz blueberries, calorie-free sweetener to taste	1½oz dried apricots	Red lentil dahl with cherry tomatoes p.197 • Chapatti p.338 • 2 tbsp riata • orange	reduced-fat whole grain cookie	Spaghetti with zucchini and toasted almonds p.155 • Summer pudding p.314 • 3 tbsp low-fat yogurt
DAY PLAN 14	2 Apple and oat pancakes p.58 • 3 tbsp low-fat yogurt • fruit	small banana	Curried parsnip soup p.86 • small container low-fat yogurt	2 sticks celery filled with 1¾oz low fat soft cheese	Slow roast pork and lentils p.261 • Cranberry and pomegranate dessert p.324

1600 CALORIES A DAY

	BREAKFAST	MID-MORNING SNACK	LUNCH	MID-AFTERNOON SNACK	EVENING MEAL
DAY PLAN 1	small glass (5fl oz) unsweetened fruit juice • 2 Apple and oat pancakes p.58 • 1 tbsp low-fat yogurt • fruit	orange	Hot and sour noodle salad with tofu p.118 • slice of melon	7fl oz skim milk	Quick turkey cassoulet p.290 • sugar snap peas • 2¾ oz fresh raspberries • 3 tbsp 2% fat Greek yogurt
DAY PLAN 2	small glass (5fl oz) unsweetened fruit juice • Rainbow muesli p.56 • 7fl oz skim milk	1½oz dried apricots	Pan-fried shrimp with lemongrass and ginger p.116 • salad with fat-free dressing • 2oz wholemeal roll • small container low-fat yogurt	1 slice Low-fat ginger tea bread p.339	Beef and bean stew p.249 • 5¼ oz new potatoes • Cranberry and pomegranate jelly p.324
DAY PLAN 3	small glass (5fl oz) unsweetened fruit juice • 2 eggs, scrambled • 1 small slice of wholemeal toast	reduced-fat wholegrain cookie	Chicken salad with fruit and nuts p.145 • 1 slice (1¼ oz) of wholemeal bread thinly spread with margarine • slice of melon	7fl oz skim milk	Pork stir-fry with cashew nuts and greens p.265 • 2½ oz (raw weight) egg noodles • Sugar-free peach sorbet p.320 • 1¾oz raspberries
DAY PLAN 4	small glass (5fl oz) unsweetened fruit juice • 1 slice Seven-grain bread p.336 thinly spread with margarine and low-sugar jam or marmalade	small container low-fat yogurt	Roast root vegetables with romesco sauce p.192 • Cranberry and pomegranate dessert p.324 • satsuma	2 sticks celery filled with 1¾ oz low-fat soft cheese	Roast lamb with flageolets p.254 • broccoli • Mango, orange, and passion fruit fool p.319
DAY PLAN 5	small glass (5fl oz) unsweetened fruit juice •1 slice of Fruit and seed soda bread p.338 topped with mashed banana	7fl oz skim milk	Chickpea, bulgur, and walnut salad p.132 • banana	7fl oz skim milk	Spanish eggs p.97 • 60g wholemeal bread • small container low-fat yogurt
DAY PLAN 6	small glass (5fl oz) unsweetened fruit juice • 2 eggs, scrambled • 1 small slice of wholemeal toast	apple	Moroccan chicken and chickpea soup p.89 • small container of low-fat yogurt	7fl oz skim milk	Salmon en papillote p.212 • broccoli • 7oz new potatoes • Cranberry and pomegranate desset p.324
DAY PLAN 7	small glass (5fl oz) unsweetened fruit juice • 1 slice Seven-grain bread p.336 thinly spread with margarine and low-sugar jam or marmalade	small container low-fat yogurt	Tabbouleh p.126 • 5oz roast chicken (skin removed) • pear	1 Oatcake p.66 with ¾oz low-fat soft cheese	Pasta puttanesca p.157 • Mango, orange, and passion fruit fool p.319

Suitable for some women as part of a weight-loss or weight-maintaining plan. Mix and match these daily menus for a balanced diet.

	BREAKFAST	MID-MORNING SNACK	LUNCH	MID-AFTERNOON SNACK	EVENING MEAL
DAY PLAN 8	small glass (5fl oz) unsweetened fruit juice • 1½oz bran flakes or other wholegrain/fiber-rich cereal • 1 banana • 5fl oz skim milk	1½oz dried apricots	Three-grain salad p.130 • pear	7fl oz skim milk	Cajun chicken with corn salsa p.283 • 7oz new potatoes • Cranberry and pomegranate dessert p.324
DAY PLAN 9	small glass (5fl oz) unsweetened fruit juice • 1 slice of Fruit and seed soda bread p.340 topped with mashed banana	reduced-fat wholegrain cookie	Mexican scrambled eggs p.62 • 1 slice (1½oz) wholemeal toast, thinly spread with polyunsaturated margarine • 2 satsumas	7fl oz skim milk	Tuna kebabs with salsa verde p.217 • 7oz new potatoes • peach
DAY PLAN 10	small glass (5fl oz) unsweetened fruit juice • Rainbow muesli p.56 • 7fl oz skim milk	1½oz dried apricots	Chicken liver paté p.71 • 2 slices wholemeal toast • low-fat yogurt • 2¾oz strawberries	2 rye crackers with 1½oz low-fat soft cheese	Brown rice, red pepper, and artichoke risotto p.167 • salad with fat-free dressing • fresh fruit salad • 4 tbsp 2% fat Greek yogurt
DAY PLAN 11	small glass (5fl oz) unsweetened fruit juice • 5½oz non-fat Greek yogurt • 1½oz oatmeal • 1¾oz blueberries (calorie-free sweetener to taste)	banana	Pea soup p.76 • 2 Oatcakes p.66 • 1¾oz low-fat cream cheese • pear	small container low-fat yogurt	Roasted snapper with new potatoes and fennel p.215 • Poached pears with toasted almonds p.317
DAY PLAN 12	small glass (5fl oz) unsweetened fruit juice • 2 small slices of wholemeal toast topped with ¾oz crunchy peanut butter and 1 small banana, sliced	7fl oz skim milk	Zucchini, feta, bean, and pea salad p.136 • Cranberry and pomegranate dessert p.324 • peach	2 rye crackers 1½oz low-fat soft cheese	Roasted pork chops with mustard rub p.267 • 7oz new potatoes • small container low-fat yogurt • 3½oz raspberries
DAY PLAN 13	small glass (5fl oz) unsweetened fruit juice • 1 boiled egg • 2 slices (2½oz) of wholemeal toast thinly spread with margarine	banana	Farfalle with fresh tomatoes and avocado p.123 • Cranberry and pomegranate dessert p.324	2 rye crackers topped with 1¾oz low-fat soft cheese	Chicken livers with kale and balsamic vinegar p.274 • 7oz new potatoes • small container low-fat yogurt
DAY PLAN 14	small glass (5fl oz) unsweetened fruit juice • 2 Apple and oat pancakes p.58 • 3 tbsp low-fat yogurt • fruit	low-fat/low-sugar cereal bar	Crab and avocado salad with vinaigrette p.144 • 1 slice wholemeal bread with thin scrape of margarine • satsuma	7fl oz skim milk	Linguine with spiced eggplant p.158 • mixed salad with fat-free dressing • slice of pineapple

1800 CALORIES A DAY

	BREAKFAST	MID-MORNING SNACK	LUNCH	MID-AFTERNOON SNACK	EVENING MEAL
DAY PLAN 1	small glass (5fl oz) fruit juice • 2 slices whole grain toast thinly spread with margarine • reduced-sugar jam or marmalade	small container of low-fat yogurt	Curried parsnip soup p.86 • 2oz whole grain roll • satsuma	banana	Roast pork chops with mustard rub p.267 • 7oz boiled new potatoes • Apple and walnut strudel p.326
DAY PLAN 2	small glass (5fl oz) fruit juice • 1 egg poached • 2 slices whole grain bread thinly spread with margarine	7fl oz skim milk	Roasted butternut squash soup p.80 • 1 slice of Seven-grain bread p.336 thinly spread with margarine • apple	1 Oatcake p.66 with 1oz Red pepper hummus p.68	Quick turkey cassoulet p.290 • 7oz boiled new potatoes • Lemon cheesecake p.331
DAY PLAN 3	small glass (5fl oz) fruit juice • 2 eggs, scrambled • 1 slice whole grain toast	7fl oz skim milk	Oven baked red pepper frittata p.113 • green salad with 1 tbsp dressing • small container of low-fat fruit yogurt	1 slice Low-fat ginger tea bread p.339	Ragout of venison with wild mushrooms p.259 • medium baked potato (7oz) • snow peas • Summer pudding p.314 • 3 tbsp fat-free Greek yogurt
DAY PLAN 4	small glass (5fl oz) fruit juice • 2 slices whole grain toast topped with mashed banana	7fl oz skim milk	Hot and sour noodle salad with tofu p.118 • small container of low-fat fruit yogurt • 1¾oz raspberries	2 rye crackers with Red pepper hummus p.68	Salmon and sweet potato pie p.220 • cabbage • Lemon cheesecake p.331
DAY PLAN 5	small glass (5fl oz) fruit juice • Rainbow muesli p.56 • 7fl oz skim milk	banana	Sweet potatoes with a smoky tomato filling p.107 • 4½oz skinless roast chicken • peach	2 rye crackers • Smoked eggplant dip p.72	Cajun chicken with corn salsa p.283 • 7oz boiled new potatoes • fruit salad
DAY PLAN 6	small glass (5fl oz) fruit juice • 1½oz whole grain cereal • 7fl oz skim milk • 2 tbsp raisins	1 slice Low-fat ginger tea bread p.339	Spiced bulgur wheat with feta and a fruity salsa p.128 • small container of low-fat fruit yogurt	1 Oatcake p.66 with Smoked eggplant dip p.72	Beef and bean stew p.249 • 7oz boiled new potatoes • carrots • fruit salad
DAY PLAN 7	small glass (5fl oz) fruit juice • 1½oz whole grain cereal • 7fl oz skim milk • banana	1 slice Low-fat ginger tea bread p.339	Falafel p.101 • mixed green salad with 1 tbsp dressing • small container of low-fat fruit yogurt	2 rye crackers with tomato salsa	Chicken, onion, and peas p.278 • Mango, orange, and passion fruit fool p.319

Suitable for some women as part of a weight-loss or weight-maintaining plan and some men as part of a weight-loss plan. Mix and match the daily menus for a balanced diet.

	BREAKFAST	MID-MORNING SNACK	LUNCH	MID-AFTERNOON SNACK	EVENING MEAL
DAY PLAN 8	small glass (5fl oz) fruit juice • 2 slices whole grain toast topped with mashed banana	low-fat fruit yogurt	Aduki bean and vegetable soup p.82 • small (2oz) whole grain roll • apple	2 rye crackers topped with 1oz low-fat soft cheese	Slow roast pork and lentils p.261 • French beans • Summer pudding p.314 • 3 tbsp non-fat Greek yogurt
DAY PLAN 9	small glass (5fl oz) fruit juice • 2 eggs, scrambled • 1 slice whole grain toast	low-fat fruit yogurt	Tabbouleh p.126 • 5⅓oz roast chicken • fresh fruit salad	7fl oz skim milk	Pasta with clams p.237 • Banana cinnamon and pistachio parcels p.327 • 3 tbsp non-fat fat Greek yogurt
DAY PLAN 10	small glass (5fl oz) fruit juice • Rainbow muesli p.56 • 7fl oz skim milk	1 slice Low-fat ginger tea bread p.339	Squash salad with avocado p.140 • 2 rye crackers with 1¾oz low-fat soft cheese • apple	low-fat fruit yogurt	Linguine with spiced eggplant p.158 • Lemon cheesecake p.331
DAY PLAN 11	small glass (5fl oz) fruit juice • 2 slices whole grain toast thinly spread with margarine and reduced-sugar jam or marmalade	banana	Tomato and bean soup p.81 • 1 slice of Rye bread p.337 spread with ¾oz low-fat soft cheese • pear	low-fat fruit yogurt	Ground pork with mushrooms and pasta p.269 • Poached pears with toasted almonds p.317
DAY PLAN 12	small glass (5fl oz) fruit juice • 2 eggs, scrambled • 1 slice whole grain toast	7fl oz skim milk	Chickpea, bulgur, and walnut salad p.132 • 3½oz roast chicken • apple	1 slice Low-fat ginger tea bread p.339	Wild rice, zucchini, fennel, and shrimp pan-fry p.230 • Chocolate and orange parfait p.329
DAY PLAN 13	small glass (5fl oz) fruit juice • 1 egg, poached • 2 slices whole grain bread thinly spread with margarine	7fl oz skim milk	Three-grain salad p.130 •3½oz cooked peeled shrimp • orange	low-fat fruit yogurt	Pork stir-fry with cashew nuts and greens p.265 • 5⅓oz boiled brown rice • Mango, orange, and passion fruit fool p.319
DAY PLAN 14	small glass (5fl oz) fruit juice • 2 slices whole grain toast topped with mashed banana	7fl oz skim milk	Mixed bean and goat cheese salad p.135 • slice of Rye bread p.337 thinly spread with margarine • plum	2 rye crackers with Smoked eggplant dip p.72	Spicy mackerel and beet roast p.208 • 3½oz boiled brown rice • small container of low-fat fruit yogurt with 2¾oz strawberries

2000 CALORIES A DAY

	BREAKFAST	MID-MORNING SNACK	LUNCH	MID-AFTERNOON SNACK	EVENING MEAL
DAY PLAN 1	small glass (5fl oz) fruit juice • Banana and pecan porridge p.60	7fl oz skim milk	Shredded pork and spring onion wrap p.98 • fruit salad • small container of low-fat fruit yogurt	1 slice Low-fat ginger tea bread p.339	Haddock and spinach gratin p.225 • 8¾oz boiled new potatoes • snow peas • Lemon cheesecake p.331
DAY PLAN 2	small glass (5fl oz) fruit juice • Rainbow muesli p.56 • 7fl oz skim milk • 1 slice whole wheat toast thinly spread with margarine and reduced-sugar jam or marmalade	7fl oz skim milk	Moroccan chicken and chickpea soup p.89 • banana • small container of low-fat fruit yogurt	banana	Bulgur wheat with lamb and chickpeas p.252 • French beans • Poached pears with toasted almonds p.317
DAY PLAN 3	small glass (5fl oz) fruit juice • Parsi eggs p.61 • 1 slice whole wheat toast thinly spread with margarine	banana	Pan-fried shrimp with ginger and lemongrass p.116 • whole wheat pita • tomato salad • small container of low-fat fruit yogurt	2 sticks celery spread with 1oz low-fat soft cheese	Griddled steak chunks with herby rice p.242 • Dark chocolate and yogurt ice cream p.322
DAY PLAN 4	small glass (5fl oz) fruit juice • 2 Apple and oat pancakes p.58 • mixed berries • 5oz 2% fat Greek yogurt	2 Oatcakes p.66 • 1oz low-fat soft cheese	Pea soup p.76 • small (2oz) whole wheat roll • mixed green salad • 3½oz roast chicken • 1 tbsp reduced-fat mayo	1 slice Low-fat ginger tea bread p.339	Pork tenderloin stuffed with chiles and tomatoes p.262 • Dark chocolate and yogurt ice cream p.322 • 2¾oz fresh raspberries
DAY PLAN 5	small glass (5fl oz) fruit juice • Mexican scrambled eggs p.62 • 1 slice whole wheat toast thinly spread with margarine	1 slice Low-fat ginger tea bread p.339	Mixed roast vegetable and mushroom soup p.77 • 1 slice Seven-grain bread p.336 thinly spread with margarine	7fl oz skim milk	Butternut squash and zucchini pasta p.162 • mixed green salad • 1 tbsp vinaigrette • Mango, orange, and passion fruit fool p.319
DAY PLAN 6	small glass (5fl oz) fruit juice • 1½oz whole grain cereal • 7fl oz skim milk • sliced banana and blueberries	7fl oz skim milk	Chorizo, chickpea, and mango salad p.147 • pear	1 Oatcake p.66 with low-fat soft cheese	Salmon and sweet potato pie p.220 • French beans • Banana, cinnamon and pistachio parcels p.327
DAY PLAN 7	Breakfast smoothie p.63 • 2 slices whole wheat toast thinly spread with margarine and reduced-sugar jam or marmalade	banana	Red lentil dahl with cherry tomatoes p.197 • 2 Chapattis p.338 • 3 tbsp riata • peach	7fl oz skim milk	Pasta with green beans and artichokes p.163 • Chocolate and orange parfait p.329

Suitable for some women as part of a weight-maintaining plan and for some men as part of a weight-loss plan. Mix and match the daily menus for a balanced diet.

	BREAKFAST	MID-MORNING SNACK	LUNCH	MID-AFTERNOON SNACK	EVENING MEAL
DAY PLAN 8	small glass (5fl oz) fruit juice • 2 Muesli pancakes with summer berry compote p.57 • 5oz 2% fat Greek yogurt	1 slice Low-fat ginger tea bread p.339	Lentil salad with lemon and almonds p.138 • 3½oz roast chicken • plum	7fl oz skim milk	Cinnamon and ginger beef with noodles p.247 • Chocolate espresso pots p.321
DAY PLAN 9	small glass (5fl oz) fruit juice • Banana and pecan porridge p.60	1 slice Low-fat ginger tea bread p.339	Carrot and ginger soup p.75 • 2 Oatcakes p.66 with 3 tbsp Red pepper hummus p.68 • low-fat yogurt	2 rye crackers with Red pepper hummus p.68	Tuna with black-eyed pea and avocado salsa p.204 • 8¾oz boiled new potatoes • Sugar-free peach sorbet p.320 • fresh raspberries
DAY PLAN 10	small glass (5fl oz) fruit juice • Banana and pecan porridge p.60	small container of low-fat fruit yogurt	Zucchini, feta, bean, and pea salad p.136 • 1 whole wheat pita • Cranberry and pomegranate dessert p.324	1 slice Fruit and seed soda bread p.340	Vegetarian cottage pie p.165 • Summer pudding p.314
DAY PLAN 11	small glass (5fl oz) fruit juice • 2 Apple and oat pancakes p.58 • mixed berries • 5oz 2% fat Greek yogurt	1 slice Low-fat ginger tea bread p.339	White bean soup p.79 • 1 whole wheat roll • fruit salad	1½oz ready-to-eat dried apricots	Pea and lemon risotto p.168 • Poached pears with toasted almonds p.317
DAY PLAN 12	small glass (5fl oz) fruit juice • Parsi eggs p.61 • 1 slice whole wheat toast thinly spread with margarine	7fl oz skim milk	Butternut squash, tomato, and pearl barley salad p.141 • small container of low-fat fruit yogurt • kiwi fruit	banana	Poached chicken with star anise, soy, and brown rice p.275 • Apricot crumble p.325
DAY PLAN 13	small glass (5fl oz) fruit juice • Mexican scrambled eggs p.62 • 1 slice whole wheat toast thinly spread with margarine	7fl oz skim milk	Moroccan tomatoes, peppers, and herbs p.133 • 1 slice Seven-grain bread p.336 thinly spread with margarine • banana • small container of low-fat fruit yogurt	1 slice Low-fat ginger tea bread p.339	Kedgeree p.228 • Sugar-free peach sorbet p.320 • fresh blueberries
DAY PLAN 14	Breakfast smoothie p.63 • 2 slices whole wheat toast thinly spread with margarine and reduced-sugar jam or marmalade	7fl oz skim milk	Spiced bulgur wheat with feta and a fruity salsa p.128 • small container of low-fat fruit yogurt	banana	Chicken jalfrezi p.289 • steamed spinach • 2 chapatti • riata • Mango, orange, and passion fruit fool p.319

MEAL PLANNER 2500 CALORIES A DAY

	BREAKFAST	MID-MORNING SNACK	LUNCH	MID-AFTERNOON SNACK	EVENING MEAL
DAY PLAN 1	small glass (5fl oz) fruit juice • Parsi eggs *p.61* • 2 slices whole grain toast thinly spread with margarine	7fl oz skim milk • plain reduced-fat cookie	Mixed bean and goat cheese salad *p.135* • slice of Rye bead *p.337* thinly spread with margarine • small container of low-fat yogurt	large banana	Linguine with spiced eggplant *p.158* • mixed green salad with 1 tbsp dressing • Chocolate espresso pots *p.321*
DAY PLAN 2	small glass (5fl oz) fruit juice • 2 slices Fruit and seed soda bread *p.340* topped with mashed banana • small container of low-fat fruit yogurt	large banana	Chicken broth with herby dumplings *p.87* • small container of low-fat fruit yogurt	low-fat cereal bar	Spaghetti with tomatoes and goat cheese *p.161* • salad with 1 tbsp dressing • Apple and walnut strudel *p.326*
DAY PLAN 3	small glass (5fl oz) fruit juice • Banana and pecan porridge *p.60* • 1 slice whole grain bead thinly spread with margarine and reduced-sugar jam or marmalade	small container of low-fat yogurt	Cinnamon and ginger beef with noodles *p.247* • small container of low-fat yogurt • banana	1 slice Fruit and seed soda bread *p.340* thinly spread with margarine	Chicken jalfrezi *p.289* • steamed spinach • 5⅓oz boiled brown basmati rice • small naan bread • riata • Mango, orange, and passion fruit fool *p.319*
DAY PLAN 4	Breakfast smoothie • 2 slices of whole grain toast topped with mashed banana	7fl oz skim milk • plain reduced-fat cookie	Roasted snapper with new potatoes and fennel *p.215* • banana with low-fat custard	1 slice Low-fat ginger tea bread *p.339* • apple	Puy lentil and vegetable pot *p.195* • Chocolate espresso pots *p.321* • summer berries
DAY PLAN 5	small glass (5fl oz) fruit juice • Rainbow muesli *p.56* • 7fl oz skim milk • banana	1 slice of whole grain toast spread with 1 tsp peanut butter	Hot and sour (tom yam) soup *p.92* • chicken salad sandwich • small container of low-fat fruit yogurt	7fl oz skim milk • plain reduced-fat cookie	Bulgur wheat with lamb and chickpeas *p.252* • snow peas • Chocolate and orange parfait *p.329*
DAY PLAN 6	small glass (5fl oz) fruit juice • Banana and pecan muffin *p.343* • small container of low-fat fruit yogurt	1 slice Fruit and seed soda bread *p.340* thinly spread with margarine	Carrot and ginger soup *p.75* • tuna and corn sandwich • small container of low-fat yogurt	2 plain reduced-fat cookies	Salmon burgers *p.104* • 8¾oz boiled new potatoes • French beans • Lemon cheesecake *p.331*
DAY PLAN 7	small glass (5fl oz) fruit juice • 1½oz whole grain cereal • 7fl oz skim milk • fresh blueberries • 1 slice whole grain toast thinly spread with margarine and reduced sugar jam	7fl oz skim milk • plain reduced-fat cookie	Curried parsnip soup *p.86* • Shredded pork and spring onion wrap *p.98*	2 rye crackers with Red pepper hummus *p.68*	Leek and tomato pilaf *p.171* • mixed green salad with 1 tbsp dressing • Apple and walnut strudel *p.326*

Suitable for some men as part of a weight-maintaining plan. Mix and match the daily menus for a balanced diet.

	BREAKFAST	MID-MORNING SNACK	LUNCH	MID-AFTERNOON SNACK	EVENING MEAL
DAY PLAN 8	small glass (5fl oz) fruit juice • 1½oz whole grain cereal • 7fl oz skim milk • fresh blueberries • 1 slice whole grain toast thinly spread with margarine and reduced-sugar jam	7fl oz skim milk • plain reduced-fat cookie	Salmon salad with raspberry dressing p.142	2 Oatcakes p.66 with Fava bean dip p.69	Pearl barley, spinach, and lamb pot p.257 • Chocolate and orange parfait p.329
DAY PLAN 9	small glass (5fl oz) fruit juice • Parsi eggs p.61 • 2 slices whole grain toast thinly spread with margarine	low-fat cereal bar	Moroccan chicken and chickpea soup p.89 • large whole grain roll thinly spread with margarine • mixed fruit salad	large banana	Vegetarian moussaka p.178 • large mixed green salad with 1 tbsp dressing • Banana, cinnamon, and pistachio parcels p.327
DAY PLAN 10	small glass (5fl oz) fruit juice • 2 slices Fruit and seed soda bread p.340 topped with mashed banana • small container of low-fat fruit yogurt	7fl oz skim milk • plain reduced-fat cookie	Mushroom lasagna p.164 • 8¾oz boiled new potatoes • salad with 1 tbsp dressing • fruit salad	1 slice Low-fat ginger tea bread p.339	Spiced lemony lentils with roast potatoes p.200 • 5½oz salmon steak, grilled • fresh fruit salad
DAY PLAN 11	small glass (5fl oz) fruit juice • Banana and pecan porridge p.60 • 1 slice whole grain bread thinly spread with margarine and reduced sugar-jam or marmalade	7fl oz skim milk • plain reduced-fat cookie	White bean soup p.79 • egg and watercress sandwich • fruit salad	small container of low-fat yogurt • kiwi fruit	Brown rice, red pepper, and artichoke risotto p.167 • Chocolate and orange parfait p.329
DAY PLAN 12	small glass (5fl oz) fruit juice • Rainbow muesli p.56 • 7fl oz skim milk • banana	low-sugar cereal bar	Mulligatawny p.91 • 2 Oatcakes p.66 with Chicken liver paté p.71 • fresh fruit salad	small container low-fat yogurt • small banana	Chicken tostada with avocado salsa p.103 • mixed green salad • Carpaccio of oranges with pistachio nuts p.316
DAY PLAN 13	Breakfast smoothie p.63 • 2 slices of whole grain toast topped with mashed banana	1½oz ready-to-eat dried apricots • 4 Brazil nuts	Lentil salad with lemon and almonds p.138 • 5½oz roast chicken • small container of yogurt	low-sugar cereal bar	Spicy udon noodles with tuna p.120 • Apricot crumble p.325 • 4 tbsp 2% fat Greek yogurt
DAY PLAN 14	small glass (5fl oz) fruit juice • Blueberry and oat muffin p.345 • small container of low-fat fruit yogurt	7fl oz skim milk • plain reduced-fat cookie	Aduki bean and vegetable soup p.82 • 1 whole grain pita • Red pepper hummus p.68 • small container of low-fat yogurt	small container of low-fat fruit yogurt • peach	Turkish-style stuffed peppers p.174 • 5½oz roast chicken • Sugar-free peach sorbet p.320 • summer berries

THE RECIPES

The delicious recipes in this book are designed to help you achieve a healthy, balanced diet that includes whole grain, low-GI carbohydrates, lean protein, dietary fiber, low-fat dairy products, and plenty of vegetables and fruit. They are also lower in sodium, fat, and sugar. A great diet—whether you have Type 2 diabetes or not.

Where this book goes further is in providing a "Guidelines per serving" chart for each recipe, telling you at a glance whether the recipe is relatively high (3 dots), medium (2 dots), or low (1 dot) in GI, calories, saturated fat, and sodium—the four key dietary areas to watch when you have Type 2 diabetes. So, if you choose a recipe with a relatively high GI, calorie count, saturated fat content, or sodium content, choose dishes that are medium or low in those areas for the rest of the day.

Each recipe also has a "Statistics per serving" breakdown that gives precise details of the number of calories, the number of grams of carbohydrate, sugar, fiber, and fat (total and saturated) in the recipe. So if you really need to crunch the numbers, you can ensure that you are getting the exact balance you need. Many recipes specify only the main part of a meal, allowing you to tailor any accompaniments (such as potatoes or rice) to your own specific needs.

Now, all that's left to do is choose, compare, cook, and enjoy!

BETTER
BREAKFASTS

⬤◯◯ GI

⬤◯◯ CALORIES

⬤◯◯ SATURATED FAT

⬤◯◯ SODIUM

RAINBOW MUESLI

MAKES 23oz   **PREP** 10 MINS
(13 SERVINGS)

This is wonderfully satisfying muesli mix, which will sustain your energy levels throughout the morning. A great breakfast to have on standby in the pantry.

3½oz (100g) rye flakes
3½oz (100g) barley flakes
3½oz (100g) rolled oats
3½oz (100g) golden raisins
3½oz (100g) ready-to-eat dried
  apricots, roughly chopped

1¾oz (50g) hazelnuts,
  roughly chopped
1¾oz (50g) pumpkin seeds
1¾oz (50g) sunflower seeds

1 Mix together all the dry ingredients in a bowl and transfer to an airtight container until needed (there are 13 servings).

2 Serve with chilled skim milk or a little plain reduced-fat yogurt. For a delicious treat, you could add some seasonal fresh fruit such as blueberries or raspberries.

STATISTICS PER SERVING:

Energy 187cals/783kJ

Carbohydrate 10g

Sugar 8g

Fiber 3g

Fat 8g
Saturated fat 1g

Sodium trace

MUESLI PANCAKES WITH SUMMER BERRY COMPOTE

MAKES 12 PANCAKES   **PREP** 10 MINS   **COOK** 15-20 MINS
(SERVES 4-6)

The combination of wholegrain cereals, buttermilk, eggs, and fruit helps to provide a balanced and nutritious start to the day.

GUIDELINES PER PANCAKE:

GI

CALORIES

SATURATED FAT

SODIUM

4½oz (125g) all-purpose wholemeal flour
1 tsp baking powder
2½oz (75g) sugar-free muesli
1 tbsp sugar
2 large eggs, separated
1¼ cups buttermilk

4oz (115g) fresh blueberries, roughly chopped
2 tbsp sunflower oil, for frying

For the summer berry compote
10oz (300g) mixed summer berries
juice and zest of 1 orange

1 Mix the flour and baking powder in a large bowl, and then stir in the muesli and sugar. Make a well in the center and beat in the egg yolks and buttermilk to make a thick batter (it should have the consistency of thick cream).

2 Whisk the egg whites until stiff but not dry, and fold into the batter. Stir in the chopped blueberries.

3 Heat a griddle pan or large, heavy, nonstick frying pan over moderate heat. Add a tiny drop of oil and then when the pan is hot, drop in a tablespoon of the batter and cook for 2–3 minutes, until bubbles start to break on the surface and the pancake is firm enough to flip. Flip it over and cook for 1–2 minutes more, until springy when prodded. Transfer to a warm oven while you cook the rest.

4 To make the compote, place the summer berries in a small saucepan, together with the orange juice and zest. Heat gently, stirring, until the berries are warmed through and have softened slightly. Arrange the pancakes on plates and serve with the compote.

STATISTICS PER PANCAKE:

Energy 117cals/493kJ

Carbohydrate 14g

Sugar 6g

Fiber 2g

Fat 4g

Saturated fat 0.8g

Sodium 0.08g

●●○ GI

●○○ CALORIES

●○○ SATURATED FAT

●●○ SODIUM

APPLE AND OAT PANCAKES

MAKES 12 PANCAKES   **PREP** 10 MINS   **COOK** 15 MINS
(SERVES 4-6)

These little pancakes are a perfect treat for the weekend. The oats used in the mixture provide soluble fiber and help to slow down the absorption of carbohydrate.

4½oz (125g) all-purpose flour
1 tsp baking powder
2½oz (75g) rolled oats
2-3 tbsp superfine sugar
pinch of ground cinnamon

2 eggs, separated
1¼ cups buttermilk
2 medium apples
sunflower oil, for frying

1 Sift the flour into a large bowl and mix with the baking powder. Stir in the oats, sugar, and cinnamon. Make a well in the center and beat in the egg yolks and buttermilk to make a thick batter (it should have the consistency of heavy cream).

2 Core the apples, coarsely grate the flesh, and stir into the batter mixture. Whisk the egg whites until stiff but not dry and fold into the batter.

3 Heat a griddle pan or large heavy-based non-stick frying pan over a moderate heat. Add a tiny drop of oil to the hot pan. When the pan is hot, drop a heaped dessertspoon of the batter into the pan and flatten slightly with the back of the spoon so that the pancakes are about 4in (10cm) in diameter and about ¼in (5mm) thick.

4 Cook for 2 minutes or until bubbles start to break on the surface and the pancakes are firm enough to flip. Flip and cook for 1–2 minutes more, until they feel springy when prodded. Transfer to a warm oven while you cook the rest, adding more oil as necessary. Try these with fresh summer fruits and low-fat Greek yogurt, or with your own favorite topping.

STATISTICS PER PANCAKE:

Energy 100cals/418kJ

Carbohydrate 14g

Sugar 5.5g

Fiber 1.1g

Fat 2g

Saturated fat 0.5g

Sodium 0.07g

GI

CALORIES

SATURATED FAT

SODIUM

BANANA AND PECAN PORRIDGE

SERVES 2   **PREP** 5 MINS   **COOK** 5-10 MINS
PLUS SOAKING

Oats are rich in slow-release carbohydrates, which help to balance blood sugar levels and keep mid-morning hunger pangs at bay.

2oz (60g) rolled oats
10fl oz (300ml) skim milk
generous pinch of ground cinnamon

2 small, very ripe bananas, mashed
½oz (15g) pecan nuts, roughly chopped
4 tbsp Greek yogurt

1 If you have time, soak the oats in the milk overnight. When ready to cook, place the oats, milk, and cinnamon in a nonstick pan.

2 Bring the oats to a boil, reduce the heat, add the bananas and simmer for 4–5 minutes, stirring occasionally. You may need to add more milk to achieve the consistency you prefer.

3 Spoon the porridge into bowls and top with the nuts and Greek yogurt. Serve immediately.

COOK'S TIP
If you soak the oats in milk overnight you may find you need more milk in the morning, as some of the liquid will be soaked up by the oats.

STATISTICS PER SERVING:

Energy 366cals/1,536kJ

Carbohydrate 32g

Sugar 28g

Fiber 4g

Fat 8g

Saturated fat 5g

Sodium 0.08g

PARSI EGGS

SERVES 4   **PREP** 10 MINS   **COOK** 30 MINS

This Indian dish has its origins in ancient Persia, and will provide a spicy start to the day—it's a whole new take on scrambled eggs.

2oz (60g) unsalted butter
4 spring onions, thinly sliced
1 tsp grated fresh ginger root
1 large red or green chile, seeded and finely chopped
2 tsp mild curry powder

4 tomatoes, seeded and chopped
8 large eggs
2 tbsp milk
salt and freshly ground black pepper
2 tbsp chopped cilantro

1 Melt 1oz (30g) of the butter in a large, nonstick frying pan. Fry the onions, ginger, and chile over low heat for 2 minutes, or until softened, stirring often.

2 Add the curry powder and tomatoes and cook for 1 minute. Remove the vegetable mixture from the pan and set aside.

3 Put the rest of the butter in the pan. Beat the eggs and milk, and season with salt and pepper. Pour into the pan, and stir until scrambled and almost set. Add the curried vegetables, stir well, and cook until just set. Scatter the chopped cilantro over the top and serve at once.

GUIDELINES PER SERVING:

● ○ ○ GI
● ● ○ CALORIES
● ● ● SATURATED FAT
● ○ ○ SODIUM

STATISTICS PER SERVING:

Energy 344cals/1,440kJ

Carbohydrate 5g

Sugar 4g

Fiber 1.7g

Fat 28g

Saturated fat 12g

Sodium 0.2g

● ○ ○   GI

● ○ ○   CALORIES

● ● ○   SATURATED FAT

● ○ ○   SODIUM

MEXICAN SCRAMBLED EGGS

SERVES 2   **PREP** 5 MINS   **COOK** 5 MINS

Eggs are a great source of protein, which helps you to feel full for longer, making this a good choice for breakfast or a light lunch.

2 tbsp vegetable oil
½ red pepper, seeded and
  finely diced
4 spring onions, finely chopped
1 small green chile, seeded
  and finely chopped

4 eggs, beaten
salt and freshly ground black pepper
1 tbsp chopped fresh cilantro,
  to serve

1 Heat the oil in a small, heavy frying pan and add the pepper, spring onion, and chile. Fry for 2–3 minutes.

2 Pour in the eggs and season to taste. Stir, with a wooden spoon, for 1–2 minutes or until the eggs are scrambled to your liking. Sprinkle with the cilantro to serve.

STATISTICS PER SERVING:

Energy 292cals/1,214kJ

Carbohydrate 4g

Sugar 4g

Fiber 4g

Fat 24g

Saturated fat 5g

Sodium 0.16g

BREAKFAST SMOOTHIE

SERVES 2   **PREP** 5 MINS

Smoothies are a great way to boost your intake of fruit, and this sustaining recipe will give you a shot of calcium as well as vitamins and minerals.

2 small, ripe bananas
16fl oz (500ml) skim milk
3 tbsp oatmeal

3½oz (100g) fresh raspberries
5½fl oz (150ml) fat-free Greek yogurt
½ tsp ground cinnamon

1 Cut the bananas into small chunks and place in a blender along with the remaining ingredients. Blend at high speed for 1–2 minutes or until smooth.

2 Pour into two glasses and drink immediately.

GUIDELINES PER SERVING:

GI

CALORIES

SATURATED FAT

SODIUM

STATISTICS PER SERVING:

Energy 336cals/1,420kJ

Carbohydrate 52g

Sugar 29g

Fiber 4g

Fat 6g
Saturated fat 3g

Sodium 0.12g

SNACKS AND SOUPS

● ○ ○ GI

● ○ ○ CALORIES

● ○ ○ SATURATED FAT

● ○ ○ SODIUM

SESAME OATCAKES

MAKES 9   **PREP** 5 MINS   **COOK** 10 MINS

These oatcakes make a tasty and low-GI alternative to crackers.

3oz (85g) fine oatmeal
4 tbsp wholemeal flour
1 tbsp sesame seeds

scant ½ tsp salt
pinch of baking soda
1 tbsp sesame oil

1 Preheat the oven to 350°F (180°C).

2 Place the oatmeal, flour, sesame seeds, salt, and baking soda in a large bowl. Stir in the oil and 2½fl oz (75ml) hot water to make a firm dough.

3 Roll the dough out on a lightly floured surface until about ⅛in (2mm) thick and cut into circles using a 3in (7.5cm) pastry cutter.

4 Bake for 8–10 minutes or until golden and crisp. Store in an airtight container. You could try these with Smoked Eggplant Dip (page 72).

STATISTICS PER OATCAKE:

Energy 72cals/303kJ

Carbohydrate 11.5g

Sugar 0.1g

Fiber 1g

Fat 2g

Saturated fat 0.2g

Sodium 0.08g

- ●○○ GI
- ●○○ CALORIES
- ●○○ SATURATED FAT
- ●○○ SODIUM

RED PEPPER HUMMUS

SERVES 4   **PREP** 5 MINS   **COOK** 5–10 MINS

Homemade hummus is quick and easy to make and this version contains considerably less fat than the store-bought variety.

2 large red peppers, halved
  and seeded
14oz can chickpeas, drained
  and rinsed
2 tbsp lemon juice
¼ tsp smoked paprika

3 tbsp olive oil
2 cloves garlic
2 tbsp tahini
2 tbsp natural yogurt
salt and freshly ground black pepper

1 Preheat the broiler to high. Place the halved peppers under the broiler for 20–25 minutes or until the skin is black. Cover with a clean, wet cloth—or place in a plastic bag—and allow to cool. Peel away and discard the skins and blot the flesh dry with paper towels.

2 Place the chickpeas in a small saucepan, cover with water and bring a the boil. Reduce the heat and simmer for 5 minutes.

3 Drain the chickpeas well and place in a food processor or blender with 3 tablespoons of hot water and process for 1–2 minutes. Add the lemon juice, paprika, olive oil, garlic, tahini, and yogurt, season to taste, and process again until smooth. Transfer to a bowl and serve—vegetable crudités or toasted pita are good accompaniments—or cover and chill until needed.

COOK'S TIP
This dip can be kept in the refrigerator, in a sealed container, for up to three days.

STATISTICS PER SERVING:

Energy 299cals/951kJ

Carbohydrate 17g

Sugar 7g

Fiber 2g

Fat 13g

Saturated fat 2g

Sodium 0.04g

FAVA BEAN PURÉE

SERVES 6   **PREP** 20 MINS   **COOK** 1¼ HOURS

Fava beans are at their best when the pods are picked while they are still young and tender. Try serving this purée with oatcakes, rye crackers, or toast.

9oz (250g) skinless dried fava beans, soaked overnight
3 onions
6 garlic cloves
bunch of cilantro, chopped, plus extra to garnish
bunch of flat-leaf parsley, chopped, plus extra to garnish

2 tbsp chopped mint
1 tsp ground cumin
salt and freshly ground black pepper
1–3 tbsp olive oil
juice of 1 lemon

1 Drain the beans and place in a large pan. Pour in enough cold water to cover. Roughly chop 1 onion and 3 garlic cloves, add to the pan and then bring to a boil. Skim off any scum and lower the heat, then cover and simmer for 1 hour, or until the beans are soft.

2 Drain the beans, reserving the cooking liquid. Place the beans in a blender or food processor with the cilantro, parsley, mint, and cumin. Add salt and pepper to taste and then blend to a smooth purée, adding enough of the reserved cooking liquid to ensure that the mixture is not too dry. Transfer to a serving dish and keep warm.

3 Slice the remaining onions. Heat 1 tablespoon of the oil in a frying pan, add the onions, and fry, stirring frequently, over medium-high heat for 10–15 minutes or until they are dark golden and slightly caramelized. Chop the remaining garlic finely, add it to the pan and stir-fry for a further minute.

4 Spread the fried onions and garlic over the top of the purée and drizzle with the lemon juice and remaining oil.

STATISTICS PER SERVING:

Energy 92cals/385kJ

Carbohydrate 7g

Sugar 0.2g

Fiber 3g

Fat 6g
Saturated fat 0.8g

Sodium 0.8g

● ○ ○ GI

● ○ ○ CALORIES

● ○ ○ SATURATED FAT

● ● ● SODIUM

TAPENADE

SERVES 6   **PREP** 15 MINS

A full-flavored Mediterranean spread made with capers and olives.

2 large garlic cloves
9oz (250g) Mediterranean black
  olives, pitted
1½ tbsp capers, drained and rinsed
4 anchovy fillets in olive oil, drained
1 tsp thyme leaves

1 tsp chopped rosemary
2 tbsp fresh lemon juice
2 tbsp extra virgin olive oil
1 tsp Dijon mustard
freshly ground black pepper

1 Place the garlic, olives, capers, anchovies, thyme, and rosemary in a food processor or blender, and process until smooth.

2 Add the lemon juice, olive oil, mustard, and black pepper to taste, and blend until a thick paste forms. Transfer to a bowl and chill until ready to use.

COOK'S TIP
Good with crudités and a spread of Mediterranean appetizers, such as olives and stuffed vine leaves.

STATISTICS PER SERVING:

Energy 97cals/405kJ

Carbohydrate 0.5g

Sugar 0.1g

Fiber 1g

Fat 10g
Saturated fat 1.5g

Sodium 0.6g

CHICKEN LIVER PÂTÉ

SERVES 4   **PREP** 10 MINS   **COOK** 15 MINS   **FREEZE** 3 MONTHS

The red wine adds flavor to this spread and cuts through the richness of the liver.

12oz (350g) chicken livers,
  thawed if frozen
1¾oz (50g) butter
¼ tsp dried thyme

5fl oz (150ml) red wine
10 chives, snipped
salt and freshly ground black pepper

GUIDELINES PER SERVING:

●○○ GI

●○○ CALORIES

●●○ SATURATED FAT

●○○ SODIUM

1 Rinse the chicken livers and pat them dry with kitchen towels. Trim away any white sinew or greenish portions from the livers with small scissors, then cut each in half.

2 Melt the butter in a large frying pan over medium heat until it foams. Add the livers and cook, stirring often, for 4 minutes, or until browned.

3 Add the thyme, wine, and chives to the pan. Bring to a boil then reduce the heat and cook, stirring occasionally for 4 minutes, or until the liquid is reduced and the livers are just cooked through.

4 Remove the pan from the heat and leave to cool for 10 minutes. Add salt and pepper to taste, then tip the livers and sauce into a blender, and blend until smooth. Adjust the seasoning if necessary. Spoon the pâté into a serving bowl, pressing it down with the back of the spoon so it is firmly packed. Leave to cool, then chill until needed.

COOK'S TIP
This is good with toasted slices of Seven-grain bread (see page 336).

STATISTICS PER SERVING:

Energy 199cals/826kJ

Carbohydrate 0g

Sugar 0g

Fiber 0g

Fat 12g

Saturated fat 7g

Sodium 0.16g

- ● ○ ○ GI
- ● ○ ○ CALORIES
- ● ○ ○ SATURATED FAT
- ● ○ ○ SODIUM

SMOKED EGGPLANT DIP

SERVES 4   **PREP** 5 MINS   **COOK** 1 HOUR

Grilled eggplant, with its delicious smoky flavor, is the basis for this tasty Middle Eastern dip.

2 eggplants, about 12oz (350g) each
3 tbsp olive oil, plus extra for greasing
3 garlic cloves, crushed
 or finely chopped
1 tbsp lemon juice

2 tsp ground cumin
1 tsp ground coriander
3 tbsp chopped fresh cilantro
salt and freshly ground black pepper

1 Preheat the oven to 400°F (200°C). Pierce the eggplants all over with a fork and place on a lightly greased baking sheet. Bake for 1 hour, or until the skin is wrinkled and the flesh is soft. Allow the eggplant to cool, then cut in half lengthwise and scoop out the flesh with a spoon.

2 Place the eggplant flesh, garlic, lemon juice, cumin, ground coriander, and olive oil in a food processor or blender and blend until smooth. Stir in the cilantro and season to taste. Chill until required.

STATISTICS PER SERVING:

Energy 86cals/361kJ

Carbohydrate 2g

Sugar 1.5g

Fiber 2g

Fat 8g
Saturated fat 1g

Sodium 0.04g

CHILI AND ROSEMARY SPICED NUTS

SERVES 4   **PREP** 5 MINS   **COOK** 20 MINS

A tasty snack, great for serving at cocktail parties as a healthier alternative to chips.

2 tsp chili powder
2 tbsp fresh rosemary,
  roughly chopped
2 tbsp olive oil
3½oz (100g) mixed whole nuts

1 Preheat the oven to 300°F (150°C). Mix the chili, rosemary, and oil in a large bowl. Add the nuts and stir until well coated.

2 Place the spiced nuts in an ovenproof dish and transfer to the oven. Cook for 20 minutes, stirring occasionally. Allow to cool slightly and then transfer to paper towels to absorb excess oil. Store in an airtight container; the nuts will keep for up to one week.

STATISTICS PER SERVING:

Energy	194cals/804kJ
Carbohydrate	3g
Sugar	1g
Fiber	1.6g
Fat	18g
Saturated fat	3g
Sodium	0.04g

CARROT AND GINGER SOUP

SERVES 4   **PREP** 15 MINS   **COOK** 50 MINS   **FREEZE** 3 MONTHS

Unlike most vegetables, which are most nutritious when eaten raw, cooking carrots increases the availability of betacarotene, which the body can convert into vitamin A.

GUIDELINES PER SERVING:

⬤⬤◯ GI

⬤◯◯ CALORIES

⬤◯◯ SATURATED FAT

⬤⬤◯ SODIUM

2 tbsp olive oil
1 large onion, peeled and
  finely chopped
1 clove of garlic, peeled and crushed
2in (5cm) piece of fresh root ginger,
  peeled and finely chopped

1lb 5oz (600g) carrots, peeled
  and roughly chopped
1½ pints (750ml) vegetable stock
zest and juice of 2 large oranges
salt and freshly ground black pepper
spring onions, chopped, to garnish

1 Heat the oil in large nonstick saucepan, add the onion and cook over medium heat for 3–4 minutes. Add the garlic, ginger, and carrots and continue to cook for a further 5 minutes, stirring occasionally.

2 Add the stock, orange zest and juice, and season to taste with salt and black pepper. Bring to a boil, then reduce the heat, cover, and simmer for 40 minutes or until the carrots are soft.

3 Transfer the soup to a food processor or liquidizer and process until smooth, then return to the pan and reheat gently. If the soup is too thick, you can thin it out with a little extra stock or water. Ladle the soup into bowls, garnish with chopped spring onions, and serve.

STATISTICS PER SERVING:

Energy 200cals/836kJ

Carbohydrate 25g

Sugar 21g

Fiber 5.5g

Fat 8g
Saturated fat 1.5g

Sodium 0.48g

● ● ○ GI

● ○ ○ CALORIES

● ○ ○ SATURATED FAT

● ● ○ SODIUM

PEA SOUP

SERVES 4   **PREP** 10 MINS   **COOK** 25 MINS   **FREEZE** 3 MONTHS

You can use frozen peas to make this tasty and filling soup in a matter of minutes.

1 tbsp olive oil
1 large onion, finely chopped
2 garlic cloves, peeled and crushed
  or finely chopped
2 celery stalks, finely chopped

1 medium potato, peeled and diced
1lb (450g) frozen peas
2 pints (1 liter) vegetable or
  chicken stock
salt and freshly ground black pepper

1 Heat the oil in a large saucepan, add the onion and cook over medium heat for 2–3 minutes, stirring. Add the garlic, celery, and potato and cook for 1 minute.

2 Add the peas, stock, and seasoning. Bring to a boil then reduce the heat, cover and simmer for 20 minutes.

3 Allow to cool slightly then transfer to a food processor or blender and purée until smooth. Return the soup to the pan, adjust the seasoning and heat until warm.

STATISTICS PER SERVING:

Energy 200cals/840kJ

Carbohydrate 35g

Sugar 5g

Fiber 7g

Fat 6g
Saturated fat 1g

Sodium 0.48g

MIXED ROAST VEGETABLE AND MUSHROOM SOUP

GUIDELINES PER SERVING:

● ○ ○ GI
● ● ○ CALORIES
● ○ ○ SATURATED FAT
● ● ○ SODIUM

SERVES 4   **PREP** 15 MINS   **COOK** 35-40 MINS   **FREEZE** 3 MONTHS

The roasted vegetables add a wonderfully intense flavor to this dish.

2 red onions, peeled and roughly
  chopped
4 small zucchini, roughly chopped
2 tbsp olive oil
few stems of rosemary
salt and freshly ground black pepper
3 medium potatoes, cubed
4 carrots, roughly chopped
2 garlic cloves, finely chopped

7oz (200g) cremini mushrooms, half
  roughly chopped and half grated
scant 1oz (25g) dried porcini
  mushrooms, soaked in boiling water
  to rehydrate
2½ pints (1.2 liters) mushroom stock
  or vegetable stock
handful of flat-leaf parsley,
  finely chopped

1 Preheat the oven to 400°F (200°C). Cook the potatoes and carrots in a large pan of boiling salted water for about 5 minutes, then drain well. Put into a roasting pan with the onions and zucchini, add half the oil, and combine with your hands. Add the rosemary stems, season with salt and pepper, and place in the oven for 15 minutes. Meanwhile, heat the remaining oil in a large saucepan, add the garlic and sweat for a few seconds over low heat, then add both the chopped and grated cremini mushrooms and cook for 5 minutes or until they begin to release their juices.

2 Using a slotted spoon, transfer the soaked porcini mushrooms to the pan along with the stock and a little salt and black pepper. Strain the soaking liquid from the mushrooms, to remove any grit, and pour into the pan. Bring to a boil, then reduce the heat and simmer for 5–10 minutes.

3 Put the roasted vegetables into the pan and cook for a further 5 minutes or until everything is cooked through. Stir through the parsley to serve.

COOK'S TIP
If you prefer, you could blend some of the vegetables to a purée to thicken the soup, but be sure to keep some chunky vegetables and mushrooms for interest.

STATISTICS PER SERVING:

Energy 312cals/1,311kJ

Carbohydrate 44g

Sugar 15g

Fiber 8g

Fat 9.5g

Saturated fat 2g

Sodium 0.6g

● ○ ○ GI

● ○ ○ CALORIES

● ○ ○ SATURATED FAT

● ○ ○ SODIUM

GAZPACHO

SERVES 4   **PREP** 15 MINS   **FREEZE** 1 MONTH

This chilled, no-cook Spanish soup is always popular when temperatures are hot outside.

2¼lb (1kg) tomatoes
1 small cucumber, peeled and finely chopped, plus extra to serve
1 small red pepper, seeded and chopped, plus extra to serve
2 garlic cloves, crushed

4 tbsp sherry vinegar
salt and freshly ground black pepper
4fl oz (120ml) extra virgin olive oil, plus extra to serve
1 hard-boiled egg, white and yolk separated and chopped, to serve

1 Bring a kettle of water to a boil. Place the tomatoes in a heatproof bowl, pour over enough boiling water to cover, and leave for 20 seconds, or until the skins split. Drain and cool under cold running water. Gently peel off the skins, cut the tomatoes in half, seed, and chop the flesh.

2 Put the tomato flesh, cucumber, red pepper, garlic, and sherry vinegar in a food processor or blender. Season to taste with salt and pepper, and process until smooth. Pour in the olive oil and process again. Dilute with a little water if too thick. Transfer the soup to a serving bowl, cover with plastic wrap and chill for at least 1 hour.

3 When ready to serve, finely chop the extra cucumber and red pepper. Place the cucumber, pepper, and egg yolk and white in individual bowls and arrange on the table, along with olive oil for drizzling. Ladle the soup into bowls and serve, letting each diner add their own garnish.

COOK'S TIP
The soup can be prepared 2 days in advance, kept covered and chilled.

STATISTICS PER SERVING:

Energy 284cals/1,176kJ

Carbohydrate 11g

Sugar 11g

Fiber 3.5g

Fat 25g

Saturated fat 4g

Sodium 0.08g

WHITE BEAN SOUP

SERVES 4   **PREP** 30 MINS   **COOK** 2 HOURS   **FREEZE** 3 MONTHS
PLUS SOAKING

This thick soup from northern Italy is guaranteed to keep out the winter chills.

GUIDELINES PER SERVING:

◕○○ GI
◕◕○ CALORIES
◕◕○ SATURATED FAT
◕◕○ SODIUM

3 tbsp olive oil
2 onions, finely chopped
2 garlic cloves, crushed
8oz (225g) dried cannellini beans,
  soaked overnight
1 celery stick, chopped
1 bay leaf
3 or 4 parsley stalks, without leaves

1 tbsp lemon juice
2 pints (1 liter) vegetable stock
salt and freshly ground black pepper
3 shallots, thinly sliced
2oz (60g) pancetta, chopped
3oz (80g) Fontina cheese or Taleggio
  cheese, chopped into small pieces

1 Heat 2 tbsp of the olive oil in a saucepan, add the onions, and fry over low heat for 10 minutes, or until softened, stirring occasionally. Add the garlic and cook, stirring, for 1 minute.

2 Drain and rinse the soaked beans and add to the pan with the celery, bay leaf, parsley stalks, lemon juice, and stock. Bring to a boil, cover, and simmer for 1½ hours, or until the beans are soft, stirring occasionally.

3 Remove the bay leaf and liquidize the soup in batches in a blender, or through a hand mill. Rinse out the pan. Return the soup to the pan and season to taste with salt and pepper.

4 Heat the remaining olive oil in a small frying pan, and fry the shallots and pancetta, until golden and crisp, stirring frequently to stop them sticking to the pan.

5 Reheat the soup, adding a little stock or water if it is too thick. Stir the Fontina or Taleggio into the soup. Ladle into individual bowls, and sprinkle each serving with the shallots and pancetta.

STATISTICS PER SERVING:

Energy 383cals/1,604kJ

Carbohydrate 34g

Sugar 8g

Fiber 12g

Fat 19g

Saturated fat 6g

Sodium 0.44g

● ● ○ GI

● ○ ○ CALORIES

● ○ ○ SATURATED FAT

● ● ○ SODIUM

ROASTED BUTTERNUT SQUASH SOUP

SERVES 4   **PREP** 15 MINS   **COOK** 50 MINS–1 HOUR

Roasting the squash helps to intensify the flavor and gives this soup a wonderfully sweet flavor.

1 medium butternut squash, peeled and diced (about 1¾lb/800g prepared weight)
2 medium red onions, peeled and thickly sliced
4 garlic cloves, unpeeled
4 tbsp olive oil
pinch of dried red pepper flakes
2 pints (1 liter) vegetable stock
salt and freshly ground black pepper

1 Preheat the oven to 400°F (200°C). Place the squash, onions, and garlic in a large roasting pan. Drizzle over the oil and stir to ensure the vegetables are well coated. Sprinkle over the red pepper flakes, then place in the oven for 45–50 minutes or until the squash is soft.

2 Gently squeeze the garlic cloves from their skins and transfer to a liquidizer or blender along with the other roasted vegetables. Add the stock and process until smooth.

3 Transfer the soup to a large saucepan and gently heat through. Season to taste and serve.

STATISTICS PER SERVING:

Energy 239cals/1,001kJ

Carbohydrate 23g

Sugar 12g

Fiber 4g

Fat 13g
Saturated fat 2g

Sodium 0.48g

TOMATO AND BEAN SOUP

SERVES 4   **PREP** 10 MINS   **COOK** 20 MINS

A flavorsome Mediterranean-style soup.

1 tbsp olive oil
1 onion, finely chopped
salt and freshly ground black pepper
2 garlic cloves, finely chopped
1 tsp fennel seeds
6 tomatoes, skinned and quartered
1 tbsp tomato purée

14oz can of chopped tomatoes
14oz can of borlotti beans, drained
  and rinsed
14oz can of cannellini beans, drained
  and rinsed
16fl oz (500ml) vegetable stock
chopped parsley, to serve

1 Heat the olive oil in a large pan, add the onion, and cook over low heat for 7–8 minutes until it softens and turns transparent. Season with a pinch of salt and some black pepper. Stir in the garlic and the fennel seeds.

2 Add the fresh tomatoes and break them up with the back of a spoon. Stir in the tomato purée and canned tomatoes.

3 Add the beans, pour in the stock and bring to a boil. Reduce the heat to a simmer and cook, uncovered, for about 20 minutes, topping up with more stock if needed. Taste and season as necessary. Stir through a little chopped parsley and serve.

GUIDELINES PER SERVING:

GI
CALORIES
SATURATED FAT
SODIUM

STATISTICS PER SERVING:

Energy 286cals/1,202kJ

Carbohydrate 40g

Sugar 12g

Fiber 4g

Fat 4g
Saturated fat 0.5g

Sodium 0.24g

● ○ ○ GI

● ● ○ CALORIES

● ○ ○ SATURATED FAT

● ○ ○ SODIUM

ADUKI BEAN AND VEGETABLE SOUP

SERVES 4   **PREP** 10 MINS   **COOK** 35 MINS   **FREEZE** 3 MONTHS

A wholesome mix of goodness, these red beans have a meaty texture to them.

1 tbsp olive oil
1 red onion, finely chopped
2 cloves of garlic, finely chopped
3 celery stalks, finely diced
3 carrots, peeled and finely diced
1 bay leaf

1 tbsp yeast extract (Marmite)
2 x 14oz cans aduki beans,
  drained and rinsed
1½ pints (750ml) vegetable stock
freshly ground black pepper

1 Heat the oil in a large saucepan, then add the onion and cook on low heat for 2–3 minutes or until soft. Stir in the garlic, celery, carrot, and bay leaf and continue to cook for a further 10 minutes until the vegetables begin to soften.

2 Stir through the yeast extract, add the beans and the stock, and bring to a boil. Reduce the heat and simmer gently for 20 minutes, adding more stock if needed.

3 Remove the bay leaf and season to taste with black pepper (you are unlikely to need salt, as the yeast extract can be salty). Spoon into bowls and serve. Chunky pieces of fresh Seven Grain Bread (see page 336) or other wholemeal bread make a good accompaniment.

STATISTICS PER SERVING:

Energy 388cals/1,632kJ

Carbohydrate 41g

Sugar 10g

Fiber 11g

Fat 6.5g

Saturated fat 2g

Sodium 0.2g

CHICKPEA AND SQUASH SOUP

SERVES 4   **PREP** 10 MINS   **COOK** 30 MINS   **FREEZE** 3 MONTHS

A delicious thick soup, livened up with cinnamon.

1 tbsp olive oil
1 onion, finely chopped
salt and freshly ground black pepper
2 garlic cloves, finely chopped
2 sage leaves, finely chopped
few sprigs of thyme, leaves only,
  chopped
1 butternut squash, peeled and
  cut into 1in (2.5cm) cubes

1 cinnamon stick
pinch of red pepper flakes
1¾ pints (900ml) mushroom stock
  or vegetable stock
2 x 14oz cans of chickpeas,
  drained and rinsed

1 Heat the olive oil in a large pan, add the onion and cook over low heat for 5 minutes or until it softens and turns transparent. Season with a pinch of salt and some black pepper. Add the garlic and cook for a few seconds, then add the fresh herbs and the squash and cook, stirring, for 10 minutes or until the squash begins to color slightly. Add the cinnamon stick and red pepper flakes and pour in a little stock. Bring to a boil, then pour in the remaining stock.

2 Add the chickpeas, bring to a simmer then cook over low heat, partially covered, for 15–20 minutes or until the squash is soft.

3 Remove the cinnamon stick, then ladle the soup into a liquidizer and blend until smooth. If the soup is too thick, add some boiling water. Taste and adjust the seasoning, reheat if necessary, and serve.

COOK'S TIP
Mushroom stock can be found in Italian delis, either ground or as cubes. It is well worth getting hold of, as it imparts a wonderful flavor into soups and casseroles.

STATISTICS PER SERVING:

Energy 314cals/1,321kJ

Carbohydrate 48g

Sugar 14g

Fiber 5g

Fat 4g

Saturated fat 0.5g

Sodium 0.16g

LENTIL AND TOMATO SOUP

SERVES 4   **PREP** 15 MINS   **COOK** 40 MINS   **FREEZE** 3 MONTHS

Plenty of vegetables are packed into this flavorful soup.

GUIDELINES PER SERVING:

●○○ GI

●○○ CALORIES

●○○ SATURATED FAT

●●○ SODIUM

2 tbsp olive oil
1 onion, peeled and finely chopped
2 garlic cloves, peeled and crushed
   or finely chopped
1 red pepper, seeded and diced
1 large carrot, peeled and finely diced
2 celery stalks, chopped
4½oz (125g) red lentils, rinsed

14oz can chopped tomatoes
2 tbsp tomato purée
1¼ pint (600ml) well-flavored chicken
   stock or vegetable stock
2oz (60g) chorizo, diced
salt and freshly ground black pepper
3 tbsp chopped fresh cilantro

1 Heat the oil in a large saucepan, add the onion and cook over medium heat for 2–3 minutes or until beginning to soften. Add the garlic, red pepper, carrot, and celery and continue to cook, stirring occasionally, for a further 5 minutes.

2 Add the lentils, tomatoes, tomato purée, stock, and chorizo. Season with salt and black pepper, stir, and bring the mixture to a boil.

3 Reduce the heat, cover, and simmer for 30 minutes or until the lentils are soft. Just before serving, stir through the chopped cilantro.

STATISTICS PER SERVING:

Energy 273cals/1,147kJ

Carbohydrate 30g

Sugar 11g

Fiber 4.5g

Fat 10g
Saturated fat 2.5g

Sodium 0.44g

● ● ○ GI

● ● ○ CALORIES

● ● ○ SATURATED FAT

● ● ○ SODIUM

CURRIED PARSNIP SOUP

SERVES 4   **PREP** 15 MINS   **COOK** 55 MINS   **FREEZE** 3 MONTHS
AFTER STEP 3

A mildly spiced soup that is perfect for a chilly winter's day. Parsnips are at their best in winter, and will boost your vitamin C, fiber, and folate intake.

2 tbsp vegetable oil
1 large onion, finely chopped
1 garlic clove, crushed or
  finely chopped
1 tbsp mild curry paste
1lb 10oz (750g) parsnips, cored
  and diced

2½ pints (1.2 liters) chicken
  or vegetable stock
salt and freshly ground black pepper
7fl oz (200ml) Greek yogurt
3 tbsp chopped fresh cilantro,
  to garnish

1 Heat the oil in a large saucepan, add the onion and cook over moderate heat, stirring occasionally, for 5 minutes. Add the garlic and cook for 1 minute.

2 Stir in the curry paste and parsnips and cook, stirring, for 5 minutes.

3 Add the stock and season to taste. Bring to a boil and then reduce the heat, cover, and simmer for about 30 minutes. Allow the soup to cool slightly, then transfer the mixture to a food processor or blender and blend until smooth.

4 Return the soup to the pan, stir in the yogurt and then gently reheat, taking care to not let it boil. Ladle into bowls and garnish with cilantro before serving.

STATISTICS PER SERVING:

Energy 318cals/1,331kJ

Carbohydrate 31g

Sugar 15g

Fiber 9g

Fat 16g

Saturated fat 5g

Sodium 0.72g

CHICKEN BROTH
WITH HERBY DUMPLINGS

SERVES 4   **PREP** 5 MINS   **COOK** 45 MINS   **FREEZE** 3 MONTHS
(BROTH ONLY)

A substantial broth for cold, rainy nights when you want to treat yourself to some comfort food.

GUIDELINES PER SERVING:

●●○ GI
●●○ CALORIES
●●● SATURATED FAT
●●● SODIUM

2 pints (900ml) chicken stock,
  plus 16fl oz (500ml) extra
2 chicken breasts, skinned
7oz (200g) baby button mushrooms,
  any larger ones halved
1¾oz (50g) flat-leaf parsley,
  finely chopped
salt and freshly ground black pepper
½oz (15g) fresh Parmesan, grated, to
  serve

For the dumplings
3½oz (100g) vegetable shortening
6oz (175g) fresh white breadcrumbs
6 sage leaves, finely chopped
1¾oz (50g) fresh thyme leaves
3 eggs

1 First, make the broth. Pour 2 pints (900ml) chicken stock into a large pan and bring to a boil. Add the chicken, reduce the heat until the stock is simmering, partially cover the pan, and cook for about 20 minutes or until the chicken is done. Remove the chicken with a slotted spoon and set aside.

2 While the chicken is cooking, prepare the dumplings. Put the shortening, breadcrumbs, herbs, and eggs into a bowl, season, and mix well. Form into a dough—add a little water if necessary for the dough to start clinging together in lumps. Shape into balls the size of a walnut, and put on a plate.

3 Top up the broth with the remaining stock, bring to a boil, part-cover, and simmer for 10 minutes. Add the dumplings and mushrooms and poach for 10 minutes. Slice or tear the chicken and return it to pan with the parsley. Heat through. Season and serve sprinkled with a little Parmesan.

COOK'S TIP
To save time, prepare the dumplings 30 minutes ahead and keep them in the refrigerator until needed.

STATISTICS PER SERVING:

Energy 527cals/2,204kJ

Carbohydrate 28g

Sugar 1g

Fiber 1.5g

Fat 31.5g

Saturated fat 14g

Sodium 0.8g

MOROCCAN CHICKEN AND CHICKPEA SOUP

SERVES 4   **PREP** 15 MINS   **COOK** 30 MINS

A hearty soup that is perfect for a light lunch.

GUIDELINES PER SERVING:

- ●○○ GI
- ●●○ CALORIES
- ●●● SATURATED FAT
- ●○○ SODIUM

2 tbsp olive oil
1lb 2oz (500g) skinless chicken thighs, chopped into bite-sized pieces
1 large onion, roughly chopped
2 garlic cloves, crushed
2 large carrots, diced
2 tsp harissa paste

2 pints (1 liter) chicken stock
1 cinnamon stick
14oz can chickpeas, rinsed and drained
salt and freshly ground black pepper
4 tbsp fresh cilantro, to garnish

1 Heat 1 tablespoon of the oil in a large saucepan, add the chicken and cook over high heat for 2–3 minutes or until beginning to brown (you may need to do this in batches). Remove from the pan and set aside.

2 Heat the remaining oil, add in the onion and cook for 1–2 minutes. Add the garlic, carrots, and harissa paste. Cook for 1–2 minutes.

3 Return the chicken to the pan, and add the stock and cinnamon stick. Bring to a boil, reduce the heat and simmer for 30 minutes.

4 Add the chickpeas and continue to cook for 1–2 minutes. Remove and discard the cinnamon stick, then season to taste with salt and black pepper. Ladle the soup into bowls and garnish with the cilantro.

STATISTICS PER SERVING:

Energy 344cals/1,440kJ

Carbohydrate 5g

Sugar 4g

Fiber 1.7g

Fat 28g
Saturated fat 12g

Sodium 0.2g

● ○ ○ GI

● ● ○ CALORIES

● ○ ○ SATURATED FAT

● ● ● SODIUM

RED LENTIL AND BACON SOUP

SERVES 4   **PREP** 10 MINS   **COOK** 40 MINS   **FREEZE** 1 MONTH

A warming meal in one; the apricots add a hint of sweetness to the earthy lentils.

1 tbsp olive oil
1 onion, finely chopped
4 slices slab bacon, fat removed
  and roughly chopped
1¾oz (50g) dried apricots, finely
  chopped

9½oz (275g) red lentils, rinsed
salt and freshly ground black pepper
10fl oz (300ml) tomato purée
3½ pints (1.7 liter) vegetable stock

1 Heat the oil in a large pan, add the onion and cook over low heat for 7–8 minutes until it softens and turns transparent. Add the bacon and cook for a further 5 minutes until the bacon begins to color. Stir through the apricots and lentils and season with a pinch of salt and some black pepper.

2 Stir through the tomato purée, increase the heat slightly and add a little of the stock. Bring to a boil, then reduce the heat to a simmer and add more stock, 1¼ pints (600ml) or so at a time, stirring and bringing to a simmer each time. Cook over low heat for 25–30 minutes until the lentils are cooked and the sauce thickens. Taste, adjust the seasoning if required, and serve.

COOK'S TIP
This soup is best left to sit awhile before serving. In fact, the flavors are even better when it is eaten the day after cooking; keep it in the refrigerator overnight and reheat gently before serving.

STATISTICS PER SERVING:

Energy 437cals/1,842kJ

Carbohydrate 54g

Sugar 9g

Fiber 6g

Fat 11g

Saturated fat 3g

Sodium 1.2g

MULLIGATAWNY

SERVES 6   **PREP** 15 MINS   **COOK** 40 MINS   **FREEZE** 3 MONTHS

A spicy, hot, filling soup for cold days.

GUIDELINES PER SERVING:

◑○○ GI

◑◑○ CALORIES

◑○○ SATURATED FAT

◑◑○ SODIUM

2 tbsp olive oil
1 large onion, finely chopped
1 carrot, peeled and finely chopped
1 potato, peeled and finely chopped
1 cooking apple, peeled, cored and
  finely chopped
1lb 2oz (500g) finely diced lean beef
1 heaped tsp curry powder
1in (2.5cm) piece of fresh ginger root,
  peeled and grated

2 green birds-eye chiles,
  seeded and finely chopped
4 garlic cloves, finely chopped
4½oz (125g) dried red lentils
4¼ pints (2 liters) chicken stock
large handful of fresh cilantro,
  finely chopped
salt and freshly ground black pepper

1 Heat the olive oil in a large pan, add the onion, carrot, potato, and apple and cook gently for a couple of minutes, then stir in the beef and curry powder and cook until the beef is no longer pink.

2 Add the ginger, chiles, and garlic and cook for 1 minute. Stir in the lentils so they are well coated in the spices then pour in the stock and bring to a boil. Reduce to a simmer and cook for 30 minutes or until the lentils are soft.

3 Stir through the cilantro, season with salt and black pepper and cook for a further 5 minutes. You could serve this with chapattis alongside (see page 338).

COOK'S TIP
Traditionally this soup is blended; do so before serving if you wish.

STATISTICS PER SERVING:

Energy 324cals/1,365kJ

Carbohydrate 27g

Sugar 7g

Fiber 3g

Fat 10g

Saturated fat 3g

Sodium 0.72g

● ○ ○ GI

● ○ ○ CALORIES

● ○ ○ SATURATED FAT

● ● ● SODIUM

HOT AND SOUR (TOM YAM) SOUP

SERVES 4 **PREP** 5 MINS **COOK** 15 MINS

A classic Thai broth, which is full of flavor and yet low in fat. This soup is perfect for a quick and healthy lunch, and its piquant ingredients are a treat for the tastebuds.

2½ pints (1.2 liters) chicken
  or vegetable stock
4 kaffir lime leaves
4 slices of fresh ginger
1 red chile, seeded and sliced
1 stalk lemongrass, bruised
3½oz (100g) shiitake mushrooms,
  sliced

3½oz (100g) rice noodles
7oz (200g) peeled shrimp, raw
4 spring onions, finely shredded
1 tsp Thai fish sauce
juice of 2 limes
1 tbsp chopped fresh cilantro

1 Put the stock, lime leaves, ginger, chile, and lemongrass in a large saucepan. Cover and bring to a boil. Add the mushrooms and simmer for 10 minutes. Break the noodles into short lengths and drop them into the soup. Simmer for 3 minutes.

2 Add the shrimp and spring onions, and simmer for 2 minutes or until the shrimp turn pink. Add the fish sauce and lime juice. Remove the lemongrass and adjust the seasoning. Sprinkle with the fresh cilantro and serve.

STATISTICS PER SERVING:

Energy 196cals/820kJ

Carbohydrate 23g

Sugar 1.5g

Fiber 0.7g

Fat 3g
Saturated fat 0.7g

Sodium 0.8g

BEEF BROTH

GUIDELINES PER SERVING:

● ● ○ GI

● ○ ○ CALORIES

● ○ ○ SATURATED FAT

● ○ ○ SODIUM

SERVES 4   **PREP** 15 MINS   **COOK** 2 HOURS 10 MINS   **FREEZE** 1 MONTH

Slow-cooked beef, left to simmer until tender, infuses this broth with rich juices to make a wholesome and satisfying soup that is a meal in itself.

1lb 2oz (500g) lean beef, diced
bouquet garni of bay leaf, parsley, and thyme
salt and freshly ground black pepper
1 tbsp olive oil

2 onions, diced
2 carrots, diced
2 small potatoes, peeled and diced
2 leeks, trimmed and chopped

1 Pour 4¼ pints (2 liters) of water into a large pan, bring to a boil, and season with salt and pepper. Add the beef and bouquet garni to the pan, return to a boil and skim off any scum that rises to the surface, then reduce to a simmer. Cook, partially covered, over very low heat for 1½ hours.

2 While the beef is cooking, heat the olive oil in a large frying pan, and add the onions, carrots, and potatoes. Cook for about 5 minutes. Add the leeks and cook for a further 5 minutes.

3 Pour the vegetable mixture into the pan with the beef, stir, season well, and cook gently for a further 30 minutes or until the vegetables are soft. Remove the bouquet garni, and serve.

STATISTICS PER SERVING:

Energy 283cals/1,191kJ

Carbohydrate 22g

Sugar 8g

Fiber 4g

Fat 8.5g
Saturated fat 2.5g

Sodium 0.12g

LIGHT LUNCHES
AND SALADS

● ○ ○ GI

● ● ○ CALORIES

● ○ ○ SATURATED FAT

● ● ○ SODIUM

YELLOW SPLIT PEAS WITH PEPPERS AND PEA SHOOTS

SERVES 2   **PREP** 15 MINS   **COOK** 35 MINS

Like all pulses, split peas provide good amounts of protein and dietary fiber. They are also a low-GI food. Here they are served as a tasty open sandwich

1 tbsp olive oil
1 small red onion, finely chopped
1 clove garlic, crushed or finely chopped
¾in (2cm) piece fresh ginger, finely chopped
3oz (85g) yellow split peas

10fl oz (300ml) vegetable stock
1 red pepper, halved
2 slices pumpernickel or toasted rye bread (about 1¾oz/50g per slice)
scant 1oz (25g) pea shoots (if unavailable, use arugula or watercress)

1 Heat the oil in a small saucepan and then scatter in the onion, garlic, and ginger. Cook, stirring, for 1–2 minutes. Add the split peas and stock, bring to a boil, then cover and reduce the heat. Simmer for 30–35 minutes or until the split peas are very soft. Add a little more stock or water if needed.

2 While the split peas are cooking, prepare the red pepper: place the two halves, skin-side up, under a hot broiler for 15–20 minutes or until the skin is charred and black. Cover with a clean, damp dish towel—or place in a plastic freezer bag—and allow to cool for 10 minutes. Remove the skin and seeds from the pepper. Blot the pepper dry with paper towels, then slice it into thick strips.

3 Place the pumpernickel bread on serving plates, spoon the split peas over it, top with the strips of red pepper, and finish with the pea shoots.

COOK'S TIP
Pea shoots are the leaves of the garden pea plant, and are high in vitamin C. They make an interesting alternative to traditional salad leaves—look out for them in the supermarket.

STATISTICS PER SERVING:

Energy 348cals/1,472kJ

Carbohydrate 53g

Sugar 5g

Fiber 6g

Fat 9g

Saturated fat 1.5g

Sodium 0.6g

SPANISH EGGS

SERVES 2   **PREP** 10 MINS   **COOK** 35 MINS

Eggs are one of the few dietary sources of vitamin D and also contain good amounts of protein and B-vitamins, making this dish a great choice for a quick, healthy lunch.

GUIDELINES PER SERVING:

● ○ ○ GI

● ● ○ CALORIES

● ● ○ SATURATED FAT

● ○ ○ SODIUM

1 tbsp olive oil
1 large red onion, diced
2 garlic cloves, crushed
  or finely chopped
½ red chile, seeded and
  finely chopped
1 small red pepper, seeded
  and diced

14oz can cherry tomatoes
2 tbsp tomato purée
½ tsp smoked paprika
5fl oz (150ml) red wine
salt and freshly ground black pepper
4 large eggs
2 tbsp chopped fresh cilantro, to
  garnish

1 Heat the oil in a nonstick frying pan. Add the onion and sauté over medium heat for 2–3 minutes, then add the garlic, chile, and red pepper. Continue to cook, stirring occasionally, for 3 minutes.

2 Add the tomatoes, tomato purée, paprika, and red wine. Season to taste. Cook, uncovered, over medium heat for 15–20 minutes or until the mixture begins to thicken.

3 Using the back of a tablespoon, make 4 egg-shaped hollows in the tomato mixture and crack an egg into each hollow. Put a lid on the pan and cook over low heat for 8–10 minutes, or until the eggs are done to your liking.

4 Sprinkle with the cilantro and serve.

STATISTICS PER SERVING:

Energy 370cals/1,542kJ

Carbohydrate 19g

Sugar 16g

Fiber 4g

Fat 19g
Saturated fat 4.5g

Sodium 0.28g

● ● ○ GI

● ● ○ CALORIES

● ○ ○ SATURATED FAT

● ● ○ SODIUM

SHREDDED PORK AND SPRING ONION WRAP

SERVES 4   **PREP** 10 MINS   **COOK** 2 HOURS

Succulent shredded pork with a Cajun-style coating.

12oz (350g) pork tenderloin, trimmed
  of fat and sinew
2 bunches spring onions,
  sliced lengthwise
4-8 Turkish flatbreads

For the marinade
1 medium onion, peeled and
  quartered

1 tsp freshly ground black pepper
½ tsp salt
1 scotch bonnet chilli, seeded
1 tsp allspice
½ tsp paprika
2 ripe peaches, pitted and quartered
2 cloves garlic, peeled and
  roughly chopped

1 Preheat the oven to 300°F (150°C). Put the marinade ingredients into a blender and process to a smooth paste. Deeply slash the pork and liberally rub all over with the marinade. Place the pork in a roasting pan and cover with any remaining marinade. Cover loosely with foil and roast for 2 hours, basting occasionally.

2 Shred the pork using two forks and toss in any remaining cooking juices. Arrange on flatbreads, each with a liberal handful of spring onions, roll or fold, and serve.

STATISTICS PER SERVING:

Energy 388cals/1,440kJ

Carbohydrate 50g

Sugar 11g

Fiber 4g

Fat 6g
Saturated fat 2g

Sodium 0.6g

○○ GI

○○ CALORIES

○○ SATURATED FAT

○○ SODIUM

MIXED BEAN BURGER

SERVES 4   **PREP** 10 MINS   **COOK** 15 MINS   **FREEZE** 3 MONTHS
PLUS CHILLING

Vegetarian burgers with a hint of Indian spice.

1 red onion, roughly chopped
2 garlic cloves, finely chopped
1 green chile, seeded and
  roughly chopped
pinch of garam masala
handful of fresh cilantro

2 x 14oz cans of mixed beans, drained
4½oz (125g) mushrooms, grated
salt and freshly ground black pepper
2 tbsp fresh breadcrumbs
1–2 eggs, lightly beaten
2 tbsp sunflower oil

1 Place the onion, garlic, chile, garam masala, cilantro, beans, and mushrooms in a food processor and pulse until well combined, but do not overblend and let it become mushy.

2 Season well with salt and black pepper then add in the breadcrumbs and a little of the egg and pulse until it all binds together but is neither too wet nor too dry—add a little more egg if needed. Shape into 8 patties, arrange on a plate and transfer to the refrigerator for 20 minutes to firm up.

3 Heat the oil in a non-stick frying pan and cook a few burgers at a time for 6–7 minutes or until the underside starts to brown. Turn over the burgers using a spatula and cook the other side for the same amount of time, adding more oil if needed. You could serve these in wholemeal bread rolls, each with a small quantity of tomato salad.

STATISTICS PER SERVING:

Energy 250cals/1,061kJ

Carbohydrate 37g

Sugar 4g

Fiber 12g

Fat 5g

Saturated fat 1g

Sodium 0.12g

FALAFEL

SERVES 4   **PREP** 25 MINS   **COOK** 15 MINS
PLUS SOAKING
PLUS CHLLING

Based on chickpeas, these tasty and substantial bites are a Middle Eastern classic.

● ○ ○   GI

● ○ ○   CALORIES

● ○ ○   SATURATED FAT

● ● ○   SODIUM

8oz (225g) dried chickpeas, soaked
  overnight in cold water
1 tbsp tahini
1 garlic clove, crushed
1 tsp salt
1 tsp ground cumin

1 tsp turmeric
1 tsp ground coriander
½ tsp cayenne pepper
2 tbsp finely chopped parsley
juice of 1 small lemon
vegetable oil, for frying

1 Drain the soaked chickpeas and place them in a food processor with the rest of the ingredients. Process until finely chopped but not puréed.

2 Transfer the mixture to a bowl and set it aside for at least 30 minutes (and up to 8 hours), covered in the refrigerator.

3 Wet your hands and shape the mixture into 12 balls. Press the tops down slightly to flatten.

4 Heat 2in (5cm) of oil in a deep pan or wok. Fry the balls in batches for 3–4 minutes, or until lightly golden. Drain on paper towels and serve. A simple green salad makes a good accompaniment.

STATISTICS PER SERVING:

Energy 277cals/1,161kJ

Carbohydrate 30g

Sugar 1.5g

Fiber 6g

Fat 13.5g

Saturated fat 1.5g

Sodium 0.4g

LIGHT LUNCHES AND SALADS   101

CHICKEN TOSTADA WITH AVOCADO SALSA

SERVES 4   **PREP** 15 MINS   **COOK** 50 MINS

A tasty and filling lunch or supper dish that is full of flavor and high in dietary fiber.

GUIDELINES PER SERVING:

●●○ GI

●●● CALORIES

●●○ SATURATED FAT

●●○ SODIUM

6 tomatoes, skinned, quartered, and seeds removed
1 large red onion, peeled and sliced into thin wedges
1 small red pepper, seeded and roughly chopped
3 cloves of garlic, unpeeled
1 red chile, seeded
3 tbsp olive oil
salt and freshly ground black pepper
14oz (400g) cooked chicken, shredded

14½oz (415g) can mixed beans, rinsed and drained
8 wholemeal flour tortillas

For the salsa
6 tomatoes, seeds removed and flesh diced
2 small ripe avocado, peeled, stones removed, and flesh diced
1 small red onion, finely chopped
3 tbsp chopped fresh cilantro
juice of 1 lime

1 Preheat the oven to 400°F (200°C). Place the tomatoes, onions, red pepper, garlic, and chile in a roasting pan, drizzle with oil, and bake for 20–30 minutes or until soft and slightly charred. Squeeze the garlic cloves from their skins and place in a food processor along with the other cooked vegetables and process until smooth. Season to taste with salt and black pepper.

2 Place the drained mixed beans in a large saucepan and cook over low heat for 2 minutes. Add the vegetable sauce, stir in the chicken, and cook for a further 2 minutes, stirring occasionally.

3 To make the salsa, mix together the tomatoes, avocado, onion, cilantro and lime juice in a bowl, and season to taste.

4 Heat the tortillas according to the packet instructions. To serve, spoon a little of the chicken mixture into each tortilla, fold, and serve with the salsa.

STATISTICS PER SERVING:

Energy 745cals/3,140kJ

Carbohydrate 90g

Sugar 17g

Fiber 13g

Fat 24g
Saturated fat 3.5g

Sodium 0.4g

● ○ ○ GI

● ● ○ CALORIES

● ● ○ SATURATED FAT

● ● ○ SODIUM

SALMON BURGERS

SERVES 6   **PREP** 10 MINS   **COOK** 10 MINS   **FREEZE** 1 MONTH
PLUS CHILLING

These tasty burgers are heavy on the fish and have no added potato—a luxurious version of the humble fishcake.

1lb 9oz (700g) salmon filets, skinned and cut into chunks
4oz (125g) breadcrumbs
bunch of spring onions, trimmed and roughly chopped

2 tsp capers, drained and rinsed
1¾oz (50g) flat-leaf parsley
salt and freshly ground black pepper
1 egg
2 tbsp sunflower oil

1 Put the salmon, breadcrumbs, spring onions, capers, and parsley into a food processor or blender. Pulse until well combined. Season with salt and black pepper, and then pulse to mix.

2 Add the egg to the food processor and pulse again so that the mixture is evenly combined. Divide the mixture into six and, one at a time, roll each lump into a ball and then pat flat to shape into a burger. Put the burgers on a plate and place in the refrigerator to firm up for 20 minutes.

3 Heat the oil in a large, nonstick frying pan and add the burgers. Cook for 3–4 minutes, or until the underside begins to turn golden, then flip them over and cook the other side for the same length of time.

COOK'S TIP
You can cook the burgers in the oven if you wish. Preheat the oven to 400°F (200°C), place the burgers in a lightly oiled roasting pan and cook for 15-20 minutes or until golden and cooked through.

STATISTICS PER SERVING:

Energy 506cals/2,118kJ

Carbohydrate 26g

Sugar 3g

Fiber 1g

Fat 27g

Saturated fat 4g

Sodium 0.4g

SHRIMP CAKES WITH MANGO SALSA

MAKES 9   **PREP** 10 MINS PLUS CHILLING   **COOK** 20 MINS   **FREEZE** 1 MONTH (SHRIMP CAKES)

Small bites with bags of flavor, complemented by a fresh and juicy mango salsa.

GUIDELINES PER CAKE:

◉○○ GI
◉○○ CALORIES
◉○○ SATURATED FAT
◉○○ SODIUM

2in (2.5cm) piece of fresh ginger root, roughly chopped
2 garlic cloves
1 red chile, halved and seeded
1 stalk lemongrass, trimmed and tough outer leaves removed
salt and freshly ground black pepper
9oz (250g) cooked shrimp

1 small egg, beaten
1–2 tbsp sunflower oil

For the mango salsa
1 mango, diced
3 spring onions, finely diced
1 tbsp finely chopped fresh cilantro
1 tsp rice vinegar

1 First, make the mango salsa. Put all the ingredients in a bowl and mix, then set aside for the flavors to develop.

2 Put the ginger, garlic, chile, and lemongrass in a food processor or blender and pulse until finely chopped. Add a pinch of salt and some black pepper and process again. Add the shrimp and pulse until the shrimp are chopped but not mushy, then taste the mixture and adjust the seasoning if needed. Add a little of the egg and process so the mixture binds together; add more of the egg if needed.

3 Using your hands to scoop up the mixture, roll it into nine balls and pat them flat into cakes. Sit them on a plate and place in the refrigerator for 30 minutes to firm up a little. The mixture will be wet and quite delicate.

4 When ready to cook, heat the oil in a nonstick frying pan and fry the cakes for a minute or so until the underside begins to crisp a little. Then, using a spatula, carefully turn the cakes over and cook the other side for a couple of minutes or until golden. Serve with the mango salsa.

STATISTICS PER CAKE:

Energy 57cals/283kJ

Carbohydrate 4g

Sugar 3g

Fiber 0.6g

Fat 2g
Saturated fat 0.4g

Sodium 0.16g

⬤⬤◯ GI

⬤◯◯ CALORIES

⬤◯◯ SATURATED FAT

⬤◯◯ SODIUM

POTATO AND THYME RÖSTI WITH MUSHROOMS

SERVES 4   **PREP** 15 MINS   **COOK** 25 MINS

This traditional Swiss favorite pleases everyone.

1¼lb (550g) potatoes (use large
  waxy ones), unpeeled
salt and freshly ground black pepper
few stems of fresh thyme, leaves only
1 onion, finely chopped

2 tbsp sunflower oil
5½oz (150g) cremini mushrooms,
  sliced
2 garlic cloves, finely chopped

1 Boil the potatoes in a large pan of salted water for 10–15 minutes until just beginning to soften. Remove with a slotted spoon and set aside until cool enough to handle. Grate the potatoes into a bowl and season with plenty of salt and black pepper. Add the thyme and onion, and stir gently.

2 Put 1 tablespoon of the oil into a medium-sized, nonstick frying pan and add the potato mixture, pressing it down so that it becomes a cake—it should be about ½in (1cm) thick. Cook over low heat for 10–12 minutes until the underside begins to turn golden and form a crust. Invert the cake onto a large plate and return it to the pan to cook the other side until golden. (Alternatively, if the handle of the pan is heatproof, you could finish it off in an oven preheated to a medium heat.)

3 Meanwhile, heat the remaining oil in another frying pan, add the mushrooms and cook for 5 minutes or until they begin to release their juices. Add the garlic and cook for a further couple of minutes, then season to taste. Using a spatula, slide the rösti out of the pan and onto a serving plate. Top with the mushrooms and slice the rösti to serve.

COOK'S TIP
You can use grated raw potato if you prefer, but do make sure you squeeze out all the water or else the rösti will become wet. You will also need to use a lower heat and cook it for longer, otherwise the inside will not cook.

STATISTICS PER SERVING:

Energy 166cals/699kJ

Carbohydrate 26g

Sugar 2g

Fiber 2.6g

Fat 6g
Saturated fat 0.7g

Sodium trace

SWEET POTATOES WITH A SMOKY TOMATO FILLING

SERVES 2   **PREP** 5 MINS   **COOK** 40 MINS

A tasty and filling light lunch, which is low in fat and salt.

4 sweet potatoes, unpeeled
2 tbsp olive oil
1 small red onion, finely chopped
1 small red pepper, seeded and diced
½ red chile, seeded and
  finely chopped

8oz (225g) cherry tomatoes, halved
5oz (150g) corn, defrosted
  if frozen
½ tsp smoked sweet paprika
salt and freshly ground black pepper

1 Preheat the oven to 350°F (180°C). Pierce the sweet potatoes in several places and put in the oven for 40 minutes or until cooked.

2 Meanwhile, heat the oil in a frying pan, add the onion and cook for 1–2 minutes. Stir in the red pepper and chile; cook for a further 1–2 minutes or until the pepper is starting to soften. Add the cherry tomatoes, corn, and paprika. Season to taste with salt and black pepper, and cook for a further 1–2 minutes.

3 Slice the potatoes in half and spoon the tomato mixture over them.

GUIDELINES PER SERVING:

GI
CALORIES
SATURATED FAT
SODIUM

STATISTICS PER SERVING:

Energy 289cals/1,226kJ

Carbohydrate 55g

Sugar 17g

Fiber 7g

Fat 7g

Saturated fat 1g

Sodium 0.08g

SWEET POTATO CAKES

SERVES 4   **PREP** 10 MINS   **COOK** 20 MINS   **FREEZE** 1 MONTH

Spring onion adds a crunchy texture to these cakes.

1lb 2oz (500g) cooked sweet potato, mashed
2in (5cm) piece of fresh ginger, peeled and grated
bunch of spring onions, finely chopped
pinch of freshly grated nutmeg
2 eggs, lightly beaten
flour for dusting
3-4 tbsp polenta
vegetable oil for shallow frying
lime wedges, to serve

1 Add the sweet potato to a large bowl then add the ginger, spring onions, and nutmeg; then add a little of the egg, a drop at time, reserving plenty for coating, until the mixture binds together.

2 Season well with salt and black pepper, then scoop up a handful of the mixture, roll into a ball, then flatten out into a cake. Repeat until all the mixture is used.

3 Dust the cakes in flour, dip in the reserved egg, then lightly coat with polenta. Heat the oil in a non-stick frying pan and add the cakes a couple at a time. Cook for 2–3 minutes or until the underside turns golden, then carefully flip and cook for a further 2–3 minutes or until evenly golden brown. Serve with lime wedges for squeezing over.

COOK'S TIP

To cook the sweet potatoes, you could bake or microwave them, then scoop out the insides and mash with a fork. Alternatively, peel them, cut into chunks, boil, and drain before mashing.

STATISTICS PER SERVING:

Energy 272cals/1,140kJ

Carbohydrate 36g

Sugar 16g

Fiber 3.5g

Fat 12g

Saturated fat 2g

Sodium 0.08g

● ○ ○ GI

● ○ ○ CALORIES

● ○ ○ SATURATED FAT

● ● ○ SODIUM

FETA AND ZUCCHINI CAKES

SERVES 4 **PREP** 15 MINS **COOK** 10 MINS **FREEZE** 1 MONTH
PLUS DRAINING
PLUS CHILLING

These moreish light and tasty cakes are perfect for spring.

1¼lb (550g) zucchini, grated
salt, for sprinkling
4½oz (125g) feta cheese, crumbled
freshly ground black pepper

pinch of paprika
1 egg, lightly beaten
1 tbsp flour, plus extra for dusting
2 tbsp olive oil

1 Add the zucchini to a colander, sprinkle with salt and leave to drain
for 20 minutes (you need as much water as possible to drain away), then
squeeze out any remaining moisture.

2 Put the zucchini into a bowl with the feta, season with black pepper and
paprika and stir. Add the egg and flour and stir until well combined.

3 Scoop up the zucchini and feta mixture, a tablespoon at a time, and pat
into cakes. Place them on a plate of flour and turn once to lightly coat. Place
in the refrigerator for 20 minutes to firm up. Heat a little of the olive oil in a
frying pan and cook the cakes, two at a time, adding the rest of the oil as
required, for a couple of minutes each side or until golden and crispy.

COOK'S TIP
For ease, you could grate your zucchini using the food processor.

Energy 160cals/657kJ

Carbohydrate 5g

Sugar 2.5g

Fiber 1.5g

Fat 10g
Saturated fat 3g

Sodium 0.4g

CAPONATA

This has a wonderful sweet–sour contrast and can be eaten hot or cold.

3 tbsp olive oil
2 medium eggplants, cut into
  bite-sized chunks
1 onion, finely chopped
3 celery stalks, roughly chopped
salt and freshly ground black pepper
14oz can of chopped tomatoes

handful of green olives, pitted
  and chopped
2 tbsp capers, drained and rinsed
2 tbsp red wine vinegar
handful of fresh basil, torn
handful of pine nuts, toasted

1 Heat 2 tablespoons of the oil in a large pan, add the eggplant, and cook—working in batches if necessary—for 6–8 minutes or until it starts to turn golden brown, adding more oil if needed. Remove with a slotted spoon and set aside.

2 Add the remaining oil to the same pan and heat for a minute. Add the onion and celery and season with salt and black pepper. Cook for 5 minutes or until the onion begins to soften, then add the tomatoes, olives, and capers and simmer gently for 15 minutes.

3 Add the vinegar and increase the heat to bring the mixture to a boil. Cook for a minute or so until the smell of the vinegar disappears, then stir in the cooked eggplant and the basil. Stir in most of the pine nuts, saving a few for the top. Spoon into a serving dish and scatter with the reserved pine nuts.

COOK'S TIP
Choose young eggplants if possible, as older ones tend to be more bitter and may need degorging–sprinkling with salt to draw out moisture and bitterness.

STATISTICS PER SERVING:

Energy 189cals/787kJ

Carbohydrate 11g

Sugar 9g

Fiber 6g

Fat 15g

Saturated fat 2g

Sodium 0.32g

OVEN-BAKED RED PEPPER AND TOMATO FRITTATA

GUIDELINES PER SERVING:

⬤◯◯ GI
⬤⬤◯ CALORIES
⬤⬤◯ SATURATED FAT
⬤◯◯ SODIUM

SERVES 2   **PREP** 15 MINS   **COOK** 30 MINS

An easy way to cook this simple vegetable and egg dish.

1 tbsp olive oil
1 onion, finely chopped
2 red peppers, seeded and finely
  chopped or sliced
salt and freshly ground black pepper
pinch of paprika

4 tomatoes, skinned, seeded,
  and flesh chopped
scant 1oz (25g) bunch of chives,
  finely chopped
4 large eggs, lightly beaten

1 Preheat the oven to 350°F (180°C). Heat the oil in a medium non-stick frying pan, add the onion and red peppers, and cook for 5–8 minutes until soft. Season with salt and pepper, add the paprika, and stir.

2 Transfer the cooked vegetables to a heatproof dish and stir in the tomatoes and chives. Add the eggs and mix gently, then place in the oven for 20–30 minutes until risen and golden.

3 Allow to cool for a few minutes before serving. A simple green salad makes a good accompaniment.

COOK'S TIP
Swap herbs to suit the seasons and add a pinch of red pepper flakes to heat things up.

STATISTICS PER SERVING:

Energy 336cals/1,402kJ

Carbohydrate 22g

Sugar 19g

Fiber 0.5g

Fat 20g
Saturated fat 5g

Sodium 0.12g

● ○ ○ GI

● ● ○ CALORIES

● ● ○ SATURATED FAT

● ○ ○ SODIUM

TORTILLA

SERVES 4   **PREP** 15 MINS   **COOK** 45 MINS

This variation of a traditional thick Spanish omelet includes broccoli and peas as well as potatoes.

4oz (115g) fresh or frozen peas
4oz (115g) broccoli florets
4 tbsp olive oil
12oz (350g) floury potatoes, such as Russet, peeled and cut into ¾in (2cm) cubes

2 small red onions, finely chopped
6 eggs, beaten
salt and freshly ground black pepper

1 Bring a large saucepan of lightly salted water to a boil over high heat. Add the peas and boil for 5 minutes, or until just tender. Use a slotted spoon to transfer the peas to a bowl of cold water. Return the pan to a boil, add the broccoli, and boil for 4 minutes or until just tender. Remove the florets and add to the peas to cool, then drain both vegetables well, and set aside.

2 Heat 3 tbsp of the oil in a non-stick frying pan over medium heat. Add the potatoes and onions, and cook for 10–15 minutes, stirring often, or until the potatoes are tender.

3 Beat the eggs in a large bowl, and season with salt and pepper, then use a slotted spoon to transfer the potatoes and onions to the eggs. Add the peas and broccoli and gently stir. Discard the excess oil from the pan and remove any crispy bits stuck to the bottom.

4 Heat the remaining oil in the pan over high heat. Add the egg mixture, immediately reduce the heat to low, and smooth the surface. Leave to cook for 20–25 minutes, or until the top of the omelet begins to set and the base is golden brown.

5 Carefully slide the tortilla on to a plate, place a second plate on top and invert so that the cooked side is on top. Slide the tortilla back into the pan and cook for 5 minutes, until both sides are golden brown and set. Remove from the heat and leave to set for at least 5 minutes. Serve warm or cooled, cut into wedges.

STATISTICS PER SERVING:

Energy 333cals/1,388kJ

Carbohydrate 20g

Sugar 3g

Fiber 4g

Fat 22g

Saturated fat 4g

Sodium 0.16g

PEAS WITH HAM

SERVES 4   **PREP** 5 MINS   **COOK** 15 MINS

Guisantes con jamón is a classic tapas dish with delicious sweet and savory flavors.

GUIDELINES PER SERVING:

⬤◯◯ GI

⬤◯◯ CALORIES

⬤◯◯ SATURATED FAT

⬤⬤◯ SODIUM

2 tbsp olive oil
1 onion, finely diced
7oz (200g) Serrano ham, diced
7fl oz (200ml) carton sieved tomatoes
1 tsp sweet paprika

1lb 2oz (500g) peas
1 garlic clove, crushed
1 tbsp finely chopped parsley
5fl oz (150ml) dry white wine
salt and freshly ground black pepper

1 Heat the oil in a frying pan and add the onion. Fry for 5 minutes, stirring frequently, until soft.

2 Increase the heat, add the ham and fry until it begins to brown, then add the tomatoes and sweet paprika. Bring to boiling point, reduce the heat, and simmer for 3 minutes, stirring frequently. Stir in the peas.

3 Mix together the garlic and chopped parsley, then stir in the wine. Pour this mixture into the pan, and season to taste with salt and pepper. Simmer for 5 minutes, then transfer to a heated serving dish and serve hot.

STATISTICS PER SERVING:

Energy	301cals/1,253kJ
Carbohydrate	20g
Sugar	4g
Fiber	6.5g
Fat	12g
Saturated fat	3.5g
Sodium	0.6g

PAN FRIED SHRIMP WITH LEMON GRASS AND GINGER

SERVES 2   **PREP** 10 MINS   **COOK** 5 MINS

A quick and simple dish with Thai-inspired flavors.

1 stalk of lemon grass, trimmed, tough outer skin removed, and finely chopped

2in (5cm) piece of fresh ginger, peeled and finely chopped

2 tsp fish sauce

pinch of palm sugar or Demerara sugar

1 tsp dried red pepper flakes

juice of 1 lime

9oz (250g) large raw shrimp, peeled, tails intact

2 tsp sunflower oil

handful of fresh cilantro leaves, finely chopped

1 tbsp dry roasted peanuts, finely chopped

lime or lemon wedges, to serve

1 Mix together the lemon grass, ginger, fish sauce, sugar, red pepper flakes, and lime juice, then add the shrimp and stir to coat.

2 Heat the sunflower oil in a wok, then use a slotted spoon to transfer the shrimp to the hot oil and stir fry for 3–5 minutes until the shrimp turn pink, then transfer them to a serving dish.

3 Pour the marinade mixture into the wok, heat, and allow to bubble for 1–2 minutes, then pour it over the shrimp. Sprinkle with the cilantro and peanuts and serve with wedges of lime or lemon to squeeze over. A simple tomato salad makes a good accompaniment for this dish.

STATISTICS PER SERVING:

Energy 171cals/717kJ

Carbohydrate 2g

Sugar 1.7g

Fiber 0.5g

Fat 7g

Saturated fat 1.2g

Sodium 0.6g

● ○ ○ GI

● ● ○ CALORIES

● ○ ○ SATURATED FAT

● ● ○ SODIUM

HOT AND SOUR NOODLE SALAD WITH TOFU

SERVES 4   **PREP** 25 MINS   **COOK** 20 MINS

An easy, Asian-style salad. Tofu, which is made from soy beans, is a good source of protein and calcium.

2 tbsp sunflower oil
7oz (200g) firm tofu, cut into
  ½ x 1¼in (1 x 3cm) cubes
1 tbsp soy sauce
9oz (250g) medium rice noodles
2 red peppers, seeded and cut
  into strips
1 white cabbage, shredded
1 red chile, seeded and cut
  into strips
2 tbsp fresh cilantro leaves, roughly
  chopped

3 spring onions, trimmed and
  finely chopped

For the dressing
3 tbsp rice vinegar
1 tbsp soy sauce
1in (2.5cm) piece of fresh ginger,
  finely chopped
juice of 1 lime
salt and freshly ground black pepper

1 First, make the dressing. Put all the ingredients in a small bowl and whisk together. Season with a little salt and black pepper to taste. Set aside.

2 Put 1 tablespoon of the oil in a wok and, when hot, add half of the tofu and half of the soy sauce (it is easiest to cook the tofu in batches). Stir-fry for 5–10 minutes (depending on the type of tofu being used) until golden all over. Add the remaining 1 tablespoon of oil and fry the rest of the tofu, with the other half of the soy sauce, in the same way. Set aside on a plate covered with paper towels.

3 Put the rice noodles in a large bowl and cover with boiling water. Leave for a few minutes, or according to the instructions on the package, until soft. Drain well.

4 Put the peppers, cabbage, and chile in a large, shallow serving dish. Top with the drained noodles, and then add the dressing and toss to coat. Arrange the tofu on top and sprinkle with the cilantro and spring onions.

STATISTICS PER SERVING:

Energy 381cals/1,590kJ

Carbohydrate 63g

Sugar 10g

Fiber 3g

Fat 9g

Saturated fat 1g

Sodium 0.56g

FARFALLE WITH FRESH TOMATOES AND AVOCADO

GUIDELINES PER SERVING:

GI

CALORIES

SATURATED FAT

SODIUM

SERVES 4 **PREP** 10 MINS **COOK** 15 MINS

A really simple dish—a fresh-tasting no-cook sauce tossed
with pasta bows.

5 tomatoes, diced
1 avocado, halved, stoned
  and diced
juice of 1 lemon

salt and freshly ground black pepper
3 tbsp olive oil
12oz (350g) dried farfalle bows
2½oz (75g) arugula leaves

1 Place the tomatoes in a bowl with the avocado and lemon juice and
season well with salt and pepper. Gently stir to combine, then add the
olive oil and stir again. Set aside to allow the flavors to develop.

2 Meanwhile, cook the pasta in a large pan of boiling salted water for 10–12
minutes or according to packet instructions. Drain, return to the pan, and
stir in the tomato mixture. Add the arugula and serve immediately.

STATISTICS PER SERVING:

Energy 387cals/1,628kJ

Carbohydrate 52g

Sugar 5.5g

Fiber 4.5g

Fat 17g

Saturated fat 3g

Sodium trace

● ● ○ GI

● ○ ○ CALORIES

● ○ ○ SATURATED FAT

● ● ○ SODIUM

LEMON, GARLIC, AND PARSLEY LINGUINE

SERVES 4 **PREP** 5 MINS **COOK** 10 MINS

An instant meal when there is little in the fridge: you just need fresh parsley, garlic, olive oil, and lemon to transform pasta into something special.

12oz (350g) linguine
3 tbsp olive oil
2 garlic cloves, finely chopped
juice of 1 lemon and zest of ½ lemon

handful of fresh flat-leaf parsley, finely chopped
pinch of red pepper flakes (optional)
salt and freshly ground black pepper

1 Add the linguine to a large pan of salted boiling water and cook for 8–10 minutes or according to the instructions on the package. Drain, then return to the pan with a little of the cooking water and toss together.

2 While the pasta is cooking, heat the oil in a frying pan, add the garlic and cook on very low heat, being very careful not to burn the garlic. Cook for about 1 minute, then add the lemon zest and juice and cook for a couple more minutes.

3 Stir in the parsley and red pepper flakes, if using. Season with salt and black pepper and then add the mixture to the pasta and toss to coat. A tomato and basil salad would work well with this dish.

STATISTICS PER SERVING:

Energy 350cals/1,477kJ

Carbohydrate 65g

Sugar 3g

Fiber 2.5g

Fat 7g
Saturated fat 1g

Sodium trace

AVOCADO AND BROWN RICE SALAD

SERVES 4   **PREP** 15 MINS   **COOK** 35 MINS

The creamy texture of avocado complements brown rice; this salad also provides vitamins B6 and E, and heart-friendly essential fats.

6oz (175g) brown basmati rice
10oz (300g) skinless roast
  chicken, diced
2 ripe avocados, peeled, stoned
  and diced
6 spring onions, finely sliced
9oz (250g) cherry tomatoes,
  cut in half

pinch of red pepper flakes (optional)
salt and freshly ground black pepper

For the dressing
3 tbsp olive oil
1 tbsp balsamic vinegar
1 small garlic clove, crushed

1 Cook the rice in a pan of boiling water according to the instructions on the package. Once the rice is cooked, drain well and allow to cool.

2 To make the dressing, combine the oil, vinegar, and garlic.

3 Transfer the rice to a serving bowl, stir in the chicken, avocado, spring onions, tomatoes, and red pepper flakes, if using. Pour the dressing over the salad and serve immediately.

GUIDELINES PER SERVING:

●○○ GI
●●○ CALORIES
●●○ SATURATED FAT
●○○ SODIUM

STATISTICS PER SERVING:

Energy 511cals/2,126kJ

Carbohydrate 40g

Sugar 4g

Fiber 3.5g

Fat 26g
Saturated fat 5g

Sodium 0.08g

◖◖◯ GI

◖◯◯ CALORIES

◖◯◯ SATURATED FAT

◖◯◯ SODIUM

TABBOULEH

SERVES 4   **PREP** 20 MINS

This Lebanese speciality of parsley, mint, tomatoes, and bulgur is refreshing all year-round.

4oz (115g) bulgur wheat
juice of 2 lemons
2½fl oz (75ml) extra virgin olive oil
freshly ground black pepper
8oz (225g) flat-leaf parsley, coarse
  stalks discarded

2½oz (75g) mint leaves, coarse
  stalks discarded
4 spring onions, finely chopped
2 large tomatoes, seeded
  and diced
1 head of Romaine lettuce

1 Put the bulgur wheat in a large bowl, pour over cold water to just cover, and leave to stand for 15 minutes, or until the wheat has absorbed all the water and the grains have swollen.

2 Add the lemon juice and olive oil to the wheat, season to taste with pepper, and stir to mix.

3 Just before serving, finely chop the parsley and mint. Mix the parsley, mint, spring onions, and tomatoes into the wheat.

4 Arrange the lettuce leaves on a serving plate and spoon the salad into the leaves to serve.

STATISTICS PER SERVING:

Energy 241cals/1,000kJ

Carbohydrate 25g

Sugar 3g

Fiber 1g

Fat 14.5g

Saturated fat 2g

Sodium trace

QUINOA TABBOULEH

SERVES 4   **PREP** 10 MINS   **COOK** 20 MINS

In this healthy salad, the quinoa has a creamy, nutty taste with a slight crunch once it is cooked.

GUIDELINES PER SERVING:

●○○ GI
●○○ CALORIES
●○○ SATURATED FAT
●●○ SODIUM

7oz (200g) quinoa
½ tsp salt
juice of 1 large lemon
9fl oz (125ml) olive oil
1 large cucumber, peeled, seeded and chopped
1 large red onion, chopped

1½oz (45g) chopped parsley
1½oz (45g) chopped mint
4oz (115g) reduced-fat feta cheese, crumbled
3½oz (100g) Kalamata olives, pitted
salt and freshly ground black pepper

1 Rinse the quinoa thoroughly in a fine mesh strainer. Drain and place it in a heavy pan. Heat, stirring constantly until the grains separate and begin to brown.

2 Add 1¼ pint (600ml) water and the salt and bring to a boil, stirring. Reduce the heat and cook for 15 minutes, or until the liquid is absorbed. Transfer to a bowl and set aside to cool.

3 Whisk together the lemon juice and 1 tbsp of the oil in a small bowl. Set aside.

4 Place the remaining oil, cucumber, onion, parsley, and mint in a separate, larger bowl. Add the quinoa and the lemon and oil dressing and toss. Sprinkle with the feta cheese and olives. Season to taste with salt and pepper.

STATISTICS PER SERVING:

Energy 260cals/1,096kJ

Carbohydrate 32g

Sugar 6g

Fiber 1.5g

Fat 9g

Saturated fat 2.5g

Sodium 0.52g

● ● ○ GI

● ● ○ CALORIES

● ○ ○ SATURATED FAT

● ○ ○ SODIUM

SPICED BULGUR WHEAT WITH FEATA AND A FRUITY SALSA

SERVES 4   **PREP** 15 MINS   **COOK** 10 MINS

A tasty grain mixed with salty feta and fresh beans.

10oz (280g) bulgur wheat
10fl oz (300ml) hot vegetable stock
5½oz (150g) fine green beans,
  chopped into ½in (1cm) pieces
salt and freshly ground black pepper
4½oz (125g) reduced fat Feta
  cheese, crumbled

For the salsa
½ fresh pineapple, diced
1 mango, diced
juice of ½–1 lime
1 red chile, seeded and
  finely chopped

1 First, make the salsa: mix all the ingredients together in a small bowl and leave to sit for a while to allow the flavors to develop.

2 Put the bulgur wheat into a large heatproof bowl and pour over the stock; it should just cover it—if not, add a little extra hot water. Allow to sit for 8–10 minutes then fluff up with a fork, separating the grains.

3 Add the beans to a pan of salted boiling water and cook for 3–5 minutes until they just soften but still have a bite to them. Drain and stir into the bulgur wheat. Season well with salt and pepper, then stir in the Feta. Add a spoonful of the fruity salsa on the side and serve. You can enjoy this on its own, with a few salad leaves, or for a more substantial meal you could add a piece of grilled chicken.

STATISTICS PER SERVING:

Energy 370cals/1,547kJ

Carbohydrate 70g

Sugar 16g

Fiber 2.5g

Fat 4g

Saturated fat 2g

Sodium 0.2g

COOK'S TIP
Bulgur wheat needs lot of flavor added to it otherwise it can be bland, so make sure you use a well-flavoured stock.

THREE-GRAIN SALAD

SERVES 6   **PREP** 5 MINS   **COOK** 35 MINS

A real good-for-you, wholesome salad mix. The mixture of grains is rich in B-vitamins, minerals, and fiber.

5½oz (150g) brown rice
4½oz (125g) bulgur wheat
125g (4½oz) couscous
4 tomatoes, diced
½ cucumber, peeled and diced

1¾oz (50g) fresh mint, finely chopped
1¾oz (50g) fresh parsley, finely chopped
1oz (30g) raisins
salt and freshly ground black pepper

1 Cook the rice in a pan of salted water for about 35 minutes until tender, or follow the instructions on the package. Drain and set aside to cool.

2 Put the bulgur wheat into a bowl and pour boiling water over it until it is just covered. Leave to stand for 5 minutes while you prepare the couscous in another bowl in the same way; leave this also for 5 minutes. Fluff up both the grains with a fork and then mix them together with the rice.

3 Stir the tomatoes, cucumber, herbs, and raisins into the grain mixture. Taste and then season if needed.

STATISTICS PER SERVING:

Energy 381cals/1,385kJ

Carbohydrate 73g

Sugar 6g

Fiber 2g

Fat 2g

Saturated fat 0.5g

Sodium trace

BULGUR WHEAT WITH EGGPLANT AND POMEGRANATE

GUIDELINES PER SERVING:

●●○ GI
●●○ CALORIES
●○○ SATURATED FAT
●○○ SODIUM

SERVES 4   **PREP** 5 MINS   **COOK** 25 MINS

A nutritious dish, full of color and texture. The nuts and seeds add a crunch as well as a vitamin and mineral boost.

2 tbsp olive oil
2 eggplants, chopped into
  bite-sized pieces
pinch of paprika
9½oz (275g) bulgur wheat

10fl oz (300ml) hot vegetable stock
salt and freshly ground black pepper
3oz (75g) hazelnuts, toasted
3oz (75g) pomegranate seeds

1 Put half the oil in a large frying pan set over low heat, and toss the eggplant in the oil. Cook on a fairly high heat for 10–15 minutes or until the eggplant starts to turn golden, adding the remaining oil when needed (you may need to add extra oil as the eggplant will soak it up quickly). Add the paprika, toss, and cook for a few more minutes. Remove from the heat and set aside.

2 Put the bulgur wheat into a large bowl and pour the stock over it so that it is just covered; use extra stock if needed. Cover with plastic wrap and leave for 8–10 minutes, then fluff up with a fork to separate the grains.

3 Stir the bulgur wheat into the pan with the eggplant and mix well. Taste and season as required. Stir in the hazelnuts and sprinkle with the pomegranate seeds.

COOK'S TIP
Buy pomegranate seeds in a vacuum pack, if available, because they are far easier to use than having to extract them from a fresh pomegranate. However, if you prefer to use a fresh fruit, keep the juice and use it in a salad dressing.

STATISTICS PER SERVING:

Energy 454cals/1,891kJ

Carbohydrate 59g

Sugar 5g

Fiber 4g

Fat 20g
Saturated fat 2g

Sodium 0.16g

● ○ ○ GI

● ● ○ CALORIES

● ○ ○ SATURATED FAT

● ○ ○ SODIUM

CHICKPEA, BULGUR, AND WALNUT SALAD

SERVES 4   **PREP** 10 MINS

A hearty and filling salad with nuts, fruits, and grains.

4½oz (125g) bulgur wheat
salt and freshly ground black pepper
14oz can of chickpeas, drained
  and rinsed
1 sweet crisp apple, cored,
  and diced

handful of walnuts, roughly chopped
scant 1oz (25g) dried cranberries
juice of 1 lemon
½ tsp paprika
2–3 tbsp olive oil

1 Put the bulgur wheat in a bowl and pour over enough hot water to cover. Set aside and leave to stand for about 5 minutes, then fluff up the grains with a with fork. Season with salt and black pepper.

2 Put the chickpeas in another bowl, then add the apple, walnuts, and cranberries and stir to combine.

3 Add the bulgur wheat and lemon juice, sprinkle over the paprika, and stir. Drizzle over a little olive oil and serve.

COOK'S TIP
You could gently warm the chickpeas in a pan, still in their water, as it softens them and helps to bring out their flavor.

STATISTICS PER SERVING:

Energy 331cals/1,379kJ

Carbohydrate 40g

Sugar 4g

Fiber 5g

Fat 11g

Saturated fat 1g

Sodium trace

MOROCCAN TOMATOES, PEPPERS, AND HERBS

SERVES 4   PREP 15 MINS   COOK 30 MINS

A colorful vegetarian dish scented with herbs and spices.

2 onions, sliced
14oz (400g) cherry tomatoes, halved
2 red peppers, seeded and
  roughly chopped
2 green peppers, seeded
  and roughly chopped
pinch of dried oregano
pinch of red pepper flakes

pinch of ground cinnamon
salt and freshly ground black pepper
2 tbsp olive oil
juice of 1 lemon
handful of fresh flat-leaf
  parsley, finely chopped
handful of fresh mint, finely chopped

1 Preheat the oven to 350°F (180°C). Put the onions, tomatoes, and peppers in a roasting pan and sprinkle over the oregano, red pepper flakes, and cinnamon. Season with salt and black pepper. Add 1 tablespoon of the oil and toss together using your hands to coat the vegetables evenly. Roast for 30 minutes or until they are soft and just beginning to char.

2 Remove the vegetables from the oven, drizzle over the remaining olive oil, squeeze over the lemon juice and add the parsley and mint. Toss it all together and serve.

COOK'S TIP
You could use different herbs such as cilantro or dill, if you prefer.

STATISTICS PER SERVING:

Energy 142cals/593kJ

Carbohydrate 18.5g

Sugar 15g

Fiber 4.5g

Fat 7g
Saturated fat 1g

Sodium trace

CARROT AND ORANGE SALAD

GUIDELINES PER SERVING:

● ● ○ GI
● ○ ○ CALORIES
● ○ ○ SATURATED FAT
● ○ ○ SODIUM

SERVES 4   **PREP** 20 MINS

This light, colorful salad is excellent as a refreshing summer lunch.

2 large carrots
2 large navel oranges
1 fennel bulb
3oz (85g) watercress

1 tbsp lemon juice
3 tbsp orange juice
1 tsp clear honey
salt and freshly ground black pepper
2 tsp sesame seeds, lightly toasted

For the dressing
3 tbsp light olive oil
3 tbsp grapeseed oil or sunflower oil

1 Trim and peel the carrots using a vegetable peeler to make thin strips.

2 Cut away the peel and pith from the oranges and divide into segments. Do this over a bowl to catch any juice, and use this in the dressing. Trim the fennel and thinly slice. Remove any yellow leaves or tough stalks from the watercress.

3 Put the carrot, orange, fennel, and watercress into a serving bowl. Whisk together the dressing ingredients and pour over. Toss lightly so all the ingredients are coated in the dressing, and serve.

STATISTICS PER SERVING:

Energy 231cals/957kJ

Carbohydrate 14g

Sugar 13g

Fiber 4g

Fat 18.5g
Saturated fat 2.5g

Sodium trace

● ○ ○   GI

● ● ○   CALORIES

● ● ○   SATURATED FAT

● ○ ○   SODIUM

SQUASH SALAD WITH AVOCADO

SERVES 4   **PREP** 15 MINS   **COOK** 25 MINS

A wonderful combination of sweet squash, peppery leaves, and hot chile.

1 butternut squash, chopped into chunks
1 tbsp olive oil
salt and freshly ground black pepper
1–2 tsp red pepper flakes
9oz (250g) arugula leaves
9oz (250g) spinach leaves
2 ripe avocados, peeled, stoned, and sliced

2 tomatoes, skinned and finely chopped
1 tbsp flat-leaf parsley

For the dressing
3 tbsp olive oil
1 tbsp lemon juice
zest of ½ lemon
½ tsp mayonnaise

1 Preheat the oven to 400°F (200°C). First, make the dressing: put all the ingredients in a small bowl or pitcher and whisk to combine. Season to taste and set aside.

2 Put the butternut squash in a large roasting pan, drizzle with the olive oil and mix well with your hands. Season with salt and black pepper, and sprinkle with the red pepper flakes. Roast in the oven for 20–30 minutes or until soft and beginning to char. Remove from the oven and allow to cool slightly (this will prevent the spinach from wilting).

3 Put the arugula and spinach leaves into a large serving bowl and add the avocado pieces. Top with the squash and toss gently to combine, then scatter the chopped tomatoes on top. When ready to serve, whisk the dressing and drizzle it over the salad. Finish with a sprinkling of parsley.

COOK'S TIP
Squeeze a little lemon juice over the avocados to prevent them from discoloring.

STATISTICS PER SERVING:

Energy 345cals/1,434kJ

Carbohydrate 19g

Sugar 11g

Fiber 8g

Fat 27g

Saturated fat 5g

Sodium 0.12g

BUTTERNUT SQUASH, TOMATO, AND PEARL BARLEY SALAD

SERVES 2   PREP 20 MINS   COOK 40 MINS

Barley is a low-GI food and its deliciously chewy texture works well in salads.

½ small butternut squash, cut into ½in (1cm) cubes (about 10oz/300g prepared weight)
2 tbsp olive oil
salt and freshly ground black pepper
pinch of red pepper flakes

3oz (85g) pearl barley
16fl oz (500ml) vegetable stock
4 plum tomatoes
3 spring onions, finely sliced
2½oz (75g) arugula

1 Preheat the oven to 400ºF (200ºC). Place the squash in a roasting pan and drizzle 1 tablespoon of the oil over it. Season with salt and black pepper and scatter the red pepper flakes on top. Put in the oven and cook for 30–40 minutes until the squash is soft and starting to brown around the edges.

2 Place the barley in a small saucepan and pour in the stock. Bring to a boil and then reduce the heat, cover, and simmer for 20–30 minutes. Add a little more stock or water if needed.

3 Slice the tomatoes into quarters and remove the seeds. Pat the flesh dry with paper towels and place the segments in a clean roasting pan. Drizzle with the remaining oil and cook in the oven for 20–30 minutes until soft and beginning to brown.

4 Allow the barley to cool for 10 minutes, then stir in the squash, tomatoes, spring onions, and arugula.

STATISTICS PER SERVING:

Energy	345cals/1,442kJ
Carbohydrate	28g
Sugar	14g
Fiber	2g
Fat	11g
Saturated fat	2g
Sodium	0.16g

SALMON SALAD WITH RASPBERRY DRESSING

SERVES 4   **PREP** 10 MINS   **COOK** 25 MINS

The fruity dressing adds a bit of glamour to this dish and cuts through the rich salmon.

4 salmon fillets, about 14oz
  (400g) in total
1 tbsp olive oil
few stalks of fresh thyme,
  leaves only
salt and freshly ground black pepper
2½oz (75g) fava beans, fresh (out of
  their pods) or frozen
9oz (250g) baby spinach leaves

scant 1oz (25g) hazelnuts, toasted
  and roughly chopped
2½oz (75g) reduced-fat Feta cheese,
  crumbled

For the dressing
3 tbsp olive oil
1 tbsp raspberry vinegar

1 Preheat the oven to 350ºF (180ºC). To make the dressing, mix the olive oil and raspberry vinegar together, season well with salt and pepper, and leave for the flavors to develop.

2 Arrange the salmon fillets in a roasting pan, drizzle over the olive oil, and scatter the thyme leaves over. Season with salt and pepper and bake in the oven for 15 minutes until the fish is cooked and flakes easily. Remove from the oven and set aside to cool.

3 Cook the fava beans in a pan of boiling salted water for 8 minutes or until tender, then drain, refresh with cold water, and drain again. Arrange the spinach leaves on a platter, flake over the fish and add the fava beans. Sprinkle over the hazelnuts and Feta and drizzle with the dressing when ready to serve.

COOK'S TIP
You can toast hazelnuts in a small frying pan over medium-high heat: cook for 5 minutes, moving them around regularly to prevent burning. Alternatively, roast them in a hot oven for 5 minutes, again keeping a close eye on them.

STATISTICS PER SERVING:

Energy 752cals/3,118kJ

Carbohydrate 6g

Sugar 3g

Fiber 6g

Fat 56g

Saturated fat 10g

Sodium 0.44g

SIMPLE DINNERS—
VEGETARIAN

● ● ○ GI

● ○ ○ CALORIES

● ○ ○ SATURATED FAT

● ● ○ SODIUM

UDON NOODLES WITH SWEET AND SOUR TOFU

SERVES 4   **PREP** 5 MINS   **COOK** 10 MINS

Pickled ginger gives noodles and tofu an unusual twist, complemented by a tangy sweet and sour sauce.

2 tbsp sunflower oil
1 tbsp pickled ginger
9oz (250g) firm tofu, cut into cubes
salt and freshly ground black pepper
10oz (300g) udon noodles

For the sweet and sour sauce
1 tbsp sunflower oil
3 garlic cloves, finely chopped

2in (5cm) piece of fresh ginger root, cut into fine strips
pinch of brown sugar
10 cherry tomatoes, halved
4 spring onions, finely chopped
1 tbsp dark soy sauce
1 tbsp rice vinegar
1 tbsp Chinese cooking wine

1 First, make the sauce. Pour 1 tablespoon of sunflower oil into a wok, then add the garlic and fresh ginger and cook for 1 minute. Add in the sugar and stir for a few seconds, then add the tomatoes and spring onions. Keep stirring for a few more minutes, until the tomatoes start to break down (you can squash them with the back of a fork).

2 Add the soy sauce, vinegar, and cooking wine. Bring to a boil, reduce to a simmer and cook for a couple of minutes.

3 Fry the tofu in 2 tablespoons of sunflower oil until golden. Stir the tofu and pickled ginger into the sweet and sour sauce. Taste, and season with salt and black pepper if required.

4 To finish, stir in the noodles and wait until they soften (about 2 minutes), then serve.

STATISTICS PER SERVING:

Energy 281cals/1,173kJ

Carbohydrate 30g

Sugar 3g

Fiber 0.5g

Fat 13.5g
Saturated fat 2g

Sodium 0.4g

SPAGHETTI WITH ZUCCHINI AND TOASTED ALMONDS

GUIDELINES PER SERVING:

GI

CALORIES

SATURATED FAT

SODIUM

SERVES 4   **PREP** 10 MINS   **COOK** 15 MINS

Lemony zucchini add a real zing to this quick pasta dish, which is sprinkled with crunchy toasted almonds.

10oz (300g) spaghetti
2 tbsp olive oil
2 zucchini, diced
2 zucchini, grated
salt and freshly ground black pepper

2 garlic cloves, finely chopped
juice of 1 lemon
pinch of dried oregano
scant 1oz (25g) flaked almonds,
  toasted (see Cook's Tip)

1 Cook the pasta in a large pan of salted boiling water for 8–10 minutes, or according to the instructions on the package.

2 Meanwhile, heat the olive oil in a large frying pan. Add all the zucchini, together with a pinch of salt and some black pepper. Cook for 5–8 minutes until soft and just beginning to turn golden at the edges. Stir in the garlic and cook for a few more seconds, then add the lemon juice and oregano and simmer for about 5 minutes.

3 Drain the pasta, reserving some of the cooking water, then return it to the pan with a little of the water. Add the zucchini mixture and toss well. Transfer to a serving dish, or dishes, and top with the toasted almonds.

COOK'S TIP
To toast the almonds, put them onto a baking tray and place it in the oven, which has been preheated to 400°F (200°C). Cook for 3–5 minutes until golden, turning them halfway through cooking. Alternatively, cook them in a small frying pan for a few minutes until golden, stirring occasionally so they don't burn.

STATISTICS PER SERVING:

Energy 362cals/1,528kJ

Carbohydrate 58g

Sugar 4g

Fiber 3.5g

Fat 11g
Saturated fat 1g

Sodium trace

● ● ○ GI

● ● ○ CALORIES

● ○ ○ SATURATED FAT

● ○ ○ SODIUM

PASTA WITH ROASTED FENNEL

SERVES 4   **PREP** 10 MINS   **COOK** 30 MINS

Roasted fennel, partnered by sweet cherry tomatoes, adds a stylish flair to spaghetti or linguine.

2 fennel bulbs, trimmed and
  sliced lengthwise
9oz (250g) cherry tomatoes, halved
2 tbsp olive oil
salt and freshly ground black pepper

1 red onion, finely chopped
2 garlic cloves, finely chopped
12oz (350g) spaghetti or linguine
1 tbsp flat-leaf parsley,
  finely chopped

1 Preheat the oven to 400°F (200°C). Put the fennel in a pan of salted boiling water, bring back to a boil and cook for about 5 minutes until softened, then drain well.

2 Put the fennel into a roasting pan, add the tomatoes, drizzle with half the olive oil and sprinkle with salt and black pepper. Combine thoroughly, using your hands. Roast in the oven for about 20 minutes or until soft and beginning to char very slightly.

3 Put a pan of salted water on to boil for the pasta. Meanwhile, heat the remaining oil in a frying pan, add the onion and cook for about 5 minutes until soft. Stir in the garlic and cook for a few more seconds, then remove the pan from the heat and set aside.

4 Cook the pasta in the boiling water for 8–10 minutes or according to the instructions on the package. Drain, reserving some of the cooking water, then return the pasta to the pan with a little of the water. Toss together with the onion mixture, fennel, and tomatoes. Transfer to a serving dish (or dishes) and sprinkle with the parsley to serve.

STATISTICS PER SERVING:

Energy 382cals/1,617kJ

Carbohydrate 71g

Sugar 6g

Fiber 5g

Fat 7.5g

Saturated fat 1g

Sodium trace

COOK'S TIP
You don't have to boil the fennel first, but it does soften it and stops it from becoming too brittle when roasted.

PASTA PUTTANESCA

SERVES 4   **PREP** 15 MINS   **COOK** 20 MINS

A rich, elegant, and satisfying sauce makes this pasta dish perfect for entertaining.

GUIDELINES PER SERVING:

⬤⬤◯ GI

⬤⬤◯ CALORIES

⬤◯◯ SATURATED FAT

⬤◯◯ SODIUM

1 tbsp olive oil
1 red onion, finely chopped
2 garlic cloves, finely chopped
4 salted anchovy filets, chopped
1 red chile, seeded and
  finely chopped
2 tbsp black olives, chopped

3 tsp capers (rinsed, if salty), chopped
6 tomatoes, diced
10oz (300g) spaghetti
1 tbsp flat-leaf parsley, finely
  chopped, to garnish

1 Heat the oil in a large frying pan, add the onion and cook for a few minutes until beginning to soften. Add the garlic and cook for a few more seconds. Stir in the anchovy filets and chile, and cook until the anchovies have melted.

2 Stir in the olives, capers, and tomatoes. Simmer over low heat for about 15 minutes, partially covered. (If the sauce becomes too dry while simmering, loosen it with a little of the pasta cooking water.)

3 Meanwhile, cook the pasta in a pan of salted boiling water for 8–10 minutes or according to the instructions on the package. Drain, reserving some of the cooking water, then return it to the pan with a little of the water and toss with half the sauce. Transfer the pasta to a serving dish (or dishes) and top with the remaining sauce. Sprinkle with the parsley.

STATISTICS PER SERVING:

Energy 333cals/1,412kJ

Carbohydrate 62g

Sugar 8g

Fiber 4g

Fat 6g
Saturated fat 1g

Sodium 0.32g

● ● ○ GI

● ○ ○ CALORIES

● ○ ○ SATURATED FAT

● ○ ○ SODIUM

LINGUINE WITH SPICED EGGPLANT

SERVES 4   **PREP** 15 MINS   **COOK** 25 MINS

A fiery sauce for this elegant pasta.

6 tbsp olive oil
2 onions, peeled and finely chopped
2 eggplants, one cut into ½in
  (1cm) dice, the other grated
4 cloves of garlic, peeled and chopped

½ tsp red pepper flakes
16fl oz (500ml) passata
1 tsp dried oregano
salt and freshly ground black pepper
14oz (400g) linguine

1 Pour the olive oil into a large frying pan and heat, add the onion and cook over low heat for 3 minutes until soft, then add the diced eggplant and cook for 3 minutes more. Add the grated eggplant, garlic, and red pepper flakes and cook for a further 3 minutes. Pour in the passata, add the oregano, and season well with salt and pepper. Bring to a simmer and allow to cook, uncovered, for 15 minutes.

2 Meanwhile add the pasta to a large pan of boiling salted water and cook for 8–10 minutes or according to pack instructions. Drain and return to the pan.

3 Add half the eggplant mixture to the pasta and toss, then transfer to a large serving dish, or individual dishes, and top with the remaining sauce.

STATISTICS PER SERVING:

Energy 518cals/2,186kJ

Carbohydrate 90g

Sugar 7g

Fiber 2g

Fat 13g

Saturated fat 2g

Sodium trace

ZUCCHINI AND FRESH TOMATO PENNE

SERVES 4   **PREP** 5 MINS   **COOK** 15 MINS

A fresh summer sauce with uncooked tomatoes and basil is a simple, yet truly tasty crowning glory for pasta. Enjoy it at its best when the vegetables are in season.

1 tbsp olive oil
3 zucchini, diced
salt and freshly ground black pepper
3 garlic cloves, finely chopped

4 tomatoes, diced
1 tbsp fresh basil, chopped
12oz (350g) penne pasta

1 Heat the olive oil in a large frying pan, add the zucchini and cook for about 5 minutes until tender. Season with salt and black pepper, stir in the garlic and cook for 2 minutes, then remove from the heat.

2 Add the tomatoes and basil, and stir to combine. Allow to cool a little.

3 Cook the pasta in a pan of salted boiling water for 10–12 minutes or according to the instructions on the package. Drain, reserving some of the cooking water, then return it to the pan with a little of the water. Add the zucchini and tomato mixture and stir. Season again, if needed. You can serve this dish hot or cold

COOK'S TIP
This is best made with plump, juicy tomatoes when they are in season and full of flavor.

STATISTICS PER SERVING:

Energy 360cals/1,528kJ

Carbohydrate 70g

Sugar 6g

Fiber 4g

Fat 5g
Saturated fat 0.8g

Sodium trace

SPAGHETTI WITH TOMATO AND GOAT CHEESE

SERVES 4   **PREP** 10 MINS   **COOK** 10 MINS
PLUS STANDING

Fresh cherry tomatoes are the basis for an instant cheesy topping that doesn't need cooking: just heap it on plates of steaming spaghetti.

20 cherry tomatoes, halved
1 tbsp capers, rinsed and dried
3 tbsp fruity extra virgin olive oil
2 garlic cloves, finely chopped
5½oz (150g) semi-hard goat cheese,
  broken or sliced into chunks

1 tsp dried oregano
1 tbsp fresh basil, chopped
salt and freshly ground
  black pepper
12oz (350g) spaghetti

1 Put all the ingredients except for the spaghetti in a bowl. Season well with salt and black pepper, and set aside for about 20 minutes for the flavors to mingle and develop.

2 When ready to serve, cook the spaghetti in a pan of salted boiling water for 8–10 minutes or according to the instructions on the package. Drain, then return to the pan with a little of the cooking water.

3 Add the tomato mixture to the spaghetti and toss well to coat. Serve immediately.

GUIDELINES PER SERVING:

GI
CALORIES
SATURATED FAT
SODIUM

STATISTICS PER SERVING:

Energy 498cals/2,099kJ

Carbohydrate 66g

Sugar 5g

Fiber 3g

Fat 19g
Saturated fat 8g

Sodium 0.24g

● ● ○ GI

● ● ○ CALORIES

● ○ ○ SATURATED FAT

● ○ ○ SODIUM

BUTTERNUT SQUASH AND ZUCCHINI PASTA

SERVES 4   **PREP** 15 MINS   **COOK** 30 MINS

Sweet butternut squash makes an excellent sauce for spaghetti and is a good source of vitamins A and C.

2 tbsp olive oil
½ butternut squash
  (about 12oz/ 350g), cut into
  ½in (1cm) dice
salt and freshly ground black pepper
2 zucchini, cut into ½in (1cm) dice

3 garlic cloves, finely chopped
1 tbsp fresh thyme stems,
  leaves only
14oz can chopped tomatoes
12oz (350g) spaghetti

1 Heat the oil in large frying pan, add the squash and season with salt and black pepper. Cook for 5 minutes, then add the zucchini and cook for 5–10 minutes until soft and beginning to turn golden (you may need to add a little more oil).

2 Stir in the garlic and thyme, cook for a minute, then add the tomatoes and simmer for about 10–15 minutes. Taste and then season if needed.

3 Meanwhile, put the pasta in a large pan of salted boiling water and cook for 8–10 minutes or according to the instructions on the package. Drain, reserving some of the cooking water, then return the pasta to the pan with a little of the water. Combine with the sauce and put onto plates.

STATISTICS PER SERVING:

Energy 410cals/1,738kJ

Carbohydrate 77g

Sugar 10.5g

Fiber 5g

Fat 7.5g

Saturated fat 1g

Sodium 0.08g

COOK'S TIP

Chop up the remaining squash, put it in a plastic freezer bag and seal, then store in the freezer. It will keep for up to three months.

PASTA WITH GREEN BEANS AND ARTICHOKES

SERVES 4   **PREP** 5 MINS   **COOK** 15 MINS

Green vegetables tossed with basil and pasta make a speedy supper that can be on the table in no time.

GUIDELINES PER SERVING:

⬤⬤◯ GI

⬤⬤◯ CALORIES

⬤◯◯ SATURATED FAT

⬤◯◯ SODIUM

7oz (200g) green beans, trimmed
1 tbsp basil leaves
scant 1oz (25g) pine nuts

9oz jar artichokes in oil, drained and roughly chopped (reserve the oil)
12oz (350g) trofi or penne pasta

1 Drop the green beans into a pan of salted boiling water and cook for 3–4 minutes, then drain and refresh in cold water (this will help them to keep their color and stop them from cooking any longer). Set aside.

2 Put the basil and pine nuts in a food processor or blender and pulse until chopped, then drizzle in a little of the oil from the artichokes and pulse again to form a paste.

3 Cook the pasta in a pan of salted boiling water for 8–10 minutes or according to the instructions on the package. Drain, reserving some of the cooking water, and then return the pasta to the pan with a little of the water. Toss the pasta with the basil paste, green beans, and artichokes.

STATISTICS PER SERVING:

Energy 419cals/1,774kJ

Carbohydrate 70g

Sugar 3g

Fiber 4g

Fat 12g
Saturated fat 0.5g

Sodium trace

⬤⬤◯ GI

⬤⬤◯ CALORIES

⬤⬤◯ SATURATED FAT

⬤◯◯ SODIUM

MUSHROOM LASAGNA

SERVES 4   **PREP** 20 MINS   **COOK** 45 MINS   **FREEZE** 3 MONTHS

A meatless lasagna made with robust mushrooms and flavor-packed leeks.

1 tbsp olive oil
2 leeks, trimmed and finely chopped
14oz (400g) white and cremini
  mushrooms, half of them chopped,
  half grated
3 garlic cloves, finely chopped
1 tbsp all-purpose flour
10fl oz (300ml) skim milk

salt and freshly ground black pepper
pinch of dried oregano
3½oz (100g) fresh Parmesan cheese,
  grated
6 tomatoes, seeded and diced
10 lasagna sheets (no need for
  precooked ones)

1 Preheat the oven to 400°F (200°C). Heat the olive oil in a large pan, add the leeks and cook for 5–8 minutes until soft. Add all the mushrooms plus the garlic, and cook for a further 5–8 minutes until the mushrooms begin to release their juices.

2 Stir in the flour and combine it well with the juices in the pan. Remove from the heat, add a little of the milk and stir until smooth. Return to the heat and add the remaining milk, little by little, until you have a smooth sauce. Season well with salt and black pepper, then add the oregano and Parmesan. Stir in the tomatoes.

3 Coat the bottom of an ovenproof baking dish with some of the sauce, then a layer of lasagna; continue adding alternate layers, ending with some sauce as the topping. Put the dish in the oven to bake for 15–20 minutes, or until the sauce is golden and bubbling.

COOK'S TIP
Lasagna is a great reheat-and-eat dish, so make it ahead to save time later.

STATISTICS PER SERVING:

Energy 312cals/1,316kJ

Carbohydrate 35g

Sugar 10g

Fiber 4.5g

Fat 13g

Saturated fat 6g

Sodium 0.28g

VEGETARIAN COTTAGE PIE

GUIDELINES PER SERVING:

- ●●○ GI
- ●●○ CALORIES
- ●○○ SATURATED FAT
- ●●○ SODIUM

SERVES 4   **PREP** 15 MINS   **COOK** 30–35 MINS   **FREEZE** 3 MONTHS

Canned lentils are a fantastic low-GI ingredient to have on standby in your pantry.

2 tbsp olive oil
2 leeks, trimmed and finely chopped
3 stalks celery, finely chopped
2 large carrots, diced
1 red pepper, seeded and diced
4½oz (125g) cremini mushrooms, roughly chopped
2 cloves garlic, crushed
10fl oz (300ml) vegetable stock
2 tsp soy sauce
pinch of red pepper flakes
salt and freshly ground black pepper
2 x 14oz cans brown lentils, drained and rinsed

1 tbsp sunflower or pumpkin seeds, or a mixture of the two

For the mash
1lb (450g) white potatoes, peeled and cut into even-sized chunks
1lb 5oz (600g) sweet potatoes, peeled and cut into even-sized chunks
5fl oz (150ml) warmed skim milk
scant 1oz (25g) polyunsaturated margarine

1 Preheat the oven to 400°F (200°C). Heat the oil in a large, deep, heavy, nonstick frying pan. Add the leeks, celery, carrots, red pepper, mushrooms, and garlic and cook, stirring, for 5 minutes.

2 Add the stock, soy sauce, and red pepper flakes. Season to taste with salt and black pepper. Bring to a boil, then reduce the heat, cover and simmer for 15 minutes, adding more stock if necessary. Remove from the heat and stir in the lentils.

3 To make the mash, boil the potatoes and sweet potatoes in a large pan of salted water for 15–20 minutes or until tender. Drain well, then return to the pan and add the milk and margarine. Mash well and season to taste.

4 Pour the vegetable and lentil mixture into a large ovenproof dish. Spread the mashed potato evenly over the top and smooth the surface. Scatter with the seeds and transfer to the oven. Bake for 20–25 minutes or until the top is golden.

STATISTICS PER SERVING:

Energy	594cals/2,506kJ
Carbohydrate	90g
Sugar	18g
Fiber	15g
Fat	17g
Saturated fat	2g
Sodium	0.48g

BROWN RICE, RED PEPPER, AND ARTICHOKE RISOTTO

GUIDELINES PER SERVING:

● ● ○ GI
● ● ○ CALORIES
● ○ ○ SATURATED FAT
● ● ○ SODIUM

SERVES 4   **PREP** 10 MINS   **COOK** 50 MINS–1 HOUR

Not a risotto in the true sense, but a great mix of flavors and textures.

1 tbsp olive oil
1 onion, finely chopped
salt and freshly ground black pepper
2 sweet pointed red peppers, halved,
  seeded and chopped
pinch of red pepper flakes

10oz (280g) brown rice
2 pints (1 liter) vegetable stock
10oz (280g) jar of artichoke hearts,
  drained and roughly chopped
handful of flat-leaf parsley,
  finely chopped

1 Heat the oil in a large frying pan then add the onion and cook on low heat until soft and transparent. Season with a pinch of sea salt and some freshly ground black pepper. Add the red peppers and cook for a few minutes until they soften.

2 Add the red pepper flakes, then stir in the rice. Raise the heat a little, pour in a ladleful of the stock, and bring to a boil. Reduce to a simmer and cook gently for 40–50 minutes, adding a little more stock each time the liquid is absorbed, until the rice is cooked.

3 Stir through the artichokes and cook for a couple of minutes to heat through, then taste and season as required. Cover with a lid, remove from the heat and leave for 10 minutes, then stir through the chopped parsley and transfer to plates or bowls. You could serve this with an arugula salad on the side.

COOK'S TIP
Artichokes bought in a jar will taste far better than the canned ones. Do save the oil as you can use it for a dressing. If you can't find the pointed peppers, just use regular peppers—they're just as tasty but not quite as sweet.

STATISTICS PER SERVING:

Energy 406cals/1,713kJ

Carbohydrate 67g

Sugar 9g

Fiber 4g

Fat 13.5g

Saturated fat 1g

Sodium 0.48g

⬤⬤◯ GI

⬤⬤◯ CALORIES

⬤⬤◯ SATURATED FAT

⬤⬤◯ SODIUM

PEA AND LEMON RISOTTO

SERVES 4   **PREP** 5 MINS   **COOK** 30-40 MINS

Frozen peas contain just as much vitamin C as fresh peas, so it's a good idea to keep a bag in the freezer for a convenient way to boost the nutritional content of meals.

2 tbsp olive oil
1 large onion, finely chopped
2 garlic cloves, crushed
  or finely chopped
10oz (300g) arborio (risotto) rice
5fl oz (150ml) white wine
1¼-1½pints (600-750ml) hot
  vegetable stock

14oz (400g) frozen peas
zest and juice of 1 lemon
salt and freshly ground black pepper
2oz (60g) freshly grated Parmesan
  cheese, plus some shavings
  to garnish

1 Heat the oil in large saucepan, add the onion and cook over medium heat for about 2 minutes or until beginning to soften. Stir in the garlic and rice and continue to cook, stirring, for 1–2 minutes. Add the wine and cook until the liquid has evaporated.

2 Pour in just enough stock to cover the rice and continue to cook, stirring frequently, until most of the liquid has been absorbed. Continue adding the stock in this way until the rice is tender.

3 Stir in the peas, lemon juice and zest, and season to taste. Cook, stirring, for 2–3 minutes.

4 Remove from the heat and stir in the Parmesan cheese. Garnish with shavings of fresh Parmesan and serve immediately.

STATISTICS PER SERVING:

Energy 537cals/2,337kJ

Carbohydrate 76g

Sugar 5.5g

Fiber 6g

Fat 13g
Saturated fat 4.5g

Sodium 0.4g

MUSHROOM AND CILANTRO RICE

SERVES 4   **PREP** 5 MINS   **COOK** 30 MINS

This fragrant rice dish combines earthy-tasting mushrooms with plenty of spice.

1 tbsp olive oil
2 tsp mustard seeds
9oz (250g) basmati rice
2½oz (75g) shredded coconut
2 tbsp fresh cilantro

1 green chile, seeded
1 tsp turmeric
9oz (250g) cremini mushrooms
salt and freshly ground black pepper

1 Heat the oil in a large frying pan, add the mustard seeds and cook for a few minutes until they pop. Set aside.

2 Pour the rice into a large saucepan, cover with water and cook for 10–15 minutes until tender, or according to the instructions on the package. Put the lid on the pan and set aside.

3 Put the coconut, cilantro, chile, and turmeric into a food processor or blender and pulse until ground together. Add the mixture to the mustard seeds and return the pan to low heat. Cook, stirring, for about 5 minutes.

4 Pulse the mushrooms in the food processor a few times until they are just broken up, then stir them into the coconut and cilantro mixture. Cook for 5–10 minutes or until the mushrooms begin to release their juices. Add in the cooked rice and stir well, then taste and season as required.

GUIDELINES PER SERVING:

●●○ GI
●●○ CALORIES
●●● SATURATED FAT
●○○ SODIUM

STATISTICS PER SERVING:

Energy 383cals/1,623kJ

Carbohydrate 52g

Sugar 2g

Fiber 1g

Fat 17g
Saturated fat 12g

Sodium 0.2g

⬤⬤◯ GI

⬤◯◯ CALORIES

⬤◯◯ SATURATED FAT

⬤⬤◯ SODIUM

MUSHROOM AND CHILE PILAF

SERVES 4   **PREP** 10 MINS   **COOK** 50 MINS

Nutty-flavored rice with an added zing of chile.

1 tbsp olive oil
1 red onion, finely chopped
salt and freshly ground black pepper
2 green chiles, seeded and
  finely chopped

1lb (450g) mushrooms, chopped
8oz (225g) brown basmati rice
1¼ pints (600ml) vegetable
  or chicken stock

1 Heat the olive oil in a large, heavy pan, add the onion and cook for 7–8 minutes over low heat until soft. Season with a pinch of salt and some black pepper. Add the chiles and cook for a few minutes more. Add in the mushrooms and cook, stirring, until they release their juices (about 5 minutes). Add a little more oil if necessary.

2 Pour in the rice and stir until it is coated with the juices in the pan, then add the stock, increase the heat and bring to a boil. Reduce to a simmer, cover, and cook gently for 30 minutes or until the rice is tender but retains some bite. Stir occasionally and add extra water, a little at a time, if needed.

3 Remove from the heat and set aside, still covered with the lid, for a further 10 minutes. Taste, season as needed, and serve.

COOK'S TIP
Brown rice takes longer to cook than white, so be patient; it will continue cooking as it steams while set aside with the lid on.

Energy 294cals/1,243kJ

Carbohydrate 50g

Sugar 3g

Fiber 3g

Fat 7g
Saturated fat 1g

Sodium 0.44g

LEEK AND TOMATO PILAF

SERVES 2   **PREP** 5 MINS   **COOK** 30 MINS

This version of a pilaf uses pearl barley instead of rice.

GUIDELINES PER SERVING:

● ○ ○ GI
● ● ○ CALORIES
● ● ○ SATURATED FAT
● ● ○ SODIUM

2 tbsp olive oil
1 large leek, trimmed and roughly
  chopped
3oz (85g) pearl barley, rinsed
14oz can chopped tomatoes
1 tbsp tomato purée
pinch of smoked paprika

16fl oz (500ml) vegetable stock
5½oz (150g) frozen soybeans
pinch of red pepper flakes
salt and freshly ground black pepper
½oz (15g) Parmesan cheese shavings,
  to serve

1 Heat the oil in a large, deep frying pan, put the leek in and fry it for
2–3 minutes. Stir in the pearl barley and cook for a further minute.

2 Add the tomatoes, tomato purée, paprika, and 14fl oz (400ml)
of the stock. Cover and simmer for 20 minutes, stirring occasionally
and adding more stock as it is absorbed.

3 Stir in the soybeans and red pepper flakes, and season to taste with
salt and pepper. Cook for a further 5 minutes or until the barley is soft
and the soybeans are heated through. Serve immediately, sprinkled with
Parmesan shavings.

STATISTICS PER SERVING:

Energy 490cals/2,048kJ

Carbohydrate 55g

Sugar 8g

Fiber 6g

Fat 20g
Saturated fat 4.4g

Sodium 0.56g

● ○ ○   GI

● ○ ○   CALORIES

● ○ ○   SATURATED FAT

● ○ ○   SODIUM

KASHA PILAF

SERVES 6   **PREP** 5 MINS   **COOK** 25 MINS

Kasha is a healthy and delicious wholegrain cereal that is prepared similarly to risotto.

2 tbsp polyunsaturated margarine
1 large onion, chopped
2 celery sticks, sliced
1 large egg
7oz (200g) coarse kasha
  (buckwheat groats) or whole kasha

1 tsp ground sage
1 tsp ground thyme
4oz (115g) raisins
4oz (115g) walnut pieces,
  coarsely chopped
salt

1 In a large frying pan, melt the margarine and gently fry the onion and celery for 3 minutes, or until the vegetables begin to soften.

2 In a small bowl, mix the egg with the kasha, then add the mixture to the pan. Cook, stirring constantly, for 1 minute, or until the grains are dry and separated. Add 16fl oz (500ml) water, the sage, and the thyme to the kasha. Bring to a boil, then reduce the heat, cover, and simmer for 10–12 minutes.

3 Stir the raisins and walnuts into the kasha. Cook for a further 4–5 minutes, or until the kasha is tender and all the liquid has been absorbed. Season to taste with salt.

STATISTICS PER SERVING:

Energy	370cals/1,537kJ
Carbohydrate	45g
Sugar	15g
Fiber	2g
Fat	19g
Saturated fat	2.5g
Sodium	0.08g

KASHA WITH VEGETABLES

GUIDELINES PER SERVING:

● ○ ○ GI

● ○ ○ CALORIES

● ○ ○ SATURATED FAT

● ○ ○ SODIUM

SERVES 4   **PREP** 10 MINS   **COOK** 40 MINS

Added vegetables and goat's cheese make this kasha dish a hearty vegetarian main course.

2 tbsp olive oil
1 onion, finely chopped
1 carrot, finely chopped
1 garlic clove, finely chopped
2 flat mushrooms, sliced
1 celery stick, finely chopped
1¼lb (550g) kasha

4fl oz (120ml) dry white wine
2 pints (1 liter) hot vegetable
  stock or water
1 beet, steamed or roasted
  until tender, chopped
2 tbsp chopped parsley
2oz (60g) goat's cheese, crumbled

1 Heat the oil in a large saucepan. Add the onion, carrot, garlic, mushrooms, and celery and sauté for 8–10 minutes, stirring frequently, until brown. Add the kasha and cook, stirring for another 2–3 minutes. Add the wine and continue stirring until all the liquid has been absorbed.

2 Gradually add the hot vegetable stock, 4fl oz (120ml) at a time, and stirring until it has been absorbed before adding more. Cook for a further 20 minutes, or until the kasha is soft and chewy.

3 Toss in the chopped cooked beet and remove from the heat. Sprinkle over the parsley and goat's cheese, and serve.

STATISTICS PER SERVING:

Energy 362cals/1,521kJ

Carbohydrate 55g

Sugar 8g

Fiber 4.5g

Fat 11.5g

Saturated fat 4g

Sodium 0.28g

TURKISH-STYLE STUFFED PEPPERS

SERVES 2   **PREP** 15 MINS   **COOK** 1 HOUR

A good dish to make use of leftover rice.

4½oz (125g) basmati rice
1 tbsp olive oil, plus extra
 for drizzling
1 red onion, peeled and finely
 chopped
salt and freshly ground black pepper
small handful of flat-leaf parsley,
 finely chopped
small handful of fresh thyme
 leaves, chopped

pinch of dried oregano
1 tomato, diced
½ tsp paprika
2 tsp pine nuts, toasted (see
 Cook's Tip, below)
1 tbsp pitted and chopped
 black olives
2 red peppers, tops removed
 and retained, seeds removed

1 First cook the rice according to pack instructions, drain and put to one side. Preheat the oven to 400°F (200°C).

2 Heat the olive oil in a frying pan, add the onion and season with salt and black pepper. Cook over low heat for 3–4 minutes until soft, add the garlic and cook for a few seconds more, then remove from the heat and allow to cool. Stir in the herbs, tomato, paprika, pine nuts, and olives, then add the cooked rice and stir again. Taste and season if needed.

3 Spoon the mixture into the peppers, packing them tightly so they hold together while cooking. Place them upright in a roasting pan, topped with the lids, drizzle with olive oil, and cook for 30–45 minutes until the peppers begin to soften and char slightly. Cover with foil toward the end of cooking if the rice is beginning to dry out too much. Serve hot.

COOK'S TIP
Toast the pine nuts on a baking sheet in a hot oven or in a small dry frying pan over moderate heat. Cook for a few minutes, keeping a close eye on them to make sure they don't burn.

STATISTICS PER SERVING:

Energy 535cals/1,475kJ

Carbohydrate 67g

Sugar 14.5g

Fiber 4g

Fat 6g

Saturated fat 0.5g

Sodium 0.08g

● ○ ○ GI

● ○ ○ CALORIES

● ○ ○ SATURATED FAT

● ● ○ SODIUM

TANDOORI PANEER KEBABS

SERVES 4   **PREP** 20 MINS   **COOK** 10 MINS
PLUS MARINATING

Paneer is a firm Indian cheese that takes on the flavor of other ingredients.

5½oz (150g) thick natural yogurt
1 tbsp tandoori curry paste
1 tbsp lemon juice
9oz (250g) paneer, cut into
  1in (2.5cm) cubes
1 red pepper, seeded and cut
  into 1in (2.5cm) chunks

12 button mushrooms
1 large zucchini, cut into
  ½in (1cm) slices
2 tbsp vegetable oil

1 In a bowl, mix the yogurt, curry paste, and lemon juice. Add the paneer, and stir well. Cover, chill, and marinate for up to 24 hours.

2 Thread the paneer cubes on to skewers, alternating with the pepper, mushrooms, and zucchini. Brush with oil and grill or barbecue for 10 minutes, or until the vegetables are cooked.

COOK'S TIP
If using wooden skewers, soak them in cold water for 30 mins before using to prevent them burning.

STATISTICS PER SERVING:

Energy 172cals/715kJ

Carbohydrate 8g

Sugar 8g

Fiber 1g

Fat 10g

Saturated fat 3g

Sodium 0.28g

MUSHROOM, LEEK, AND RED PEPPER FILO PIE

SERVES 4   **PREP** 15 MINS   **COOK** 40 MINS

A layered pie to be eaten hot or cold.

GUIDELINES PER SERVING:

⬤⬤◯ GI
⬤◯◯ CALORIES
⬤◯◯ SATURATED FAT
⬤◯◯ SODIUM

1 tbsp oil, plus extra for brushing
1 onion, finely chopped
salt and freshly ground black pepper
small handful fresh thyme,
   finely chopped
1 leek, finely sliced
2 red peppers, finely chopped

9oz (250g) mushrooms (chestnut
   and oyster varieties; keep them
   separate), chopped
5fl oz (150ml) vegetable stock
about 18 sheets filo pastry
butter, melted, for brushing

1 Preheat the oven to 375°F (190°C). Heat the oil in a large frying pan then add the onion, season with salt and black pepper, and add the thyme. Cook over low heat for 2–3 minutes until the onion begins to soften, then stir in the leek and red peppers and cook for 5–8 minutes more.

2 Add the chestnut mushrooms and cook for 5 minutes or until they begin to release their juices, then add the oyster mushrooms and cook for 2 minutes more. Pour in a little stock, increase the heat and allow to bubble, then gradually add the rest and cook until the liquid is almost absorbed.

3 Lay a double layer of filo pastry sheets in a small–medium oblong pie dish or roasting pan to cover the base (about 6 sheets), and brush with oil. Spoon over half the mixture, then arrange another double layer of pastry sheets on top and brush with oil. Repeat with the remaining mixture and a third double layer of pastry, tucking the edges down the sides of the dish. Brush liberally with melted butter and transfer to the oven to cook for 20–25 minutes until golden and crispy. Cut into 4 portions and serve. You could try this with a dressed mixed salad on the side.

COOK'S TIP
This brittle pastry requires oiling so it doesn't break up. If you prefer not to oil, work quickly between layering and keep the filo wrapped in plastic wrap.

STATISTICS PER SERVING:

Energy 259cals/1,078kJ

Carbohydrate 35g

Sugar 10g

Fiber 3g

Fat 10g
Saturated fat 2.5g

Sodium 0.28g

VEGETARIAN SAUSAGES

SERVES 4   **PREP** 20 MINS   **COOK** 25 MINS

These vegetarian sausages are rich in flavor and provide a less fatty alternative to meat sausages.

2 tbsp olive oil, plus extra for greasing
1 onion, finely diced
1 leek, trimmed and finely sliced
1 zucchini, finely diced
salt and freshly ground black pepper
1 egg

5½oz (150g) lightly toasted
   breadcrumbs
2½oz (80g) Parmesan cheese,
   finely grated
pinch of paprika

1 Preheat the oven to 350°F (180°C). Heat the oil in a large frying pan and add in the onion, leek, and zucchini. Season with salt and black pepper and then cook over low heat for about 10 minutes until soft.

2 Allow to cool, then put in a mixing bowl and add the egg, half the breadcrumbs, the Parmesan cheese, and the paprika. Stir until the mixture is evenly combined (you don't need more seasoning because the Parmesan is salty-tasting).

3 Using your hands, form the mixture into 8 sausages and roll each one in the remaining breadcrumbs. Place the sausages on an oiled baking sheet and cook in the oven for 15–20 minutes until just beginning to turn golden.

STATISTICS PER SERVING:

Energy 306cals/1,285kJ

Carbohydrate 32g

Sugar 3g

Fibre 2g

Fat 14g

Saturated fat 5g

Sodium 0.44g

MUSHROOM STRUDEL

SERVES 4   **PREP** 15 MINS   **COOK** 35 MINS

Reduced-fat cream cheese gives this dish a creamy taste
without adding too many calories or a lot of fat.

2 tbsp olive oil
1lb (450g) mixed mushrooms,
  roughly chopped
2 stalks celery, finely chopped
1 bunch of spring onions, trimmed
  and roughly chopped
8oz (225g) reduced-fat soft cheese
  with garlic and herbs

4 tbsp chopped fresh chives
salt and freshly ground black pepper
8 large sheets of filo pastry
  (about 7oz/200g)
1oz (30g) polyunsaturated margarine,
  melted

1 Preheat the oven to 350°F (180°C). Heat the oil in a large frying pan and
add the mushrooms, celery, and spring onions. Cook over medium heat,
stirring occasionally, for 5 minutes or until the mushrooms are soft and all
the liquid has evaporated.

2 Allow the mushroom mixture to cool thoroughly, then stir in the soft
cheese and chives. Season the filling to taste.

3 Lay 4 pieces of filo pastry side by side on a clean dish towel, overlapping
the long edges by about 2in (5cm). Brush with a little melted margarine.
Place the 4 remaining sheets of pastry on top and brush with a little more
margarine. Cover the pastry with a clean, damp dish towel to help prevent
it from drying out; uncover when you are ready to add the filling.

4 Carefully spread the mushroom mixture over the pastry, leaving a
border of 1in (2.5cm) around the edges, then roll it up from a short edge,
just as you would a Swiss roll. Carefully transfer to a baking sheet, making
sure that the seam is underneath. Using a sharp knife, make light diagonal
slashes across the top of the pastry.

5 Brush the strudel with the remaining margarine and bake in the oven
for 20 minutes or until the pastry is crisp and golden. Leave to stand for
5 minutes and then cut into slices. Serve warm.

STATISTICS PER SERVING:

Energy 274cals/1,139kJ

Carbohydrate 15g

Sugar 4g

Fiber 2g

Fat 20g

Saturated fat 6g

Sodium 0.28g

⬤◯◯ GI

⬤◯◯ CALORIES

⬤◯◯ SATURATED FAT

⬤◯◯ SODIUM

BUTTERNUT SQUASH AND SPINACH CURRY

SERVES 6   **PREP** 15 MINS   **COOK** 30-35 MINS   **FREEZE** 3 MONTHS

A mildly spiced, low-fat curry, rich in B vitamins and betacarotene, which the body can convert to Vitamin A.

2 tbsp vegetable oil
1 large onion, peeled and chopped
1 medium butternut squash, about
  2¾lb (1.25kg), peeled and cut into
  ¾in (2cm) cubes
2 cloves garlic, peeled and crushed
2-3 tbsp curry paste

14oz (400g) can chopped tomatoes
12fl oz (360ml) vegetable stock
  or chicken stock
8oz (225g) bag fresh washed
  baby spinach
salt and freshly ground black pepper

1 Heat the oil in a large, deep pan, add the onion and cook gently for 2–3 minutes. Add the butternut squash, garlic, and curry paste and cook for a further 2–3 minutes.

2 Add the tomatoes and stock. Bring to a boil, then reduce the heat, cover, and simmer for 15 minutes, stirring occasionally. Remove the lid and simmer for a further 10 minutes. Add a little extra stock or water if it becomes too dry.

3 Stir in the spinach, cover and cook for 1–2 minutes until just wilted. Season to taste with salt and pepper and spoon into serving bowls. If desired, you could add a spoonful of yogurt to serve.

STATISTICS PER SERVING:

Energy 194cals/817kJ

Carbohydrate 26g

Sugar 16g

Fiber 6g

Fat 8g
Saturated fat 0.8g

Sodium 0.24g

MEDITERRANEAN VEGETABLES WITH FARRO

SERVES 4   **PREP** 15 MINS   **COOK** 40 MINS   **FREEZE** 1 MONTH

A hearty mix of chunky vegetables thickened with grains.

GUIDELINES PER SERVING:

◕○○ GI

◕○○ CALORIES

◕○○ SATURATED FAT

●○○ SODIUM

1 tbsp olive oil
1 onion, chopped
salt and freshly ground black pepper
3 celery stalks, chopped
pinch of dried oregano
1 red pepper, chopped

2 zucchini, chopped
dollop of tomato purée
2 x 14oz cans of tomatoes
2 pints (900ml) vegetable stock
1¾oz (50g) farro

1 Heat the oil in a large pan then add the onion and cook over low heat for 5 minutes or until soft and transparent. Season with salt and black pepper and add the celery and oregano and cook for 5 minutes or until the celery is soft.

2 Add the red pepper and zucchini and cook for 5 more minutes. Stir in the tomato purée, add the canned tomatoes and stock, and bring to a boil. Reduce the heat to a simmer, add the farro, and cook for 30–40 minutes, stirring occasionally and topping up with hot water or more stock if needed. Taste, season as required, and serve hot.

COOK'S TIP

Farro is a delicious healthy grain with a chewy texture. Used a lot in Italian cooking, you will find it in health food stores or in the international section of some supermarkets.

STATISTICS PER SERVING:

Energy 237cals/1,000kJ

Carbohydrate 25g

Sugar 11g

Fiber 3g

Fat 3g

Saturated fat 1.5g

Sodium 0.12g

◐○○ GI

◐◐○ CALORIES

◐○○ SATURATED FAT

◐◐○ SODIUM

BEANS, SWISS CHARD, AND ARTICHOKES

SERVES 4   **PREP** 15 MINS   **COOK** 30 MINS   **FREEZE** 1 MONTH

A simple and hearty one-pot dish. Swiss chard contains vitamin K, which is good for bone health.

1 tbsp olive oil
1 onion, finely chopped
3 garlic cloves, finely chopped
2 red peppers, seeded and
  finely chopped
pinch of ground cumin
pinch of paprika
1 bay leaf
salt and freshly ground black pepper
½ tbsp white wine vinegar

2 pints (900ml) vegetable
  or chicken stock
14oz can each of butter beans,
  cannellini beans, and red kidney
  beans, drained and rinsed
9oz (250g) Swiss chard, stems and
  leaves separated and roughly
  chopped
7oz jar artichoke hearts in oil,
  drained, rinsed, and halved

1 Heat the olive oil in a large, heavy pan, add the onion and cook for about 5 minutes or until soft. Stir in the garlic and red peppers along with the cumin, paprika, and bay leaf. Season well with salt and black pepper.

2 Add the vinegar and increase the heat a little, stirring the contents of the pan, then pour in a little stock and bring to a boil. Reduce to a simmer, add the beans, stir, pour in the rest of the stock, and simmer gently for about 15 minutes with the pan partially covered.

3 Add the stems of the chard and cook for 5 more minutes. Add the leaves and the artichokes, and cook for a couple of minutes or until the leaves have wilted. Taste and, if needed, add more seasoning and a little more stock. Remove the bay leaf, then ladle into bowls.

STATISTICS PER SERVING:

Energy 421cals/1,776kJ

Carbohydrate 12g

Sugar 10g

Fiber 15g

Fat 12g

Saturated fat 1g

Sodium 0.6g

COOK'S TIP
Swiss chard is grown in varieties that have green, red, or multicolored stems. Choose a colorful variety to add drama to the dish.

EGGPLANT AND ZUCCHINI TAGINE WITH COUSCOUS

●●○ GI
●●○ CALORIES
●○○ SATURATED FAT
●●○ SODIUM

SERVES 4   **PREP** 10 MINS   **COOK** 35-40 MINS   **FREEZE** 3 MONTHS
(TAGINE ONLY)

A colorful dish that is packed with aromatic Middle Eastern spices.

1 tbsp olive oil, plus 2-3 tbsp
  extra for frying
1 red onion, sliced
1 tsp coriander seeds, ground
2 tsp dried mint
1 heaped tsp paprika
salt and freshly ground black pepper
1 eggplant, chopped into bite-sized
  pieces
2-3 small zucchini, chopped into
  bite-sized pieces

1¼ pint (600ml) vegetable stock,
  plus extra for the couscous
4 preserved lemons, halved, pith
  and skin removed and discarded,
  chopped
8oz (225g) couscous
2oz (50g) pine nuts, toasted
1 tbsp chopped cilantro leaves,
  to garnish

1 Heat 1 tablespoon of olive oil in a large, wide, heavy pan and add the onion, ground coriander, dried mint, paprika, and salt and black pepper. Cook over low heat for about 5 minutes or until the onion starts to soften. Put in the eggplant and, adding more oil as needed, cook until golden. Add the zucchini and continue cooking until they begin to color.

2 Add a little of the stock and bring to a boil, then reduce to a simmer and add the remaining stock. Cook gently, partially covered, for about 20 minutes or until the liquid has reduced, adding a little more hot water if needed. Stir in the preserved lemons for the last 10 minutes of cooking.

3 Put a lid on the pan of tagine and set it aside while you prepare the couscous. Put the couscous into a bowl and pour in just enough stock to cover it, leave for 5 minutes, then fluff up with a fork to separate the grains. Season well and then pile onto individual plates and spoon the vegetable mixture over it. Sprinkle with the pine nuts and cilantro leaves.

STATISTICS PER SERVING:

Energy 370cals/1,537kJ

Carbohydrate 37g

Sugar 5g

Fiber 3g

Fat 20g

Saturated fat 2.5g

Sodium 0.48g

●●○ GI

●●○ CALORIES

●○○ SATURATED FAT

●○○ SODIUM

ROAST ROOT VEGETABLES WITH ROMESCO SAUCE

SERVES 4   **PREP** 20 MINS   **COOK** 45-50 MINS   **FREEZE** 3 MONTHS

The delicious smoky flavor of the romesco sauce complements the roasted vegetables perfectly.

2 sweet potatoes, cut into
  ½in (1cm) cubes
2 large carrots, cut into
  ½in (1cm) cubes
2 parsnips, cut into
  ½in (1cm) cubes
1 small celery root, cut
  into ½in (1cm) cubes
4 garlic cloves
4 tbsp olive oil
salt and freshly ground black pepper

For the romesco sauce
2 red peppers, seeded and roughly
  chopped into ¾in (2cm) chunks
3 large tomatoes, seeded and cut
  into quarters
3 tbsp olive oil
scant 1oz (25g) blanched almonds
2 garlic cloves, crushed or finely
  chopped
½ tsp smoked paprika
½ tsp cayenne pepper, or to taste
1-2 tbsp red wine vinegar

1 Preheat the oven to 425°F (220°C). Toss all the root vegetables and the 4 garlic cloves in 3 tablespoons of the olive oil, season to taste with salt and black pepper, and transfer to a large roasting pan. Roast in the oven for 40–50 minutes, or until tender.

2 To make the romesco sauce, place the peppers and tomatoes in a separate roasting pan. Drizzle with 1 tablespoon of the oil and cook in the oven for 20 minutes, then add the almonds and cook for a further 5 minutes. Remove from the oven and set aside to cool.

3 Place the cooled peppers and tomatoes in a food processor or a blender with the garlic, paprika, cayenne pepper, and vinegar. Process until smooth. Transfer to a small bowl and adjust the seasoning.

4 Arrange the roasted vegetables on a serving plate and drizzle the romesco sauce over them.

STATISTICS PER SERVING:

Energy 390cals/1,622kJ

Carbohydrate 37g

Sugar 20g

Fiber 13g

Fat 25g

Saturated fat 3g

Sodium 0.16g

PUY LENTIL AND VEGETABLE HOTPOT

GUIDELINES PER SERVING:

● ○ ○ GI
● ● ○ CALORIES
● ○ ○ SATURATED FAT
● ● ○ SODIUM

SERVES 4   **PREP** 20 MINS   **COOK** 1 HOUR   **FREEZE** 3 MONTHS

Sweet potatoes and cinnamon add a delicious sweetness to this tasty hotpot.

1 tbsp olive oil
2 onions, roughly chopped
1 cinnamon stick
1 bay leaf
3 celery stalks, finely diced
salt and freshly ground black pepper
2 garlic cloves, finely chopped
3 carrots, roughly chopped

14oz (400g) puy lentils, well rinsed
  and any grit removed
2½ pints (1.2 liters) vegetable stock
handful of curly kale or dark green
  cabbage, roughly chopped
2 sweet potatoes, diced
handful of flat-leaf parsley, finely
  chopped

1 Heat the oil over low heat in a large, heavy saucepan, add the onions and cook for a few minutes or until the onions soften a little. Add the cinnamon stick, bay leaf and celery and cook for a further 5 minutes to sweat the celery. Season with salt and some black pepper.

2 Stir in the garlic and carrots, cook for a couple of minutes, then add the lentils and stir until coated. Pour in the stock, bring it to a boil then reduce the heat to a simmer and cook, partially covered, for about 40 minutes or until the lentils are done. Stir occasionally and top up with more hot water if the mixture begins to dry out.

3 Add the cabbage and sweet potatoes to the pan, cover, and cook for a final 10 minutes or until the potato is soft and the cabbage is cooked. Remove the cinnamon stick and bay leaf, then stir through the parsley. Taste and season as needed, ladle into bowls, and serve.

COOK'S TIP
Curly kale is a member of the cabbage family and is full of nutrients. Trim away any tough bits of stalk before using and rinse the leaves well to remove dirt. Kale requires a slightly longer cooking time than cabbage, so do check that it is cooked before serving.

STATISTICS PER SERVING:

Energy 523cals/2,214kJ

Carbohydrate 84g

Sugar 17g

Fiber 15g

Fat 8g

Saturated fat 1g

Sodium 0.64g

RED LENTIL DHAL WITH CHERRY TOMATOES

SERVES 4   **PREP** 10 MINS   **COOK** 40 MINS

A quick and tasty lunch or supper. Unlike other pulses, lentils don't need to be soaked before cooking.

2 tbsp vegetable oil
1 large onion, peeled and
  finely chopped
3 cloves of garlic, peeled and
  crushed or finely chopped
¼in (5mm) piece of fresh ginger,
  peeled and finely chopped
7oz (200g) red lentils, rinsed

1 red chile, seeded and
  finely chopped
½ tsp salt
freshly ground black pepper
7oz (200g) cherry tomatoes, halved
1 tsp black mustard seeds (optional)
3 tbsp chopped fresh cilantro

1 Heat the oil in a large saucepan, add the onion and cook over low heat, stirring occasionally, for 5 minutes. Add the garlic and ginger and continue to cook for 1–2 minutes.

2 Add the lentils, chile, salt, and 1½ pints (750ml) water. Bring to a boil, reduce the heat, and simmer for 30 minutes or until the lentils are soft. Season to taste with freshly ground black pepper.

3 Stir in the tomatoes, mustard seeds if using, and cilantro. Serve with chapattis (see page 338) and riata.

see page 338

GUIDELINES PER SERVING:

- ●○○ GI
- ●○○ CALORIES
- ●○○ SATURATED FAT
- ●○○ SODIUM

STATISTICS PER SERVING:

Energy 231cals/965kJ

Carbohydrate 33g

Sugar 4.5g

Fiber 3.5g

Fat 7g

Saturated fat 1g

Sodium 0.04g

LENTIL LOAF

SERVES 6   **PREP** 15 MINS   **COOK** 1 HOUR 20 MINS

Lentils are a good source of protein and iron, and this substantial loaf can be eaten hot or cold.

6oz (175g) red lentils
15fl oz (450ml) vegetable stock
1 tbsp olive oil
1 onion, sliced
2 stalks celery, finely chopped
1 red pepper, seeded and diced
1 clove garlic, crushed
1 small red chile, seeded and finely chopped

4½oz (125g) shiitake mushrooms, finely chopped
5½oz (150g) low-fat Cheddar cheese, grated
8oz (225g) wholemeal breadcrumbs
3 tbsp chopped fresh cilantro
1 egg, beaten
salt and freshly ground black pepper

1 Put the lentils in a saucepan and add the stock. Bring to a boil, then reduce the heat, cover and simmer over low heat for 15–20 minutes or until the lentils are very soft.

2 Preheat the oven to 350°F (180°C). Grease and line the bottom of a 2½ pints (1.2 liter) loaf pan. Heat the oil in a frying pan, add the onion and cook for 2–3 minutes or until softened. Add the celery, red pepper, garlic, chile, and mushrooms. Cook, stirring, for 10 minutes.

3 Add the vegetables into the lentil mixture, then stir in the cheese, breadcrumbs, cilantro, and egg. Mix well and season to taste with salt and pepper.

4 Spoon the mixture into the prepared loaf pan and bake for 1 hour or until firm to the touch.

5 Cool in the pan for 10 minutes before turning out. Cut into thick slices and serve hot or cold.

STATISTICS PER SERVING:

Energy 300cals/1,265kJ

Carbohydrate 35g

Sugar 3.5g

Fiber 4g

Fat 9g

Saturated fat 3.5g

Sodium 0.52g

LENTILS WITH TURNIPS AND CHESTNUTS

SERVES 4   **PREP** 10 MINS   **COOK** 50 MINS   **FREEZE** 3 MONTHS

A chunky vegetable dish with versatility: serve it as a soup or a casserole.

1 tbsp olive oil
1 onion, finely chopped
salt and freshly ground black pepper
2 garlic cloves, finely chopped
2 turnips, cut into chunks
7oz vacuum pack of chestnuts

3 sage leaves, roughly chopped
1 tbsp fresh parsley,
  roughly chopped
12oz (350g) Puy lentils, rinsed
  and any grit removed
2½ pints (1.2 liters) vegetable stock

1 Heat the oil in a large, heavy pan, put in the onion and cook until soft. Season with salt and black pepper, then stir in the garlic, turnips, chestnuts, sage, and parsley.

2 Stir in the lentils so they are coated with the vegetable mixture, then pour in the stock and bring to a boil. Reduce to a simmer, partially cover the pan and cook gently for about 40 minutes or until the lentils are soft, topping up with more stock if needed.

3 Season to taste, then ladle into bowls and serve.

GUIDELINES PER SERVING:

● ○ ○ GI
● ● ○ CALORIES
● ○ ○ SATURATED FAT
● ● ○ SODIUM

STATISTICS PER SERVING:

Energy 442cals/1,872kJ

Carbohydrate 67g

Sugar 8g

Fiber 11g

Fat 8g
Saturated fat 1.5g

Sodium 0.56g

SPICED LEMONY LENTILS WITH ROAST POTATOES

SERVES 4   **PREP** 15 MINS   **COOK** 40-50 MINS   **FREEZE** 3 MONTHS

A tasty vegetarian dish, made extra substantial by the inclusion of chickpeas and roast potatoes.

6oz (175g) Puy lentils, rinsed and any grit removed
2 pints (900ml) vegetable stock
salt and freshly ground black pepper
3 potatoes, peeled and cut into 1in (2.5cm) cubes
2 tbsp olive oil
2 red chiles, seeded and finely chopped
2 tsp cumin seeds

2 garlic cloves, finely chopped
zest of 1 lemon
1 onion, finely chopped
1 red pepper, seeded and finely chopped
14oz can chickpeas, drained and rinsed
juice of 2 lemons
1 tbsp flat-leaf parsley, finely chopped

1 Preheat the oven to 400°F (200°C). Put the lentils in a large pan and cover with the stock. Season well and bring to a boil, remove any scum on the surface of the liquid, and then simmer gently for 30–40 minutes or until the lentils are soft. (If the lentils look as if they are drying out, top up with a little more stock.) Drain and set aside.

2 While the lentils are cooking, toss the potatoes in 1 tablespoon of the olive oil and put them in a large roasting pan along with the chiles and cumin seeds. Season well with salt and black pepper. Roast in the oven for 30–35 minutes, giving them a shake or a stir halfway through, and add the garlic and lemon zest at the same time.

3 Heat 1 tablespoon of the oil in a large, heavy, deep frying pan. Add the onion and red pepper, and cook for about 5 minutes or until the pepper softens. Add in the chickpeas and the cooked lentils, stir well, and then stir in the lemon juice and parsley. If you prefer a wetter mixture, add a little hot stock and let it cook for a few minutes. Serve topped with a spoonful of the crispy roast potatoes.

STATISTICS PER SERVING:

Energy 456cals/1,925kJ

Carbohydrate 67g

Sugar 7g

Fiber 7g

Fat 9g

Saturated fat 1.5g

Sodium 0.44g

SIMPLE DINNERS— FISH

● ○ ○ GI

● ● ○ CALORIES

● ● ○ SATURATED FAT

● ○ ○ SODIUM

TUNA WITH BLACK-EYED PEA AND AVOCADO SALSA

SERVES 4   **PREP** 10 MINS   **COOK** 15 MINS

Serving fish or meat with a spicy salsa like this one is a great way to add to your intake of fruit and vegetables.

14oz can black-eyed peas,
  rinsed and drained
2 ripe avocados, peeled, stoned,
  and diced
7oz (200g) plum tomatoes, cut into
  quarters, seeded and diced
1 small red onion, finely chopped

4 tbsp chopped fresh cilantro
zest and juice of 2 limes
salt and freshly ground black pepper
4 fresh tuna steaks (about
  5½oz/150g each)
1 tbsp olive oil

1 To make the salsa, mix together the beans, avocados, tomatoes, and onion in a large bowl. Stir in the cilantro, lime zest and juice, and season to taste.

2 Brush the tuna steaks with oil. Place on a hot griddle pan and sear for 4–5 minutes each side.

3 Transfer the tuna to a warm serving plate and serve with the salsa.

STATISTICS PER SERVING:

Energy 480cals/2,014kJ

Carbohydrate 20g

Sugar 5g

Fiber 9g

Fat 25g
Saturated fat 6g

Sodium 0.08g

STEAMED SEA BASS WITH SOY, GINGER, AND LEMONGRASS

GUIDELINES PER SERVING:

⬤◯◯ GI

⬤◯◯ CALORIES

⬤◯◯ SATURATED FAT

⬤⬤⬤ SODIUM

SERVES 4   **PREP** 5 MINS   **COOK** 15 MINS

Sea bass is a delicate-tasting fish; here it is enhanced with aromatic spices and cooked in foil to seal in all the juices.

4 sea bass filets, skin on
4 tbsp soy sauce
2in (5cm) piece of fresh ginger root, finely sliced
2 stalks lemongrass, trimmed and finely sliced

1 bunch of spring onions, trimmed and sliced on the diagonal
1 tbsp fresh cilantro, leaves only

1 Preheat the oven to 350°F (180°C). Rinse the fish and pat dry. Lay a large piece of foil in a roasting pan and place the fish on it. Pour the soy sauce over it and sprinkle with the ginger and lemongrass.

2 Bring the edges of the foil together and squeeze so they are secure, but leave plenty of room around the fish. Put in the oven and cook for 8–10 minutes until the fish flakes when poked with a sharp knife.

3 Remove the fish to a serving dish and top with the spring onions and cilantro, then pour the soy sauce from the foil over it.

STATISTICS PER SERVING:

Energy 165cals/697kJ

Carbohydrate 3.5g

Sugar 3g

Fiber 0.4g

Fat 4g
Saturated fat 0.6g

Sodium 1.16g

● ○ ○ GI

● ● ○ CALORIES

● ○ ○ SATURATED FAT

● ○ ○ SODIUM

ROASTED MONKFISH WITH ROMESCO SAUCE

SERVES 4   **PREP** 15 MINS   **COOK** 20-25 MINS

A meaty fish such as monkfish works so well with this piquant red pepper sauce.

2 red peppers
1 bulb of garlic
2½lb (1.1kg) monkfish tails, washed
  and thin membrane removed,
  patted dry
4 tbsp olive oil
salt and freshly ground black pepper

2 tomatoes, quartered
2 tbsp breadcrumbs
scant 1oz (25g) blanched almonds
  or hazelnuts
2 tbsp red wine vinegar
pinch of red pepper flakes

1 Preheat the oven to 400°F (200°C). Put the peppers and garlic in a roasting pan and place in the oven for 20 minutes or until the peppers begin to soften and char very lightly. Remove the peppers, put them in a plastic bag and leave to cool. Set the garlic aside to cool. Leave the oven on.

2 While the vegetables are cooling, lightly rub the fish with a little olive oil and season with salt and black pepper. Put in a roasting pan and cook in the oven for 20–25 minutes or until the fish is cooked through.

3 Remove the skin from the red peppers and discard it along with the stem and seeds. Heat a little of the olive oil in a frying pan, add the tomatoes and cook for a couple of minutes until they soften. Put into a food processor or blender and process until blended. Add the breadcrumbs and blend again. Squeeze the garlic cloves from their skins and put them in the mixture along with the peeled red peppers, then blend again. Add the nuts, vinegar, remaining oil, and red pepper flakes. Season well with salt and black pepper. Blend to a smooth paste. Taste and adjust the seasoning if needed, and serve with the roasted fish.

COOK'S TIP
For ease, you could use ready-roasted peppers from a 12oz jar, drained and blended as per the recipe.

STATISTICS PER SERVING:

Energy 345cals/1,450kJ

Carbohydrate 13g

Sugar 6g

Fiber 2g

Fat 16g

Saturated fat 2g

Sodium 0.12g

SWORDFISH WITH A SPICY COATING

SERVES 4   **PREP** 5 MINS   **COOK** 10 MINS

This firm, rich-textured fish is perfect for griddling and here's a quick and zesty way to enjoy it at its freshest.

1 tsp cayenne pepper
1 tbsp olive oil
1 tbsp fresh flat-leaf parsley, finely chopped
juice and zest of 1 lime
salt and freshly ground black pepper
4 x 7oz (200g) swordfish steaks
4 lime segments, to serve

1 In a small bowl, mix together the cayenne pepper, olive oil, parsley, lime juice and zest. Season with salt and black pepper.

2 Lay the swordfish steaks on a plate, pour the spicy mixture over them and rub to coat. Heat a griddle pan over high heat, then pop in the steaks, two at a time if there is not enough room for all of them, and cook for 3–5 minutes each side until cooked through. Remove and serve with a squeeze of lime.

STATISTICS PER SERVING:

Energy   243cals/1,018kJ

Carbohydrate 0g

Sugar 0g

Fiber 0g

Fat 11g

Saturated fat 2g

Sodium 0.24g

● ● ○ GI

● ● ○ CALORIES

● ● ○ SATURATED FAT

● ○ ○ SODIUM

SPICY MACKEREL AND BEET ROAST

SERVES 4   **PREP** 15 MINS   **COOK** 10 MINS

Mackerel, an oily fish that is rich in essential fatty acids, marries well with sweet beets and Indian spices.

4 whole fresh mackerel, cleaned, gutted, and slashed
10oz (300g) cooked beets
1 tbsp olive oil
1 tbsp fresh cilantro, to garnish

For the spice rub
1 tsp cumin seeds
1 tsp coriander seeds

2 garlic cloves, roughly chopped
1 red chile, seeded and chopped
½ tbsp sherry vinegar or red wine vinegar
1 tbsp olive oil
salt and freshly ground black pepper

1 Preheat the oven to 400°F (200°C). First, make the spice rub. Put all the ingredients in a food processor or blender and process until ground. Alternatively, grind in a pestle and mortar.

2 Rub the paste all over the fish and into the slashes. Put the beets in a roasting pan and toss in 1 tablespoon of oil. Add the fish and place in the oven for 8–10 minutes or until cooked and crispy. Sprinkle with the cilantro to serve. You could accompany this with a little brown or basmati rice.

STATISTICS PER SERVING:

Energy 414cals/1,730kJ

Carbohydrate 7g

Sugar 6g

Fiber 1.5g

Fat 29g

Saturated fat 6g

Sodium 0.2g

COOK'S TIP
Mackerel needs to be cooked and eaten as soon as possible after purchase.

● ○ ○ GI

● ○ ○ CALORIES

● ○ ○ SATURATED FAT

● ○ ○ SODIUM

MONKFISH WITH SALSA VERDE

SERVES 4   **PREP** 15 MINS   **COOK** 15 MINS

Salsa verde, or green sauce, is a piquant Italian recipe that can work magic with roasted or grilled fish and meat.

2 x 12oz (350g) pieces of chunky
  prepared monkfish, outer film
  removed
1 tbsp olive oil

For the salsa verde
1 tbsp fresh flat-leaf parsley
1 tbsp fresh basil

1 tbsp fresh mint leaves
2 tbsp capers, rinsed
2 anchovy filets
2 garlic cloves
1 tbsp red wine vinegar
3½fl oz (100ml) good-quality,
  fruity olive oil

1 Preheat the oven to 400°F (200°C). First, make the salsa verde. Put all the ingredients for the sauce in a food processor or blender and pulse until the mixture is well combined but still fairly coarse.

2 Slash the monkfish a few times, then spoon a little of the salsa verde into the slashes, making sure that it includes some of the oil.

3 Heat the olive oil in a large frying pan over gentle heat, add the monkfish, and cook for about 4 minutes each side. Carefully remove the fish from the pan and transfer to a roasting pan. Cook in the oven for 6–8 minutes, depending on the thickness of the pieces, until done.

4 Spoon a little of the salsa verde over the monkfish and put the remainder in a small bowl to serve alongside.

COOK'S TIP
Monkfish is covered with a thin film. To remove it, simply use a small, sharp knife to peel it away.

STATISTICS PER SERVING:

Energy 303cals/1,263kJ

Carbohydrate 0.5g

Sugar 0g

Fiber 0g

Fat 22g

Saturated fat 3g

Sodium 0.32g

COD IN A RICH TOMATO SAUCE

GUIDELINES PER SERVING:

● ○ ○ GI
● ○ ○ CALORIES
● ○ ○ SATURATED FAT
● ● ○ SODIUM

SERVES 4   **PREP** 10 MINS   **COOK** 40-45 MINS   **FREEZE** 3 MONTHS
(SAUCE ONLY)

Like all white fish, cod is low in fat, making it an excellent choice for anyone watching their weight.

2 tbsp olive oil
1 large red onion, finely chopped
2 stalks celery, finely chopped
2 cloves garlic, crushed
large pinch of red pepper flakes
1 tsp ground coriander
1 tsp ground cumin

2 x 14oz cans chopped tomatoes
2 tbsp tomato purée
5fl oz (150ml) red wine
salt and freshly ground black pepper
4 skinless cod filets
1¾oz (50g) pitted black olives

1 Heat half the oil in large saucepan, add in the onion and cook for 2–3 minutes. Add the rest of the oil, the celery, garlic, red pepper flakes, coriander, and cumin. Cook for 5 minutes or until the onion is beginning to soften.

2 Empty in the tomatoes, tomato purée, and red wine. Season to taste, bring to a boil and then simmer for about 30 minutes or until the sauce is reduced by about half.

3 Bury the fish in the tomato sauce and scatter with the olives. Cover and cook gently for 10 minutes or until the fish is done. Check the seasoning and serve immediately.

STATISTICS PER SERVING:

Energy 269cals/1,130kJ

Carbohydrate 11g

Sugar 9g

Fiber 3g

Fat 9g

Saturated fat 1g

Sodium 0.32g

● ○ ○ GI

● ● ○ CALORIES

● ○ ○ SATURATED FAT

● ○ ○ SODIUM

SALMON EN PAPILLOTE

SERVES 4   **PREP** 25 MINS   **COOK** 15 MINS

Cooking in a tightly sealed parchment packet or *papillote* ensures that the cooking juices are retained and keeps the fish moist.

olive oil, for greasing
4 tomatoes, sliced
4 salmon steaks or fillets,
  6oz (175g) each

2 lemons, sliced
8 sprigs of tarragon
freshly ground black pepper

1 Cut 8 circles of wax paper large enough for the salmon steaks to fit on half of a circle. Place 2 circles on top of each other to create a double thickness of paper. Lightly grease the top circle's surface with olive oil. Repeat with the other circles.

2 Preheat the oven to 325°F (160°C). Divide the tomato slices among the circles, placing them on one half. Place the salmon on the tomatoes, then top with the lemon slices and tarragon and season to taste with pepper. Fold up the paper to enclose the fish. Crimp the edges to create a tight seal. Place the parcels on a baking tray and bake for 15 minutes.

3 Place the salmon on warm plates, and serve immediately.

COOK'S TIP
The salmon parcels can be prepared several hours in advance and chilled until needed.

STATISTICS PER SERVING:

Energy 345cals/1,441kJ

Carbohydrate 3g

Sugar 3g

Fiber 1g

Fat 21g

Saturated fat 3.5g

Sodium 0.08g

MEDITERRANEAN-STYLE GRILLED SARDINES

GUIDELINES PER SERVING:

⬤◯◯ GI
⬤◯◯ CALORIES
⬤◯◯ SATURATED FAT
⬤◯◯ SODIUM

SERVES 4   **PREP** 15 MINS   **COOK** 5 MINS
PLUS MARINATING

Popular in coastal regions all over southern Europe, this is the way to enjoy these oily fish at their very best.

8 large whole sardines, cleaned
8 sprigs of thyme or lemon thyme, plus extra to garnish
4 lemons

3 tbsp olive oil
2 garlic cloves, crushed
1 tsp ground cumin

1 Rinse the sardines inside and out, and pat dry. Put a sprig of thyme or lemon thyme inside each fish, and place them in a shallow non-metallic dish. Grate the zest and squeeze the juice from 3 of the lemons and place in a small bowl. Add the oil, garlic, and cumin, and whisk together. Pour this mixture over the sardines, cover, and leave to marinate in the refrigerator for at least 2 hours.

2 Preheat the broiler on its highest setting. Transfer the sardines to a grill pan and broil for 2–3 minutes on each side, basting with the marinade.

3 Cut the remaining lemon into 8 wedges. Transfer the sardines to a heated serving plate and serve immediately, garnished with lemon wedges and sprigs of thyme.

STATISTICS PER SERVING:

Energy 322cals/1,341kJ

Carbohydrate 0g

Sugar 0g

Fiber 0g

Fat 22g
Saturated fat 3g

Sodium 0.16g

ROASTED SNAPPER WITH NEW POTATOES AND FENNEL

GUIDELINES PER SERVING:

●●○ GI

●○○ CALORIES

●○○ SATURATED FAT

●○○ SODIUM

SERVES 4   **PREP** 15 MINS   **COOK** 30 MINS

An easy and healthy all-in-one roast.

10oz (300g) baby new potatoes
2 tbsp olive oil
salt and freshly ground black pepper
8 cherry tomatoes, finely chopped
1 fennel bulb, finely chopped
2 tsp capers, rinsed

4 filets of snapper (about 5oz/140g
    each), skin on
1 tbsp fresh flat-leaf parsley, finely
    chopped
1 tbsp fresh dill, finely chopped

1 Preheat the oven to 400°F (200°C). Put the potatoes in a roasting pan and drizzle with 1 tablespoon of the olive oil. Mix to coat, using your hands, and arrange so that they have plenty of room around them. Season well with salt and black pepper, then roast for about 15 minutes.

2 While the potatoes are cooking, combine the tomatoes, fennel, and capers with the remaining olive oil. Season to taste. Smother the fish filets with the tomato mixture. Remove the pan of potatoes from the oven, sit the coated fish on top, and return the pan to the oven to cook for a further 15 minutes, or until the potatoes and fish are done.

3 Sprinkle with the parsley and dill and serve immediately.

STATISTICS PER SERVING:

Energy 244cals/1,028kJ

Carbohydrate 13g

Sugar 2g

Fiber 1.5g

Fat 8g

Saturated fat 1.5g

Sodium 0.24g

MONKFISH WITH SPICY WILTED GREENS

SERVES 4   **PREP** 15 MINS   **COOK** 25 MINS

Earthy greens livened up with red pepper flakes and sherry are an excellent accompaniment to white fish.

2 tbsp olive oil
2½lb (1.1kg) monkfish tails, washed, thin membrane removed and patted dry
salt and freshly ground black pepper

1lb 2oz (500g) young spinach leaves
3 garlic cloves, finely chopped
1 tsp red pepper flakes
1 tbsp dry sherry
lemon wedges, to serve

1 Preheat the oven to 400°F (200°C). Heat 1 tablespoon of the oil in a large frying pan. Season the fish with salt and black pepper, add to the pan, and cook for 5 minutes on each side or until it is sealed. Transfer the fish to a roasting pan and bake in the oven for 15 minutes or until cooked through.

2 While the fish is cooking, wipe out the pan with a piece of paper towel and heat the remaining olive oil. Add the spinach and cook for a minute then add the garlic and red pepper flakes and cook for a further 2–3 minutes or until the spinach begins to wilt. Increase the heat, add the sherry and a little salt and pepper, and cook for 2–3 minutes more or until the sherry has evaporated.

3 Divide up the spinach onto plates, then slice the monkfish and arrange on top. Serve with lemon wedges for squeezing over.

STATISTICS PER SERVING:

Energy 267cals/1,126kJ

Carbohydrate 2g

Sugar 1.5g

Fiber 2.5g

Fat 7.5g

Saturated fat 1g

Sodium 0.24g

TUNA KEBABS WITH SALSA VERDE

GUIDELINES PER SERVING:

● ○ ○ GI

● ● ○ CALORIES

● ● ○ SATURATED FAT

● ○ ○ SODIUM

SERVES 4   **PREP** 15 MINS   **COOK** 10 MINS

Tuna's firm, meaty texture makes it good for kebabs.

1lb (450g) tuna, cut into
  12 bite-sized pieces
2½oz (75g) Parma ham,
  cut into 12 strips
12 small cherry tomatoes
olive oil, for brushing

For the salsa verde
1 tsp Dijon mustard
8 tbsp olive oil

2 anchovy fillets
handful of flat-leaf parsley
handful of mint
handful of basil
1 tbsp capers, rinsed
2 garlic cloves, peeled
juice of 1 lemon

1 First make the salsa verde: place all the ingredients in a food processor and blend for 30 seconds or until smooth.

2 Preheat the broiler to high. Wrap each piece of tuna in a strip of Parma ham and thread onto 4 skewers, alternating with cherry tomatoes. Brush the kebabs with a little oil and place under the broiler for 3–4 minutes, then turn and cook for a further 3 minutes or until cooked to your liking. Serve with the salsa verde.

STATISTICS PER SERVING:

Energy 345cals/1,432kJ

Carbohydrate 1g

Sugar 1g

Fiber 0.5g

Fat 27g

Saturated fat 4g

Sodium 0.24g

SEAFOOD CEVICHE

SERVES 4   **PREP** 20 MINS
PLUS MARINATING

"Ceviche" describes a brief, light pickling of raw fish in citrus juice, which brings out its true flavor.

1lb (450g) very fresh, firm-fleshed
  fish such as salmon, turbot, halibut,
  or monkfish
1 red onion, thinly sliced
juice of 2 lemons or limes

1 tbsp olive oil
½ tsp pimentón picante
1 chile, seeded and finely chopped
salt and freshly ground black pepper
2 tbsp finely chopped parsley

1 With a sharp knife, slice the fish into very thin slivers.

2 Spread the onion slices evenly in the bottom of a shallow, nonmetallic dish. Pour the lemon juice over the onion, then sprinkle the pimentón picante and chile on top.

3 Place the fish slivers on the layer of onion slices, gently turning them so that they are all fully coated with the marinade.

4 Leave to marinate in the refrigerator for at least 20 minutes, preferably for over 1 hour. Season to taste with salt and pepper, then sprinkle with parsley and serve.

COOK'S TIP
Pimentón picante is a medium-hot paprika pepper.

STATISTICS PER SERVING:

Energy 238cals/988kJ

Carbohydrate 2g

Sugar 1.5g

Fiber 0.3g

Fat 15g

Saturated fat 2.5g

Sodium 0.08g

HADDOCK AND GREEN BEAN PIE

SERVES 4   **PREP** 10 MINS   **COOK** 30 MINS   **FREEZE** 1 MONTH

Flakes of fish in a creamy tarragon sauce, topped with crispy breadcrumbs.

2 slices of wholemeal bread
1 tbsp olive oil
1 onion, finely chopped
salt and freshly ground black pepper
7oz (200g) green beans, trimmed and halved
3 garlic cloves, finely chopped

1 tbsp white wine vinegar
1 tbsp all-purpose flour
10fl oz (300ml) milk
few tarragon leaves, finely chopped
1lb 2oz (500g) haddock filets, skinned

1 Preheat the oven to 400°F (200°C). Put the bread in a food processor or blender and pulse until it forms breadcrumbs, then set aside.

2 Heat the olive oil in a large frying pan, add the onion and cook for about 3 minutes until soft and translucent. Season with some salt and black pepper, then add the beans and garlic and cook for a further minute. Add the vinegar, increase the heat and cook for 1 minute.

3 Remove the pan from the heat, stir in the flour to combine, add a little milk and stir again until all the flour is mixed in. Reduce the heat, return the pan to the burner and slowly pour in the rest of the milk, stirring continuously to make a smooth sauce (you can use a balloon whisk to prevent lumps forming).

4 Remove the pan from the heat and stir in the tarragon. Season to taste. Lay the fish in an ovenproof baking dish, pour the sauce over it and stir to combine. Sprinkle with the breadcrumbs and cook in the oven for about 20 minutes or until the fish is done and the breadcrumbs are golden.

STATISTICS PER SERVING:

Energy 246cals/1,037kJ

Carbohydrate 17g

Sugar 6g

Fiber 2g

Fat 7g
Saturated fat 2.5g

Sodium 0.2g

SALMON AND SWEET POTATO PIE

SERVES 4   **PREP** 25 MINS   **COOK** 40-45 MINS   **FREEZE** 1 MONTH

Salmon topped with a golden, sweet mash makes a flavorsome mix that is rich in nutrients.

4 salmon filets, skinned (about 1lb/450g in total)
1lb 10oz (750g) sweet potatoes, sliced
scant 1oz (25g) polyunsaturated margarine

1 tbsp flour
16fl oz (500ml) skim milk
salt and freshly ground black pepper
2½oz (75g) frozen or fresh peas
1 bunch of chives, snipped

1 Preheat the oven to 400°F (200°C). Put the salmon in a roasting dish and cook for 10–15 minutes or until it flakes when you poke it. Don't let it dry out too much. Meanwhile, boil the sweet potatoes in a pan of lightly salted water for 10–15 minutes, until soft when pierced with a knife. Drain and mash using a potato masher.

2 Next, make the sauce. Melt the margarine in a pan, remove from the heat and stir in the flour. Add a little of the milk and stir with a wooden spoon until smooth. Put the pan back on the heat, and gradually add the remaining milk, stirring all the time. Cook, stirring, until it thickens into a smooth sauce. Season well with salt and black pepper. Stir the peas and chives into the sauce.

3 Put the cooked fish in an ovenproof dish and flake it slightly. Pour or spoon the sauce over it, then mix gently to combine. Top with the sweet potato mash, patterning the surface with the back of a fork. Put the pie in the oven to cook for about 30 minutes or until golden brown.

STATISTICS PER SERVING:

Energy 500cals/2,096kJ

Carbohydrate 50g

Sugar 16g

Fiber 6g

Fat 21g

Saturated fat 5g

Sodium 0.2g

● ○ ○ GI

● ● ○ CALORIES

● ○ ○ SATURATED FAT

● ○ ○ SODIUM

CURRIED SALMON KEBABS

SERVES 4 **PREP** 5 MINS **COOK** 10 MINS
PLUS CHILLING

These kebabs are perfect for an easy supper. You could also make miniature versions and serve as canapés with a tzatziki dip (see opposite).

3 tbsp tandoori curry paste
5½oz (150g) plain yogurt
4 skinless salmon filets, sliced
  into bite-sized cubes
1 lemon, cut into 4 wedges, to serve

1 Stir the curry paste into the yogurt and mix well. Add the salmon to the yogurt mix and cover the dish. Set aside in the refrigerator for 15 minutes.

2 Thread the salmon cubes onto metal kebab skewers.

3 Preheat the broiler to a medium-high temperature. Line a broiler pan with foil and put the kebabs under the broiler for 7–10 minutes, or until cooked through. Serve with the lemon wedges.

STATISTICS PER SERVING:

Energy 318cals/1,331kJ

Carbohydrate 3.5g

Sugar 3g

Fiber 0g

Fat 19g
Saturated fat 3g

Sodium 0.28g

SALMON AND SWEET POTATO FISHCAKES

SERVES 4   **PREP** 15 MINS   **COOK** 30 MINS
PLUS CHILLING

Salmon is a great source of omega-3 fats, which help to keep your heart healthy.

1lb 2oz (500g) sweet potatoes, cut into even-sized chunks
2 tbsp reduced-fat mayonnaise
14oz can red salmon, drained
3oz (85g) smoked salmon, roughly chopped
all-purpose flour, for dusting
1 large egg, beaten
4oz (115g) fresh wholemeal breadcrumbs

3 tbsp sunflower oil
4 lemon wedges, to serve

For the tzatziki
1 small cucumber
7fl oz (200ml) reduced-fat Greek yogurt
2 tbsp chopped fresh mint
salt and freshly ground black pepper

1 Put the sweet potatoes in a pan of salted water, bring to a boil and cook for 20 minutes, or until tender. Drain well, add the mayonnaise and mash.

2 To make the tzatziki, slice the cucumber in half lengthwise and, using a teaspoon, remove the seeds. Dice the flesh and mix with the yogurt and mint. Season with salt and black pepper to taste, cover and set aside.

3 Place the canned salmon in a large bowl and mash it. Add the mashed sweet potato and smoked salmon, and season to taste. Mix well, then cover and place in the refrigerator for 1 hour.

4 Preheat the oven to its lowest setting. Turn out the mixture onto a lightly floured surface and shape it into 8 fishcakes. Dip each one into the beaten egg, then into the breadcrumbs, making sure that they are evenly coated.

5 Heat half the oil in a large frying pan over high heat and cook half the fishcakes for 4 minutes each side, or until golden brown. Drain the fishcakes on paper towels, then transfer to a plate and keep warm in the oven while you cook the rest. Serve with the tzatziki and lemon wedges.

STATISTICS PER SERVING:

Energy 580cals/2,456kJ

Carbohydrate 54g

Sugar 10g

Fiber 4g

Fat 25g

Saturated fat 4.5g

Sodium 1g

PAELLA

◑ GI

◑ CALORIES

◑ SATURATED FAT

◑ SODIUM

SERVES 4   **PREP** 10 MINS   **COOK** 30 MINS

This Spanish rice dish has many regional variations. This version contains a delicious mix of seafood.

2 pints (1 liter) hot fish stock
large pinch of saffron threads
2 tbsp olive oil
1 onion, finely chopped
2 garlic cloves, crushed
2 large tomatoes, skinned and diced
12 large shrimp, peeled

8oz (225g) squid, sliced into rings
14oz (400g) paella rice
3oz (85g) fresh or frozen peas
4 langoustines
12-16 mussels, scrubbed and
  debearded
1 tbsp chopped parsley, to garnish

1 Pour a little of the hot fish stock into a cup or jug, add the saffron threads, and set aside to infuse. Heat the oil in a paella pan or large frying pan, and fry the onion and garlic until softened. Add the tomatoes and cook for 2 minutes, then add the shrimp and squid and fry for 1–2 minutes, or until the shrimp turn pink.

2 Stir in the rice, then add the saffron liquid, peas, and 2 pints (1 liter) of the stock. Simmer, uncovered, without stirring, over low heat for 12–14 minutes, or until the stock has evaporated and the rice is just tender (add a little extra stock if necessary).

3 Meanwhile, cook the langoustines in 5fl oz (150ml) simmering stock for 3–4 minutes, or until cooked through. Transfer to a warm plate with a slotted spoon. Add the mussels to the stock, cover, and cook over high heat for 2–3 minutes, or until open. Remove from the pan with a slotted spoon, discarding any that have not opened.

4 Reserve 8 mussels for garnish. Remove the rest from their shells and stir into the paella. Arrange the reserved mussels and langoustines on top, and garnish with parsley.

COOK'S TIP
Tap the mussels prior to cooking and discard any that do not close.

STATISTICS PER SERVING:

Energy 552cals/2,312kJ

Carbohydrate 88g

Sugar 5g

Fiber 3.5g

Fat 8g
Saturated fat 1g

Sodium 0.36g

WILD RICE, ZUCCHINI, FENNEL, AND SHRIMP PAN-FRY

SERVES 4   **PREP** 15 MINS   **COOK** 35 MINS

Wild rice adds a delicate, nutty flavor to this pan-fry.

2 tbsp olive oil
1 red onion, finely chopped
3 zucchini, diced
salt and freshly ground black pepper
1 fennel bulb, trimmed and finely
  chopped
8oz (225g) mixed long-grain and
  wild rice.

2 pints (900ml) vegetable stock
7oz (200g) peeled shrimp, raw
2 garlic cloves, chopped
1 tbsp flat-leaf parsley,
  finely chopped
4 lemon wedges, to serve

1 Heat half the oil in a large frying pan and add the onion. Cook over low heat for 5 minutes, or until it softens. Stir in the zucchini and cook for 5 minutes, or until they begin to color slightly. Season well with salt and black pepper.

2 Add the fennel and continue cooking over low heat for 5 minutes, or until it softens. Stir in the mixed rice. Pour in a little of the stock and bring to a boil. Reduce the heat to a simmer, then add most of the remaining stock and cook for 20–25 minutes or until the wild rice starts to split. Add more hot stock if needed.

3 Meanwhile, heat the remaining oil in a frying pan, add the shrimp, and cook for a few minutes until they turn pink. Throw in the garlic and toss with the shrimp. Remove from the heat and stir in the parsley. Spoon the rice mixture into a large serving dish, and scatter the shrimp over it. Serve with the lemon wedges.

COOK'S TIP

Alternatively, you could use cooked shrimp for ease; once the rice is cooked, just stir them in and warm through.

STATISTICS PER SERVING:

Energy 366cals/1,528kJ

Carbohydrate 52g

Sugar 4g

Fiber 2g

Fat 8g

Saturated fat 1.5g

Sodium 0.56g

○ ○ ○ GI

● ● ○ CALORIES

● ○ ○ SATURATED FAT

● ○ ○ SODIUM

MOROCCAN FISH TAGINE

SERVES 4   **PREP** 10 MINS   **COOK** 25 MINS

This dish is just the thing to warm you up on a cold winter's night. It is healthy, low in fat, and can be put together in a matter of minutes.

4 cloves garlic, crushed
½ tsp ground cumin
½ tsp ground turmeric
¼ tsp paprika
¼ tsp hot chili powder
zest and juice of 1 lemon
3 tbsp olive oil
4 skinless cod filets or any
  firm white fish
1 large red onion, thinly sliced
2 tsp harissa paste
3oz (85g) dried apricots,
  roughly chopped

2 large carrots, thickly sliced
1 red pepper, seeded
  and roughly chopped
salt and freshly ground black pepper
14fl oz (400ml) hot fish
  stock or vegetable stock
14oz can chickpeas, drained
  and rinsed
8oz (225g) cherry tomatoes,
  sliced in half
2 tbsp roughly chopped fresh cilantro

1 Combine half the garlic with the cumin, turmeric, paprika, chili powder, lemon zest and juice, and 1 tablespoon of olive oil. Rub the mixture over the fish filets.

2 Heat the remaining oil in a large saucepan, add the onion and cook for 2–3 minutes or until beginning to soften. Add the remaining garlic and harissa paste, and cook for a further minute.

3 Add the apricots and all the vegetables to the pan and stir. Pour in the stock and bring to a boil. Season to taste, cover and simmer for 15 minutes.

4 Add the chickpeas and cherry tomatoes, and stir to combine. Place the fish on top of the vegetables, cover the pan and cook for a further 10 minutes or until the fish is done. Scatter with the cilantro to serve.

STATISTICS PER SERVING:

Energy 389cals/1,631kJ

Carbohydrate 36g

Sugar 19g

Fiber 8g

Fat 12g

Saturated fat 1.5g

Sodium 0.2g

SWEET POTATO AND MUSSEL STEW

GUIDELINES PER SERVING:

⬤⬤◯ GI

⬤◯◯ CALORIES

⬤◯◯ SATURATED FAT

⬤⬤◯ SODIUM

SERVES 4   **PREP** 20 MINS   **COOK** 30 MINS

The chile cuts through the richness with a subtle underlying heat. Portion sizes are on the small side—you might consider serving this as an impressive starter.

2 tbsp olive oil
1 onion, finely chopped
2 celery stalks, finely chopped
salt and freshly ground black pepper
2 leeks, trimmed and chopped
1 tsp paprika
½ tsp red pepper flakes

3 garlic cloves, finely chopped
few fresh thyme stems
16fl oz (500ml) vegetable stock
2 sweet potatoes, cut into
  bite-sized pieces
2½lb (1.1kg) fresh mussels, scrubbed
  and debearded

1 Heat the olive oil in a large, deep pan. Put in the onion and celery, and cook over low heat for a couple of minutes until they soften. Season with salt and black pepper, then add the leeks and cook for about 3 minutes.

2 Add the paprika, red pepper flakes, garlic, and thyme. Cook for 1 minute. Pour in a little of the vegetable stock and let it boil, then add the remaining stock and simmer gently for 8–10 minutes, partially covered. Taste, and add a little more seasoning if needed.

3 Put the sweet potatoes into the pan and cook for about 10 minutes until they are just beginning to soften. Add the mussels, put the lid on and cook for 5–8 minutes until the mussels start to open. Remove the thyme stems before serving.

COOK'S TIP
Do not cook mussels if the shells are already open—throw them away. After cooking mussels, don't eat any that haven't opened.

STATISTICS PER SERVING:

Energy 242cals/1,013kJ

Carbohydrate 27g

Sugar 8g

Fiber 4g

Fat 9g

Saturated fat 1g

Sodium 0.6g

FISHERMAN'S TUNA STEW

SERVES 4   **PREP** 10 MINS   **COOK** 35 MINS

This fish stew, which Basque fisherman call *marmitako de bonito,* was originally made at sea to provide for a hungry crew.

2lb (900g) potatoes
1lb 10oz (750g) fresh tuna
12oz (350g) jar roasted red peppers, drained
3 tbsp olive oil
1 large onion, finely sliced

2 garlic cloves, crushed
1 bay leaf
salt and freshly ground pepper
14oz (400g) can chopped tomatoes
10oz (300g) frozen green peas
2 tbsp chopped parsley

1 Peel the potatoes and cut into thick rounds. Cut the tuna into pieces roughly the same size as the potatoes, and slice the red peppers into strips.

2 Heat the oil in a flameproof casserole, stir in the onion, garlic, and bay leaf, and cook, stirring, until the onions are translucent. Add the potatoes, stir well, season to taste with salt and pepper, then cover with water. Boil for 10 minutes, or until the potatoes are almost cooked, then add the tomatoes, and continue to cook for a further 5 minutes.

3 Reduce the heat to low, add the tuna, and cook for a further 5 minutes, then add the green peas and the red peppers, and cook very gently for 10 minutes. Sprinkle with the parsley and serve.

STATISTICS PER SERVING:

Energy 625cals/2,630kJ

Carbohydrate 50g

Sugar 6g

Fiber 10g

Fat 24g

Saturated fat 3.5g

Sodium 0.2g

FISH SOUP WITH SAFFRON AND FENNEL

⬤⬤◯ GI

⬤◯◯ CALORIES

⬤◯◯ SATURATED FAT

⬤◯◯ SODIUM

SERVES 6   **PREP** 10 MINS   **COOK** 1 HOUR

This rustic, Mediterranean-style fish soup is simple to prepare and sure to please.

5 tbsp olive oil
1 large fennel bulb, finely chopped
2 garlic cloves, crushed
1 small leek, sliced
4 ripe plum tomatoes, chopped
3 tbsp brandy
¼ tsp saffron threads, infused in a little hot water
zest of ½ orange
1 bay leaf
3½ pints (1.7 liters) fish stock

10oz (300g) potatoes, diced and parboiled for 5 minutes
4 tbsp dry white wine
1lb 2oz (500g) fresh black mussels, scrubbed and debearded
salt and freshly ground black pepper
1lb 2oz (500g) monkfish or firm white fish, cut into bite-sized pieces
6 raw whole large shrimp
parsley, chopped, to garnish

1 Heat 4 tbsp of the oil in a large, deep pan. Stir in the fennel, garlic, and leek, and fry over moderate heat, stirring occasionally, for 5 minutes, or until softened and lightly browned.

2 Stir in the tomatoes, add the brandy, and boil rapidly for 2 minutes, or until the juices are reduced slightly. Stir in the saffron, orange zest, bay leaf, fish stock, and potatoes. Bring to a boil, then reduce the heat and skim off any scum from the surface. Cover and simmer for 20 minutes, or until the potatoes are tender. Remove the bay leaf.

3 Meanwhile, heat the remaining oil with the wine in a large deep pan until boiling. Add the mussels, cover, and continue on high heat for 2–3 minutes, shaking the pan often. Discard any mussels that do not open. Strain, reserving the liquid, and set the mussels aside. Add the liquid to the soup and season to taste. Bring to a boil, add the monkfish and shrimp, then reduce the heat, cover, and simmer gently for 5 minutes, or until the fish is just cooked and the shrimp are pink. Add the mussels to the pan and bring almost to a boil. Serve the soup sprinkled with chopped parsley.

STATISTICS PER SERVING:

Energy 265cals/1,112kJ

Carbohydrate 15g

Sugar 5g

Fiber 4g

Fat 11g

Saturated fat 1.5g

Sodium 0.28g

⬤⬤◯ GI

⬤⬤◯ CALORIES

⬤◯◯ SATURATED FAT

⬤◯◯ SODIUM

LINGUINE WITH SARDINES

SERVES 4   **PREP** 5 MINS   **COOK** 10 MINS

A classic combination that can be made with pantry ingredients.

10oz (300g) linguine
1 tbsp olive oil
1 red onion, finely chopped
salt and freshly ground black pepper
2 garlic cloves, finely chopped

4oz can sardines in oil, drained
3 tsp capers (rinsed, if salty)
juice of 1 lemon
1 tbsp flat-leaf parsley,
    finely chopped

1 Put the pasta in a pan of salted boiling water and cook for 8–10 minutes, or according to the instructions on the package.

2 Meanwhile, heat the olive oil in a large frying pan, add the onion and cook for about 5 minutes over low heat until it begins to soften. Season with a little salt and black pepper. Stir in the garlic and cook for a few seconds, then add the sardines and stir gently to break them up. Add the capers and lemon juice, and cook for about 5 minutes.

3 Drain the pasta, reserving some of the cooking water, then return it to the pan with a little of the water. Add the sardine sauce and the parsley and toss to combine.

COOK'S TIP
You can, of course, use fresh sardines if you wish: broil until cooked, then flake them and serve with the pasta.

STATISTICS PER SERVING:

Energy 362cals/1,530kJ

Carbohydrate 60g

Sugar 3g

Fiber 3g

Fat 8.5g

Saturated fat 1.5g

Sodium 0.24g

PASTA WITH CLAMS

GUIDELINES PER SERVING:

⬤⬤◯ GI

⬤⬤◯ CALORIES

⬤◯◯ SATURATED FAT

⬤◯◯ SODIUM

SERVES 4   **PREP** 10 MINS   **COOK** 15 MINS

Salty, meaty clams tossed with delicate linguine pasta and aromatic fresh parsley.

2½lb (1.1kg) clams
1 tbsp olive oil
1 onion, finely chopped
2 garlic cloves, finely chopped
1 red chile, seeded and finely chopped

12oz (350g) linguine
1 tbsp flat-leaf parsley,
  finely chopped
freshly ground black pepper

1 First, wash the clams, throwing away any that are already open. Set aside.

2 Pour the olive oil into a large frying pan, add the onion and cook for 5 minutes until soft. Put a pan of salted water on to boil for the pasta.

3 Stir the garlic and chile into the onion and cook for a minute or two, being careful not to burn the garlic. Add 2 tablespoons of water, add in the clams, cover the pan and cook for 3–5 minutes.

4 Put the pasta in the pan of boiling water and cook for 8–10 minutes, or according to the instructions on the package. Drain, reserving some of the cooking water, then return the pasta to the pan with a little of the water. Add the clams and the parsley, and toss to coat. Season with black pepper if needed.

COOK'S TIP
Do not cook clams that are already open: throw them away. After cooking clams, discard any that haven't opened.

STATISTICS PER SERVING:

Energy 415cals/1,764kJ

Carbohydrate 71g

Sugar 3g

Fiber 3g

Fat 6g

Saturated fat 1g

Sodium 0.28g

●●○ GI

●●○ CALORIES

●○○ SATURATED FAT

●●○ SODIUM

VERMICELLI NOODLES WITH SHRIMP AND CRAB

SERVES 4   **PREP** 10 MINS   **COOK** 20 MINS

A light, quick, Asian-style dish full of aromatic flavors, prepared in a wok.

2in (5cm) piece of fresh ginger root, roughly chopped
2 tsp Sichuan pepper
3 garlic cloves
1 stalk lemongrass, trimmed and woody outer leaf removed
salt and freshly ground black pepper
2 tbsp sunflower oil
9oz (250g) peeled shrimp, raw

¼ small pumpkin or butternut squash (about 5oz/ 140g), grated
7oz (200g) fresh white crabmeat
1 tbsp rice vinegar
14fl oz (400ml) vegetable or chicken stock
8oz (225g) vermicelli noodles
1 bunch of spring onions, finely chopped, to garnish

1 Put the ginger, Sichuan pepper, garlic, and lemongrass in a food processor or blender and pulse until chopped. Season with salt and black pepper and pulse again. Heat 1 tablespoon of oil in a wok, swirling it around to coat. When the oil is hot, add the shrimp and cook until pink (2–4 minutes). Remove and set aside.

2 Pour the remaining oil into the wok, add the ginger mixture to the pan and stir for a couple of minutes. Add the grated pumpkin and cook for a further 5 minutes, until the pumpkin has softened. Stir in the crabmeat.

3 Add the rice vinegar and the stock, and bring a the boil. Toss in the vermicelli noodles and stir for 5–8 minutes until the clump breaks down and the noodles begin to soften. Stir the cooked shrimp into the mixture. Taste, season if needed, and then sprinkle with the spring onions to serve.

COOK'S TIP
Use ready-cooked shrimp if you prefer: simply stir them in at the end of cooking.

STATISTICS PER SERVING:

Energy 392cals/1,640kJ

Carbohydrate 51g

Sugar 4g

Fiber 1g

Fat 9g

Saturated fat 1g

Sodium 0.4g

SHRIMP AND NEW POTATO BALTI

SERVES 4   **PREP** 10 MINS   **COOK** 20-25 MINS

In common with other shellfish, shrimp are low in fat, making them a good option for a healthy curry.

2 tbsp oil
1 large red onion, sliced
2 cloves garlic, crushed
14oz (400g) baby new potatoes, unpeeled, sliced in half

2 tbsp balti curry paste
14oz can plum tomatoes
7fl oz (200ml) vegetable stock
8oz (225g) peeled shrimp, raw
7oz (200g) baby spinach leaves

1 Heat the oil in a deep frying pan and cook the onion for 2–3 minutes. Add the garlic, potatoes, and curry paste. Cook, stirring, for 2 minutes.

2 Add the tomatoes and stock, bring to a simmer and cook for 15 minutes, stirring occasionally, until the potatoes are tender. Add a little more stock if necessary.

3 Gently stir in the shrimp and spinach, and simmer gently for 3 minutes until the shrimp are cooked through.

STATISTICS PER SERVING:

Energy 255cals/1,068kJ

Carbohydrate 25g

Sugar 8g

Fiber 3.5g

Fat 9g

Saturated fat 1g

Sodium 0.36g

SIMPLE DINNERS—MEAT

GRIDDLED STEAK CHUNKS WITH HERBY RICE

SERVES 4   **PREP** 10 MINS   **COOK** 30 MINS

A tasty and filling dish for red meat lovers.

2 tbsp olive oil
1 red onion, finely chopped
salt and freshly ground black pepper
2 cloves garlic, finely chopped
8oz (225g) basmati rice
2 pints (900ml) vegetable stock
4½oz (125g) frozen peas

handful of flat-leaf parsley,
  finely chopped
handful of fresh mint,
  finely chopped
handful of fresh cilantro,
  finely chopped
1lb 2oz (500g) lean steak

1 Heat 1 tablespoon of the oil in a large frying pan and add half the onion. Cook over low heat for 5 minutes or until soft. Season with salt and pepper, then stir in the garlic. Add the rice and stir to coat with the oil.

2 Pour in a little of the stock and let it bubble, add a little more, and stir again. Gradually add the rest of the stock as it is absorbed and cook for 15 minutes until the rice is soft and tender, then stir in the peas. Heat through for 1–2 minutes, then remove from the heat and stir in the herbs. Cover with a lid and set aside.

3 Coat the steak with the remaining olive oil and season. Heat a griddle pan until hot, then add the steak and grill for 3–5 minutes each side or until cooked to your liking. Remove and let rest for a few minutes, then slice and arrange over the rice. Sprinkle over the remaining onion and serve.

STATISTICS PER SERVING:

Energy 488cals/2,039kJ

Carbohydrate 52g

Sugar 2.5g

Fiber 2g

Fat 13g

Saturated fat 3.5g

Sodium 0.52g

BEEF AND GREEN BEAN STIR-FRY

SERVES 4   **PREP** 10 MINS   **COOK** 15 MINS
PLUS MARINATING

An instant meal full of punchy flavor and nutrients. Beef is a good source of protein, iron, B-vitamins, and zinc.

½ tbsp soy sauce
½ tbsp Worcestershire sauce
juice of 1 orange
2 garlic cloves, finely chopped
1 green chile, seeded and
  finely chopped

salt and freshly ground black pepper
14oz (400g) beef steak, cut into strips
1 tbsp sesame oil
10oz (300g) fine green beans,
  topped and tailed
9oz (250g) baby spinach leaves

1 Combine the soy sauce, Worcestershire sauce, orange juice, garlic, and chile. Season with salt and black pepper. Put the beef in a shallow bowl and pour the marinade over it. Leave to marinate for 15–30 minutes.

2 Meanwhile, put the beans in a pan of salted boiling water and cook for 3 minutes. Drain and refresh with cold water, then set aside. Heat the oil in a wok over high heat, then add the strips of beef, shaking them a little first to remove excess marinade.

3 Stir-fry the beef for about 5 minutes, moving it around the pan until it is no longer pink. Add the beans and stir-fry for a few more minutes. With the heat on high, add in the marinade and let it bubble and cook for a few minutes. Finally, add the spinach and stir until it wilts.

STATISTICS PER SERVING:

Energy 185cals/773kJ

Carbohydrate 4g

Sugar 3g

Fiber 3g

Fat 8g

Saturated fat 2g

Sodium 0.28g

COOK'S TIP
The key to this stir-fry is to use good-quality, tender beef, as this will require only a little cooking, and to keep everything moving over high heat.

SPICY COTTAGE PIE WITH LENTILS

SERVES 4   **PREP** 20 MINS   **COOK** 1 HOUR   **FREEZE** 1 MONTH

In this recipe, some of the meat has been replaced with lentils to reduce the fat content of the dish and boost fiber.

2 tbsp olive oil
14oz (400g) extra-lean ground beef
1 large onion, finely chopped
3 stalks celery, finely chopped
2 garlic cloves, crushed
1 red pepper, seeded and diced
2 tbsp all-purpose flour
½ tsp ground cinnamon
2 tbsp tomato purée
5fl oz (150ml) red wine
1 tsp dried thyme
10–14fl oz (300–400ml) beef stock
1 tsp Worcestershire sauce

pinch of dried red pepper flakes
14oz can lentils, rinsed and drained

For the mash
1lb (450g) white potatoes, peeled and cut into even-sized chunks
1lb 5oz (600g) sweet potatoes, peeled and cut into even-sized chunks
5fl oz (150ml) hot skim milk
scant 1oz (25g) polyunsaturated margarine
salt and freshly ground black pepper
1 tbsp sunflower or pumpkin seeds

1 Preheat the oven to 400°F (200°C). Heat 1 tablespoon of oil in a non-stick frying pan. Brown the beef over high heat for 1–2 minutes; set it aside. Using the remaining oil, cook the onion over medium heat for 2 minutes. Add the celery, garlic, and red pepper. Cook for 2 minutes.

2 Return the meat to the pan. Add the flour, cinnamon, tomato purée, and wine. Cook, stirring, for 1 minute. Add the thyme, 10fl oz (300ml) stock, the Worcestershire sauce, and red pepper flakes. Season to taste. Bring to a boil and reduce the heat. Cover and simmer for 30 minutes, adding more stock if necessary. Remove from the heat and stir in the lentils.

3 Boil the potatoes and sweet potatoes for 15–20 minutes, or until tender. Drain well, then return to the pan and dry off over low heat for 1 minute. Add the milk and margarine, and mash well. Season to taste. Spoon the meat mixture into an ovenproof dish, spread the mash on top, and sprinkle with the seeds. Place the cottage pie on a baking tray and cook in the oven for 20–25 minutes, or until the top begins to brown.

STATISTICS PER SERVING:

Energy 683cals/2,878kJ

Carbohydrate 75g

Sugar 17g

Fiber 10g

Fat 26g
Saturated fat 7g

Sodium 0.4g

CINNAMON AND GINGER BEEF WITH NOODLES

SERVES 4   **PREP** 10 MINS   **COOK** 15 MINS

A quick dish with punchy flavors.

1lb 2oz (500g) lean steak, thinly sliced
2 tsp ground cinnamon
1 tbsp sunflower oil
1 onion, sliced
2in (5cm) piece of fresh ginger,
  peeled and shredded
1 red chile, seeded and
  finely chopped
2 garlic cloves, finely chopped

1 tbsp fish sauce
1 tbsp sesame oil
7oz (200g) mixed exotic mushrooms,
  such as oyster, shiitake and hon
  shimeji, trimmed or chopped
7oz (200g) snow peas
14oz (400g) medium or thick
  straight-to-wok udon noodles

1 Put the steak in a bowl, sprinkle over the cinnamon and stir to coat. Heat the sunflower oil in a wok, add the onion, and stir-fry over high heat for 1 minute. Add the ginger and chile and stir-fry for a further minute.

2 Now add the steak, garlic, fish sauce, and sesame oil and continue to cook, stirring, until the meat is no longer pink. Add the mushrooms and snow peas and continue to stir-fry for a further 1–2 minutes.

3 Add the noodles and stir-fry for about 3 minutes until the noodles become sticky. Serve immediately.

COOK'S TIP
Always cook quickly over high heat when using a wok, and have all your ingredients to hand.

STATISTICS PER SERVING:

Energy 378cals/1,584kJ

Carbohydrate 33g

Sugar 2.5g

Fiber 2.2g

Fat 12g

Saturated fat 3g

Sodium 0.48g

LEBANESE SPICED BEEF AND OKRA

SERVES 4   **PREP** 10 MINS   **COOK** 35 MINS

A spiced and flavorful one-pot dish.

1 tbsp olive oil
1 onion, sliced
7oz (200g) okra, topped and
  halved horizontally
1lb 2oz (500g) lean steak, cut
  into ½in (1cm) pieces
1 tsp paprika

4 cloves garlic, finely chopped
juice of ½ lemon
14oz can of chopped tomatoes
handful of fresh cilantro,
  roughly chopped
salt and freshly ground black pepper

1 Heat the oil in a large frying pan, add the onion, and cook over medium heat for 2 minutes until it begins to soften, then add the okra and cook for a further minute.

2 Add the beef, paprika, and garlic and cook, stirring, until the beef is no longer pink. Add the lemon juice, tomatoes, and cilantro and season with salt and pepper. Bring to a boil then reduce to a simmer and cook, uncovered, for 20–30 minutes, stirring occasionally, until the sauce has reduced and thickened. Spoon into warmed bowls and serve. You could accompany this with some brown rice.

COOK'S TIP
Frying the okra before the other ingredients are added will prevent it from becoming gluey.

STATISTICS PER SERVING:

Energy 226cals/947kJ

Carbohydrate 7.5g

Sugar 6g

Fiber 3g

Fat 8.5g

Saturated fat 2.5g

Sodium 0.16g

BEEF AND BEAN STEW

GUIDELINES PER SERVING:

● ○ ○ GI

● ● ○ CALORIES

● ○ ○ SATURATED FAT

● ○ ○ SODIUM

SERVES 4   **PREP** 10 MINS   **COOK** 35 MINS   **FREEZE** 3 MONTHS

A hearty meal-in-one of tender beef simmered with tomatoes and beans.

2 tbsp olive oil
2 onions, roughly chopped
salt and freshly ground black pepper
1lb 2oz (500g) lean beef, diced
1 tsp hot paprika or cayenne pepper
1 tbsp cider vinegar
4 garlic cloves, finely chopped
14oz can of black-eyed beans, drained
  and rinsed

14oz can of chickpeas, drained
  and rinsed
14oz can of chopped tomatoes
10fl oz (300ml) vegetable stock
handful of fresh flat-leaf parsley,
  chopped
4 spring onions, finely chopped,
  to serve

1 Heat the oil in a large pan, add the onions and cook for about 5 minutes until soft. Season with salt and black pepper, then add the beef and paprika, stir to coat, and cook for 2–3 minutes until the beef is no longer pink. Add the vinegar and cook for a minute or two until the liquid evaporates.

2 Add the garlic and cook for 1 minute, then add the beans and chickpeas and stir to combine. Add the tomatoes and stock, bring to a boil, then reduce to a simmer and cook gently for 20–30 minutes until thickened. Top up with a little extra stock or water if it dries out too much. Stir in the parsley and adjust the seasoning if required. Scatter over the chopped spring onions and serve immediately.

STATISTICS PER SERVING:

Energy 453cals/1,910kJ

Carbohydrate 40g

Sugar 8g

Fiber 8g

Fat 14g
Saturated fat 3g

Sodium 0.24g

● ○ ○ GI

● ● ○ CALORIES

● ● ○ SATURATED FAT

● ● ○ SODIUM

CHILI CON CARNE

SERVES 4   **PREP** 5 MINS   **COOK** 50 MINS   **FREEZE** 1 MONTH

A hearty and warming Tex-Mex classic.

1 tbsp olive oil
1 onion, thinly sliced
2 tbsp chili sauce
1 garlic clove, crushed
1 tsp ground cumin

1lb 5oz (600g) extra lean ground beef
14oz (400g) can red kidney beans,
 drained and rinsed
14oz (400g) can chopped tomatoes
salt and freshly ground black pepper

1 Heat the oil in a large saucepan over medium heat. Add the onions and fry for 5 minutes, or until softened. Stir in the chili sauce, garlic, cumin, and beef, and fry for 3 minutes, or until the meat browns, stirring occasionally.

2 Stir in the kidney beans and tomatoes and bring to a boil. Reduce the heat, cover, and leave to simmer for 40 minutes, stirring occasionally. Season to taste with salt and pepper. You might want to try serving this with a spoonful of soured cream.

STATISTICS PER SERVING:

Energy 397cals/1,664kJ

Carbohydrate 20g

Sugar 8g

Fiber 6g

Fat 18g
Saturated fat 7g

Sodium 0.4g

NAVARIN OF LAMB

GUIDELINES PER SERVING:

●●○ GI

●●○ CALORIES

●●● SATURATED FAT

●○○ SODIUM

SERVES 4   **PREP** 30 MINS   **COOK** 1½ HOURS   **FREEZE** 3 MONTHS

This classic French stew is a complete one-pot meal, traditionally made with young spring vegetables.

2 tbsp olive oil
2lb (900g) middle neck of lamb,
  cut into pieces
2 small onions, quartered
1 tbsp all-purpose flour
14fl oz (400ml) lamb stock
  or beef stock

2 tbsp tomato purée
1 bouquet garni
salt and freshly ground black pepper
10oz (300g) small new potatoes
10oz (300g) small whole carrots
10oz (300g) baby turnips
6oz (175g) green beans

1 Heat the oil in a large flameproof casserole, add the lamb chunks, and fry until brown on all sides. Add the onions and fry gently for 5 minutes, stirring frequently.

2 Sprinkle the flour over the meat and stir well for 2 minutes, or until the pieces are evenly coated. Stir in the stock, then add the tomato purée and bouquet garni, and season to taste with salt and pepper. Bring to a boil, then cover and simmer for 45 minutes.

3 Add the potatoes, carrots, and turnips. Cover and cook for a further 15 minutes, then stir in the beans, cover, and cook for a further 10–15 minutes, or until all the vegetables are tender.

STATISTICS PER SERVING:

Energy	543cals/2,270kJ
Carbohydrate	32g
Sugar	15g
Fiber	7g
Fat	25g
Saturated fat	8.5g
Sodium	0.28g

●●○ GI

●●○ CALORIES

●●○ SATURATED FAT

●●○ SODIUM

BULGUR WHEAT WITH LAMB AND CHICKPEAS

SERVES 6   **PREP** 10 MINS   **COOK** 45 MINS

The classic combination of chickpeas and lamb makes a filling supper dish.

all-purpose flour, for dusting
salt and freshly ground black pepper
1lb (450g) lean lamb, cut into
  bite-sized pieces
2 tbsp oil
4½oz (125g) frozen peas
1 onion, finely chopped

1 tbsp fresh thyme, leaves only,
  chopped
2 x 14oz cans chickpeas,
  drained and rinsed
2½ pints (1.2 liters) vegetable stock
9½oz (275g) bulgur wheat
1 tbsp fresh dill, finely chopped

1 Season the flour with a pinch of salt and black pepper, and dust the meat with it until coated. Cook the meat in batches: heat 1 teaspoon of the oil in a large frying pan, add some of the meat, and cook until golden. Repeat for the rest of the meat. Remove the meat with a slotted spoon and set aside.

2 Put the peas into a bowl of boiling water, leave for few minutes, then drain and refresh with cold water and set aside.

3 Heat 1 tablespoon of oil in the pan, add the onion, and cook for 5 minutes, or until soft and transparent. Season well and stir in the thyme. Return the meat to the pan along with the chickpeas. Increase the heat, add a little of the stock, and bring to a boil. Reduce to a simmer and then add most of the remaining stock, reserving 10fl oz (300ml). Cook over low heat for about 20 minutes or until it thickens. Add more water if it needs it.

4 Meanwhile, put the bulgur wheat into a bowl, pour in the reserved stock, cover with plastic wrap, and leave for 8–10 minutes. Fluff up with a fork, stir in the peas and dill, and season to taste. Serve with the lamb mixture.

COOK'S TIP
Choose lean lamb such as leg, and dice it yourself rather than buying it already cut. It is usually cheaper to do this, and you can easily remove any fat.

STATISTICS PER SERVING:

Energy 528cals/2,203kJ

Carbohydrate 51g

Sugar 31g

Fiber 1.5g

Fat 16.5g

Saturated fat 5.5g

Sodium 0.4g

ROAST LAMB WITH FLAGEOLETS

SERVES 6   **PREP** 15 MINS   **COOK** 1 HOUR 40 MINS

A perfect Sunday lunch; the beans make a tasty change to the more traditional accompaniment of roast potatoes.

½ leg of lamb, about 3lb (1.35kg)
2–3 sprigs rosemary
1 tbsp olive oil
salt and freshly ground black pepper
4 garlic cloves, roughly chopped

9oz (250g) baby plum
  tomatoes, halved
14½oz can flageolet beans, drained
1 tbsp tomato purée
5fl oz (150ml) dry white wine

1 Preheat the oven to 350°F (180°C). With a small, sharp knife, make several deep cuts into the skin surface of the lamb. Push a few rosemary leaves into each cut. Place the lamb in a roasting pan, brush with oil, and season with salt and pepper. Roast for 1 hour.

2 Mix the remaining rosemary with the garlic, tomatoes, and flageolets. Remove the lamb from the oven and spoon the tomato and bean mixture around it. Mix the tomato purée with the wine and pour over the lamb.

3 Cover loosely with foil, then return to the oven for 30–40 minutes, or until the lamb is cooked but the juices are still slightly pink, stirring once. Allow the meat to rest for 10–15 minutes, loosely covered with foil, before carving.

COOK'S TIP

The lamb can be prepared and stuffed with the rosemary leaves, ready for roasting, a few hours in advance of cooking.

STATISTICS PER SERVING:

Energy   338cals/1,414kJ

Carbohydrate   10g

Sugar   2.5g

Fiber   3.5g

Fat   16g

Saturated fat   6g

Sodium   0.24g

LAMB CUTLETS WITH CHERMOULA

SERVES 6   **PREP** 15 MINS   **COOK** 10 MINS
PLUS MARINATING

Chermoula is a classic Moroccan spice marinade, wonderful for grilled meats and fish.

12 lamb cutlets, trimmed
4 ripe plum tomatoes, chopped
salt and freshly ground
  black pepper
1 tbsp balsamic vinegar

For the marinade
1 red onion, finely chopped
2 garlic cloves, crushed

1 tsp ground cumin
¼ tsp smoked paprika
1 tsp ground coriander
grated zest and juice of 1 lemon
6 tbsp olive oil, plus extra
  for drizzling
handful of mint, roughly chopped
handful of cilantro, chopped

1 Place the trimmed cutlets in a dish. In a mixing bowl, combine the red onion, garlic, cumin, paprika, ground coriander, lemon juice and zest, olive oil, and most of the chopped mint and cilantro. Rub the marinade over the lamb and leave to marinate for at least 30 minutes.

2 Season the chopped tomatoes with salt and pepper, drizzle with a little olive oil, the balsamic vinegar, and the remaining cilantro and mint. Set aside.

3 Preheat the broiler on its highest setting. Remove the cutlets from the marinade and broil for 5 minutes each side, or until cooked and crisp. Serve the lamb with the tomato salad alongside.

COOK'S TIP
The meat can be left to marinate for up to 24 hours.

STATISTICS PER SERVING:

Energy 350cals/1,451kJ

Carbohydrate 4g

Sugar 3.5g

Fiber 1g

Fat 23g

Saturated fat 7g

Sodium 0.12g

PEARL BARLEY, SPINACH, AND LAMB POT

GUIDELINES PER SERVING:

⬤◯◯ GI
⬤⬤◯ CALORIES
⬤⬤⬤ SATURATED FAT
⬤◯◯ SODIUM

SERVES 4   **PREP** 15 MINS   **COOK** 1 HOUR 25 MINS
PLUS SOAKING

One-pot cooking at its best, this dish is easy to make and full of flavor and goodness.

1 tbsp olive oil
1 onion, finely chopped
2 cloves of garlic, finely chopped
3 carrots, diced
3 celery stalks, diced
few stalks of thyme
1lb 10oz (750g) neck of lamb
  on the bone, trimmed of fat

2 pints (1 liter) of vegetable stock
2½oz (75g) pearl barley,
  soaked overnight
9oz (450g) spinach leaves,
  roughly chopped
salt and freshly ground black pepper

1 Heat the oil in a large heavy-based pan, add the onion and cook over low heat until it softens. Add the garlic, carrot, celery, and thyme and cook for a further 10 minutes. Add the lamb to the pan and cover with the stock. Bring to a boil and skim off any scum that comes to the surface. Reduce to a simmer, add the pearl barley, and cook gently for 1 hour until the lamb is tender and pearl barley is cooked. Top up with more stock or water if needed.

2 Remove the lamb from the pan, leave to cool slightly, and then shred the meat away from the bone. Meanwhile add the spinach to the pan and cook for 5 minutes or until it has wilted. Return the lamb to the pot and stir well then taste and season as required. Ladle into bowls and serve.

COOK'S TIP
This will taste even better the next day; put in the refrigerator once cooled and reheat when required.

STATISTICS PER SERVING:

Energy 570cals/2,731kJ

Carbohydrate 28g

Sugar 9.5g

Fiber 5g

Fat 21g
Saturated fat 8g

Sodium 0.32g

⬤◯◯　GI

⬤◯◯　CALORIES

⬤⬤⬤　SATURATED FAT

⬤◯◯　SODIUM

LAMB WITH EGGPLANT PURÉE

SERVES 6　　**PREP** 15 MINS　　**COOK** 40 MINS
PLUS MARINATING

Harissa makes a spicy crust for the lamb that goes well with the creamy eggplant.

1 tbsp harissa
2 tbsp chopped mint,
  plus extra for garnish
5 tbsp lemon juice
3 tbsp olive oil
2lb (900g) lamb loin fillet
  or noisettes of lamb

2 eggplants
2 garlic cloves, crushed
2 tbsp tahini
4fl oz (120ml) Greek yogurt
salt and freshly ground black pepper

1 Preheat the oven to 425°F (220°C). Place the harissa, mint, 2 tablespoons of the lemon juice, and 1 tablespoon of the olive oil in a bowl. Add the lamb and cover evenly in the marinade. Leave to marinate for at least 30 minutes.

2 Place the eggplant on a baking tray, pierce the skin with a fork several times, and bake for 30 minutes, or until the skins have charred. Remove from the oven and, when cool enough to handle, peel away the skins and discard. Place the eggplant flesh in a colander, drain for 15 minutes, then place in a food processor with the garlic, the remaining 3 tablespoons of lemon juice, the tahini, and the Greek yogurt and process until smooth. Season to taste with salt and pepper.

3 Remove the lamb from the marinade. Heat the remaining 2 tablespoons of oil in a frying pan and brown the lamb on all sides. Roast in the oven for 10 minutes, or longer if desired. Remove, and let rest for 10 minutes.

4 Carve the lamb and serve on warmed plates with the purée. Pour the pan juices over, and sprinkle with a little chopped mint.

COOK'S TIP
The eggplant purée can be made 1 day in advance and served at room temperature. The lamb can marinate for up to 24 hours, chilled and covered.

STATISTICS PER SERVING:

Energy　348cals/1,447kJ

Carbohydrate　2g

Sugar　2g

Fiber　1g

Fat　23g

Saturated fat　8g

Sodium　0.16g

RAGOUT OF VENISON WITH WILD MUSHROOMS

GUIDELINES PER SERVING:

● ○ ○ GI
● ○ ○ CALORIES
● ● ○ SATURATED FAT
● ● ○ SODIUM

SERVES 4   **PREP** 15 MINS   **COOK** 1¾–2¼ HOURS   **FREEZE** 3 MONTHS

This slowly simmered stew concentrates all the rich flavors of the venison and mushrooms.

1 tbsp olive oil
½oz (15g) butter
4 shallots, sliced
4oz (115g) smoked bacon, diced
1lb 5oz (600g) venison, diced
1 tbsp all-purpose flour
3 tbsp brandy

9oz (250g) wild mushrooms, sliced
9fl oz (250ml) beef stock
1 tbsp tomato purée
1 tbsp Worcestershire sauce
1 tsp dried oregano
salt and freshly ground black pepper

1 Heat the oil and butter in a casserole and fry the shallots and bacon over medium-high heat, stirring frequently, until beginning to brown.

2 Add the venison and fry for 3–4 minutes, or until browned on all sides, stirring frequently. Stir in the flour, then cook for 1–2 minutes, or until beginning to brown.

3 Add the brandy and stir for 30 seconds, then add the mushrooms and stock. Bring to a boil, stirring often.

4 Stir in the tomato purée, Worcestershire sauce, and oregano, and season to taste with salt and pepper. Reduce the heat to low, cover tightly with a lid, and simmer very gently for 1½–2 hours, or until the venison is tender (the cooking time will depend on the age of the meat). Serve hot, straight from the casserole.

COOK'S TIP
Leftovers can be reheated the next day. The flavor will improve with keeping.

STATISTICS PER SERVING:

Energy 362cals/1,521kJ

Carbohydrate 10g

Sugar 7g

Fiber 2.5g

Fat 16g
Saturated fat 6g

Sodium 0.8g

●○○ GI

●●○ CALORIES

●●○ SATURATED FAT

●●○ SODIUM

VENISON WITH ROAST CELERY ROOT AND RED CURRANT SAUCE

SERVES 2   **PREP** 10 MINS   **COOK** 50 MINS   **FREEZE** 3 MONTHS (SAUCE ONLY)

Venison steaks contain just 1.5g of fat per 100g, which is considerably less than even the leanest cut of beef.

½ medium celery root, cut into
  2in (5cm) chunks
4 tbsp olive oil
1 small red onion, finely chopped
1 clove garlic, finely chopped
7fl oz (200ml) chicken stock

7fl oz (200ml) fruity red wine
pinch of ground cinnamon
1 tbsp red currant jelly
salt and freshly ground black pepper
2 venison steaks, about 5½oz
  (150g) each

1 Preheat the oven to 350°F (180°C). Place the celery root in a bowl, drizzle with 2 tablespoons of oil and stir to coat. Transfer to an ovenproof dish and put in the oven for 40 minutes or until cooked through

2 To make the sauce, heat 1 tablespoon of the oil in a non-stick pan. Put in the onion and garlic and cook, stirring occasionally, for about 2–3 minutes. Add the stock, red wine, and cinnamon. Bring to a boil and allow the sauce to bubble for about 10 minutes or until reduced by half. Strain the sauce and discard the onions. Season with salt and ground black pepper, and stir in the red currant jelly.

3 Brush the venison with the remaining oil and cook on a hot griddle pan for 2–3 minutes either side, or until done to your liking.

4 Place the venison and celery root on a warm serving plate, then spoon a little of the sauce over the venison and serve.

COOK'S TIP
You can prepare the sauce up to two days in advance and keep it in the refrigerator. Simply reheat it in a small pan when needed.

STATISTICS PER SERVING:

Energy 484cals/2,022kJ

Carbohydrate 9g

Sugar 7.5g

Fiber 5.6g

Fat 25g

Saturated fat 4.5g

Sodium 0.4g

SLOW-ROAST PORK AND LENTILS

SERVES 4 **PREP** 10 MINS **COOK** 1 HOUR 10 MINS

A comforting dish made from pork tenderloin, or filet, which is a long, cylindrical cut of meat.

GUIDELINES PER SERVING:

GI
CALORIES
SATURATED FAT
SODIUM

3 sage leaves
1lb (450g) pork tenderloin,
  slashed 3 times
½ tbsp olive oil
salt and freshly ground black pepper
12oz (350g) Puy lentils, rinsed and
  any grit removed

2 celery stalks, roughly chopped
3 carrots, roughly chopped
1 onion, roughly chopped
1 sweet potato, roughly chopped
2 pints (900ml) vegetable stock

1 Preheat the oven to 400°F (200°C). Stuff the sage leaves into the cuts on the pork, drizzle with the oil and season well. Heat a large, cast-iron pot over high heat, put the pork in and cook for about 5 minutes on each side to seal.

2 Add the lentils, celery, carrots, onion, and sweet potato. Season well. Pour in the stock, push the pork down to sit snugly in the lentils, put the lid on the pot and cook in the oven for about 1 hour. Check halfway through the cooking time to make sure the pork isn't drying out; if it is, top up with a little hot water.

COOK'S TIP
You could cook the lentils and pork separately. Cook the lentils up to one day ahead and keep in the refrigerator, then reheat when required. Roast the pork for about 30 minutes. Serve together.

STATISTICS PER SERVING:

Energy 520cals/2,288kJ

Carbohydrate 63g

Sugar 11g

Fiber 11g

Fat 10g

Saturated fat 2.5g

Sodium 0.56g

PORK TENDERLOIN STUFFED WITH CHILES AND TOMATOES

SERVES 4   **PREP** 15 MINS   **COOK** 35 MINS

A fiery dish that looks impressive but is simple to make.

1–2 tbsp green jalapeños pickled
  in vinegar, drained
1 tbsp capers, rinsed if salty
8 large sun-dried tomatoes in
  oil, drained

1lb (450g) pork tenderloin
1 tbsp olive oil
salt and freshly ground black pepper

1 Preheat the oven to 400°F (200°C). Put the jalapeños, capers, and sun-dried tomatoes in a food processor or blender and blend to form a paste.

2 Slice the pork along its length, making sure that you don't cut all the way through it. Smother with the oil and season with salt and black pepper.

3 Stuff the paste into the slit in the pork, spreading it evenly. Pull the edges of the pork up around the stuffing and transfer the meat to a roasting pan, cut-side down. Roast the pork for 30–35 minutes, or until it is cooked to your liking. Allow the meat to rest for 5 minutes before slicing. Try this with green vegetables and brown basmati rice.

STATISTICS PER SERVING:

Energy 177cals/745kJ

Carbohydrate 3g

Sugar 0.5g

Fiber 0.5g

Fat 6.5g

Saturated fat 1.5g

Sodium 0.2g

⬤◯◯ GI

⬤◯◯ CALORIES

⬤◯◯ SATURATED FAT

⬤⬤◯ SODIUM

PORK CHOPS WITH SALSA VERDE

SERVES 4   **PREP** 10 MINS   **COOK** 10-12 MINS

A simple recipe for juicy pork.

large handful of flat-leaf parsley
handful of fresh basil leaves
handful of fresh mint leaves
2 tbsp red wine vinegar
2 garlic cloves, roughly chopped

2 anchovy fillets
2 tbsp capers, drained and rinsed
3-4 tbsp olive oil
4 lean pork chops, trimmed of fat
salt and freshly ground black pepper

1 Add the herbs, vinegar, garlic, anchovies, capers, and most of the olive oil to a food processor and pulse until chopped. Spoon out and transfer to a dish.

2 Rub the pork chops with a splash of the remaining oil and season well with salt and black pepper. Heat a griddle pan until hot, add the chops and leave undisturbed for 3–5 minutes, depending on their thickness, then turn them and cook the other side for the same length of time again or until they are no longer pink and are cooked through.

3 Serve the chops topped with the salsa verde and with a mixed salad.

STATISTICS PER SERVING:

Energy 266cals/1,115kJ

Carbohydrate 0.5g

Sugar 0g

Fiber 0g

Fat 15g
Saturated fat 3g

Sodium 0.44g

PORK STIR-FRY WITH CASHEWS AND GREENS

GUIDELINES PER SERVING:

GI
CALORIES
SATURATED FAT
SODIUM

SERVES 4   **PREP** 15 MINS   **COOK** 10-15 MINS

A fast and flavorsome dish.

2 tbsp sunflower oil
1 onion, chopped
1in (2.5cm) piece of fresh ginger root, peeled and finely chopped
3 garlic cloves, finely chopped
1 red chile, seeded and finely sliced

14oz (400g) pork tenderloin, finely sliced
3 tbsp soy sauce
1 tbsp sesame oil
handful of cashews
7oz (200g) bok choy, roughly sliced lengthwise

1 Heat the oil in a wok, add the onion and stir-fry quickly for a minute then add the ginger, garlic, and chile and cook, stirring continually to make sure the ingredients don't burn.

2 Throw in the pork, stir, and cook for 3–5 minutes until no longer pink, then add the remaining ingredients and cook for a further 3–5 minutes, stirring occasionally until the bok choy is tender and wilted. Serve immediately with noodles or rice.

STATISTICS PER SERVING:

Energy   265cals/1,100kJ

Carbohydrate 6g

Sugar 4g

Fiber 2g

Fat 16g
Saturated fat 3g

Sodium 0.92g

ROASTED PORK CHOPS WITH MUSTARD RUB

SERVES 4   **PREP** 10 MINS   **COOK** 40 MINS

Tasty pork chops paired with purple sprouting broccoli and roasted fennel.

4 tsp English mustard
few stalks thyme, leaves only,
  finely chopped
few stalks rosemary, leaves only,
  finely chopped
salt and freshly ground black pepper
4 chunky pork chops, trimmed of fat

2 onions, peeled and sliced
2 bulbs of fennel, trimmed and sliced
  horizontally
1 tbsp olive oil
handful of purple sprouting broccoli,
  stalks trimmed (prepared weight
  about 3½oz/100g)

1 Preheat the oven to 350°F (180°C). In a bowl, combine the mustard, thyme, and rosemary and season with salt and pepper. Rub this mixture all over the pork chops and put to one side.

2 Arrange the onions and fennel in a roasting pan, season, and drizzle over the olive oil. Add the pork chops, nestling them in among the vegetables. Transfer to the oven to cook for about 40 minutes or until the pork is cooked and the onions and fennel are starting to caramelize.

3 Meanwhile, add the purple sprouting broccoli to a pan of boiling salted water and cook for 8–10 minutes or until tender, then drain. Arrange the pork and roasted vegetables on plates with the broccoli on the side, and serve.

COOK'S TIP
Cover the pan with foil if the vegetables are beginning to brown too quickly.

STATISTICS PER SERVING:

Energy 244cals/1,026kJ

Carbohydrate 5.5g

Sugar 4g

Fiber 2.5g

Fat 9g

Saturated fat 2.5g

Sodium 0.16g

● ○ ○ GI

● ○ ○ CALORIES

● ○ ○ SATURATED FAT

● ○ ○ SODIUM

GROUND PORK WITH GREEN BEANS

SERVES 4   **PREP** 10 MINS   **COOK** 30 MINS

Choose this supper when you have had a long day at work—it's quick to make.

1 tbsp olive oil
1 large onion, finely diced
1 red chile, seeded and chopped
1lb 2oz (500g) lean ground pork
3 garlic cloves, finely chopped

1 tbsp fresh thyme stems, leaves only
7oz (200g) fine green beans, trimmed and halved
10fl oz (300ml) vegetable stock
salt and freshly ground black pepper

1 Heat the oil in a large frying pan and add the onion. Cook for about 3 minutes until soft, then add the chile and cook for 1 minute. Add the pork and cook for 3–5 minutes until no longer pink.

2 Stir in the garlic, thyme, and green beans. Cook for 1 minute, then add the stock. Season well with salt and black pepper, bring to a boil, then reduce to a simmer. Cook for about 15–20 minutes, partially covered, stirring occasionally. Top up with boiling water if it gets too dry.

STATISTICS PER SERVING:

Energy 223cals/938kJ

Carbohydrate 6g

Sugar 4g

Fiber 2g

Fat 9g
Saturated fat 2g

Sodium 0.24g

GROUND PORK WITH MUSHROOMS AND PASTA

GUIDELINES PER SERVING:

●●○ GI

●●○ CALORIES

●○○ SATURATED FAT

●○○ SODIUM

SERVES 4   **PREP** 10 MINS   **COOK** 30 MINS

An easy, everyday pasta dish: achieve tasty results with minimal effort.

1 tbsp olive oil
1 onion, finely chopped
salt and freshly ground black pepper
14oz (400g) lean ground pork
9oz (250g) cremini mushrooms,
  roughly chopped

1 chile, seeded and finely chopped
2 garlic cloves, finely chopped
1 tsp dried oregano
14oz can chopped tomatoes
12oz (350g) pappardelle pasta
1 tbsp fresh basil, chopped

1 Heat the oil in a large saucepan, add the onion and cook for about 5 minutes or until soft. Season with salt and black pepper, then add the pork and mash with the back of a fork. Cook for about 5 minutes or until no longer pink.

2 Add the mushrooms, chile, garlic, and oregano. Cook for a further 5 minutes, then add the tomatoes, stir well and bring to a boil. Reduce to a simmer and cook for about 20 minutes, adding a little hot water if it starts to dry out too much.

3 Meanwhile, put the pasta in a pan of salted boiling water and cook for 10–12 minutes, or according to the instructions on the package. Drain, reserving some of the cooking water, and return the pasta to the pan with a little of the water.

4 Add the basil to the pork, stir, and season if needed. Toss the mixture with the pasta.

COOK'S TIP
Use spaghetti, linguine, or fettucine as an alternative to pappardelle, if you wish.

STATISTICS PER SERVING:

Energy	485cals/2,059kJ
Carbohydrate	70g
Sugar	6g
Fiber	4.5g
Fat	9g
Saturated fat	2g
Sodium	0.12g

PORK AND APPLE PATTIES

SERVES 4   **PREP** 15 MINS   **COOK** 10 MINS   **FREEZE** 1 MONTH
(MAKES 8)   AFTER STEP 1

Miniature burgers made from a few simple ingredients.

1lb (450g) ground pork
2 crisp eating apples, cored
  and finely diced
salt and freshly ground black pepper
1 egg

1 tsp paprika
4-5 stems of fresh thyme, leaves only,
  finely chopped
oil for frying

1 Place the pork in a bowl with the apple, season well with salt and black pepper, and mix together. Add the egg, paprika, and thyme and mix until combined, then, using your hands, squeeze the mixture together until it is an even paste. Shape into 8 balls (2 per serving) and pat into patties.

2 Heat the oil in a large non-stick frying pan and add the patties, working in batches if necessary. Cook over medium heat for 3–4 minutes each side, until a deep golden color. Transfer to a plate lined with paper towels to drain, then serve.

COOK'S TIP
You could also oven bake these; sit them in a roasting pan and cook at 400°F (200°C) for 15-20 minutes.

STATISTICS PER SERVING:

Energy 126cals/528kJ

Carbohydrate Carbohydrate 3g

Sugar 3g

Fiber 0.4g

Fat 7g

Saturated fat 1.5g

Sodium 0.08g

BEEF BURGERS

GUIDELINES PER BURGER:

● ○ ○   GI

● ○ ○   CALORIES

● ● ○   SATURATED FAT

● ● ○   SODIUM

SERVES 4   **PREP** 10 MINS   **COOK** 15-20 MINS   **FREEZE** 3 MONTHS
PLUS CHILLING   AFTER STEP 2

Using lean beef, and oven baking rather than frying, stops these burgers being too fatty.

1lb 2oz (500g) lean ground beef
2 tbsp capers, drained, rinsed,
  and very finely chopped

1 onion, very finely chopped
2 tsp wholegrain mustard

1 Add all the ingredients to a bowl and, using your hands, mix evenly until well combined.

2 Divide the mixture into four and roll each into a ball. Flatten into patties on a sheet of wax paper set on a plate, and place in the fridge to firm up for 30 minutes.

3 Preheat the oven to 400°F (200°C). When hot, turn each patty onto a baking sheet and peel away the paper. Transfer the baking sheet to the oven for 15–20 minutes or until the burgers are cooked through. These are good served on wholemeal rolls with some fresh lettuce and tomato.

STATISTICS PER BURGER:

Energy 236cals/988kJ

Carbohydrate 3.5g

Sugar 2g

Fiber 0.8g

Fat 12g
Saturated fat 5g

Sodium 0.36g

SIMPLE DINNERS— POULTRY

CHICKEN LIVERS WITH KALE AND BALSAMIC VINEGAR

SERVES 4   **PREP** 10 MINS   **COOK** 15-20 MINS

A robust and hearty dish that is full of flavor and packed with vitamins and minerals.

1lb (450g) chicken livers
7oz (200g) kale or spinach leaves
2 tbsp olive oil
2 red onions, thickly sliced
3½oz (100g) 4 slices smoked slab
  bacon, roughly chopped

2 garlic cloves, crushed or finely
  chopped
3 tbsp balsamic vinegar
5fl oz (150ml) dry sherry
salt and freshly ground black pepper
9oz (250g) baby cherry tomatoes

1 Rinse the chicken livers and chop roughly, discarding any fibrous bits.

2 Chop the kale or spinach leaves, removing the central stalk of the kale. Heat 1 tablespoon of oil in a large, nonstick frying pan. When the oil is hot, add the chicken livers and cook over high heat for about 5 minutes or until just brown. Remove the livers from the pan and set aside.

3 Pour the remaining oil into the pan and reduce the heat. Add the onions, bacon, and garlic. Cook, stirring frequently, for about 5 minutes or until the onions are soft.

4 Add the balsamic vinegar and sherry and continue to cook for a further minute. Return the chicken livers to the pan and season with black pepper. Add the kale and tomatoes. Continue cooking over low heat for 4–6 minutes or until the kale begins to wilt.

STATISTICS PER SERVING:

Energy 318cals/1,326kJ

Carbohydrate 12g

Sugar 10g

Fiber 3g

Fat 13g

Saturated fat 3g

Sodium 0.48g

POACHED CHICKEN WITH STAR ANISE, SOY, AND BROWN RICE

SERVES 4   PREP 5 MINS   COOK 50 MINS   FREEZE 1 MONTH WITHOUT THE RICE

A light and aromatic chicken dish enjoyed with nutty brown rice.

8oz (225g) brown basmati rice
salt and freshly ground black pepper
2 tsp five-spice powder
4 chicken breasts, skinned
4 star anise
2in (5cm) piece of fresh ginger root, finely sliced

2 large red chiles, seeded and finely sliced lengthwise
3 tbsp dark soy sauce
3½oz (100g) sugarsnap peas, finely sliced lengthwise

1 Put the rice in a large pan of salted water and cook for 30–35 minutes, or according to the instructions on the package. Drain, return to the pan and set aside with the lid on.

2 Sprinkle the five-spice powder over the chicken and set it aside. Measure 3½ pints (1.7 liters) water into a large pan and add the star anise, ginger, chiles, and soy sauce. Bring to a boil, then add the chicken. Reduce to a simmer and cook until the chicken is done—about 20 minutes (pierce it with a sharp knife: the juices should run clear). Remove the chicken from the pan and set aside.

3 Bring the liquid in the pan to a boil and reduce it by half. Taste, and season with black pepper if needed—it should be salty enough because of the soy sauce. Add the sugarsnap peas for the last couple of minutes of cooking. Slice or tear the chicken into bite-sized pieces (if you wish) and return it to the broth. Remove the star anise. Serve the rice in individual bowls, topped with the chicken, and with plenty of juice ladled over it.

COOK'S TIP
You could use the star anise for a garnish, but remember that it should not be eaten.

GUIDELINES PER SERVING:

● ● ○ GI
● ● ○ CALORIES
● ○ ○ SATURATED FAT
● ● ● SODIUM

STATISTICS PER SERVING:

Energy 373cals/1,584kJ

Carbohydrate 48g

Sugar 2.5g

Fiber 1.5g

Fat 3.5g
Saturated fat 1g

Sodium 0.88g

◐○○ GI

◐◐○ CALORIES

◐○○ SATURATED FAT

◐○○ SODIUM

BENGALI SPICE RUB CHICKEN

SERVES 4   **PREP** 15 MINS   **COOK** 40 MINS

An easy Indian-style dish you can make as hot as you wish.

1 tbsp turmeric
4 chicken breasts, skinned and cut
  into chunky pieces
1 onion, roughly chopped
2in (5cm) piece of fresh ginger, peeled
1–2 green chiles, seeded
1 tsp mustard seeds
1 tsp cumin seeds
1 tsp onion seeds
1 tbsp sunflower oil
salt and freshly ground black pepper

6 tomatoes, roughly chopped
2 red peppers, roughly chopped
1 tbsp of tomato purée

For the yogurt mixture
7oz (200g) carton of thick
  natural yogurt
½ cucumber, halved lengthwise,
  peeled, seeds removed, and diced
handful of fresh cilantro leaves,
  finely chopped

1 First make the yogurt mixture: mix all the ingredients together and season with a pinch of sea salt. Put to one side. Toss the chicken pieces in the turmeric to coat and put to one side. Put the onion, ginger, and chiles in a food processor and whiz to a paste.

2 In a heavy-based deep frying pan, heat the mustard seeds over medium heat for a minute or so until they begin to pop, then add the cumin and onion seeds and fry for 1–2 minutes more, being careful not to let the seeds burn. Add the oil to the pan, then add the chicken and cook for 5–10 minutes or until golden, then remove from the pan and set aside. Spoon in the onion mixture, season with salt and black pepper, and cook for 5 minutes.

3 Add the tomatoes, red peppers, and tomato purée and cook over low heat for a further 5 minutes until softened. A little at a time, add 1¼ pints (600ml) water, stirring and allowing the mixture to bubble in between times. Return the chicken to the pan and cook on low heat for 15 minutes. Serve with basmati rice, with the yogurt on the side.

COOK'S TIP
If you prefer, you can skin the tomatoes before chopping, or use a 14oz (400g) can of chopped tomatoes instead.

STATISTICS PER SERVING:

Energy 294cals/1,240kJ

Carbohydrate 18g

Sugar 16g

Fiber 3.5g

Fat 8g

Saturated fat 2g

Sodium 0.2g

CHICKEN, ONION, AND PEAS

SERVES 4   **PREP** 5 MINS   **COOK** 40 MINS

A simple, satisfying dish made with few ingredients.

4 chicken thighs or breasts
salt and freshly ground black pepper
2 tbsp oil
1 onion, finely chopped
2 garlic cloves
1 tbsp fresh thyme leaves

1¼ pint (600ml) mushroom
  or vegetable stock
8oz (225g) frozen green peas
1 tbsp flat-leaf parsley,
  finely chopped
7oz (200g) brown rice

1 Season the chicken well with salt and black pepper. Pour 1 tablespoon of oil into a large, heavy pan and when hot, add the chicken pieces. Cook for about 5 minutes, or until golden, then turn and cook them on the other side for the same length of time. Remove with tongs and set aside.

2 Heat the remaining oil in the pan, add the onion and cook until soft. Season well, then throw in the garlic and thyme and cook for a few seconds. Return the chicken to the pan and add a small amount of stock. Let it bubble, then stir up any bits from the bottom of the pan before adding the remaining stock. Reduce to a simmer.

3 Add in the peas and continue to cook, covered, over low heat for 25–35 minutes or until the chicken is cooked (the juices should run clear when the chicken is pierced with a sharp knife). If the chicken begins to dry out, top up the pan with a little more hot stock or water.

4 Meanwhile, cook the rice according to the instructions on the package. Drain, then serve with the chicken.

COOK'S TIP
Chicken breasts will not take as long to cook as thighs.
To prevent the chicken from drying out, don't have the heat too high.

STATISTICS PER SERVING:

Energy 468cals/1,956kJ

Carbohydrate 50g

Sugar 3.5g

Fiber 4.1g

Fat 10.5g

Saturated fat 2.2g

Sodium 0.32g

WILD RICE WITH CHICKEN, SAFFRON, AND PUMPKIN

SERVES 4 **PREP** 15 MINS **COOK** 1 HOUR 15 MINS

A fruity and aromatic dish, full of color. Bring a golden glow to a winter evening.

12oz (350g) chicken breast, cut into chunky, bite-sized pieces
1 tbsp olive oil
salt and freshly ground black pepper
1 onion, roughly chopped
2 carrots, roughly chopped
6 cloves garlic, unpeeled
2 pints (900ml) vegetable stock
1 bay leaf

2½oz (75g) bacon, chopped into bite-sized pieces
½ small pumpkin (about 10oz/300g), cut into bite-sized chunks
zest and juice of 1 orange
pinch of saffron threads, soaked in a little boiling water
12oz (350g) rice and wild rice, mixed

1 Preheat the oven to 400°F (200°C). Rub the chicken with the oil and season well with salt and black pepper. Heat a large, cast-iron casserole and add the chicken. Cook for about 6–8 minutes, turning, until brown on all sides.

2 Add the onion, carrots, garlic, and a little of the stock. Bring to a boil and stir, then pour in the remaining stock. Add the bay leaf, bacon, pumpkin, orange zest and juice, and saffron in its water. Season well and stir. Transfer the casserole to the oven and cook for 1 hour, topping it up with hot water if the mixture becomes too dry.

3 Meanwhile, cook the rice in salted boiling water for 20 minutes, or according to the instructions on the package. Drain and keep warm. Remove the garlic cloves from the casserole with a slotted spoon, and then squeeze them out of their skins and back into the pot.

4 Divide the rice between 4 bowls or plates, and ladle in the chicken and pumpkin mixture.

STATISTICS PER SERVING:

Energy 558cals/2,338kJ

Carbohydrate 79g

Sugar 6.5g

Fiber 2g

Fat 10g
Saturated fat 2.5g

Sodium 0.8g

CHICKEN WITH HERBS AND CHILES

SERVES 4   **PREP** 5 MINS   **COOK** 35 MINS

A simple and healthy, but very tasty, way to serve chicken.

handful of curly parsley
handful of basil leaves
1-2 red chiles, seeded
3 garlic cloves, peeled
juice of ½ lemon

1 tbsp olive oil, plus extra
   for oiling
salt and freshly ground
   black pepper
4 skinless chicken breasts

1 Preheat the oven to 400°F (200°C). Place the parsley, basil, chiles, garlic, lemon juice, and olive oil in a food processor and blend until well combined. Season with salt and pepper and blend again.

2 Slash the chicken breasts a few times horizontally then rub the herb mixture all over, making sure it goes into the slashes. Place the chicken in an oiled roasting pan and cook in the oven for 30–35 minutes or until the chicken is cooked through.

STATISTICS PER SERVING:

Energy 184cals/775kJ

Carbohydrate 0g

Sugar 0g

Fiber 0g

Fat 4.5g
Saturated fat 0.8g

Sodium 0.12g

CHICKEN NUGGETS

SERVES 4   **PREP** 20 MINS   **COOK** 20 MINS   **FREEZE** 1 MONTH

Tender bites of moist chicken in a golden coating.

4 slices of white bread
1 tsp paprika
salt and freshly ground black pepper
1–2 eggs, lightly beaten

all-purpose flour, for dusting
2 skinless chicken breasts,
  cut into strips
olive oil, for oiling

1 Preheat the oven to 400°F (200°C). Place the bread in a food processor and pulse to crumbs, then sprinkle in the paprika, a pinch of salt and some black pepper and pulse again. Put the crumbs onto a baking sheet, spread them out evenly then bake for 3–6 minutes until golden, giving them a gentle stir halfway through.

2 Return the toasted crumbs to the food processor and pulse again until fine. Pour onto a large plate.

3 Pour the beaten egg onto another large plate and place the flour onto a third large plate. Toss the chicken pieces in the egg first, then coat them with the flour and finally the breadcrumbs. Oil a baking sheet well with olive oil and sit the coated chicken pieces on it. Bake in the oven for 15–20 minutes or until the chicken is cooked and the coating is golden.

STATISTICS PER SERVING:

Energy 208cals/880kJ

Carbohydrate 17g

Sugar 0.9g

Fiber 0.5g

Fat 6g
Saturated fat 1g

Sodium 0.24g

CAJUN CHICKEN WITH CORN SALSA

GUIDELINES PER SERVING:

● ○ ○ GI

● ● ○ CALORIES

● ● ○ SATURATED FAT

● ○ ○ SODIUM

SERVES 2   **PREP** 10 MINS   **COOK** 15 MINS

Avocados give the salsa a wonderfully creamy flavor, which helps to balance the fieriness of the chicken.

2 skinless chicken breasts
1 tbsp of Cajun seasoning
1 tbsp olive oil

For the salsa
1 large fresh corn on the cob, stripped
  of husks and threads

½ small red onion, finely chopped
½ red pepper, seeded and diced
1 red chile, seeded and
  finely chopped
1 small hass avocado, diced
1 tbsp olive oil
juice of 1 lime

1 Put the chicken breasts between 2 pieces of plastic wrap and pound with a rolling pin until flattened evenly. Mix the the Cajun seasoning with the oil and brush over the flattened chicken. Leave to marinate for at least 15 minutes.

2 To make the salsa, add the corn to a large pan of boiling water and cook for 5 minutes, then immediately transfer to a bowl of ice water to cool. Drain well, then, using a sharp knife, scrape off all the kernels. Combine with the remaining salsa ingredients, mix well, and set aside.

3 Heat a griddle pan and cook the chicken for 4–5 minutes on one side, pressing the pieces down on the griddle pan, then turn and cook for 4–5 minutes on the other side, or until cooked through.

4 Spoon the salsa onto serving plates and top with the griddled chicken.

STATISTICS PER SERVING:

Energy 442cals/1,846kJ

Carbohydrate 18g

Sugar 5g

Fiber 3.5g

Fat 23g

Saturated fat 4g

Sodium 0.12g

⬤◯◯ GI

⬤◯◯ CALORIES

⬤◯◯ SATURATED FAT

⬤◯◯ SODIUM

SAFFRON CHICKEN BROCHETTES

SERVES 6   **PREP** 10 MINS   **COOK** 10 MINS
PLUS MARINATING

Simple, prepare-ahead food, also suitable for a barbecue.

6 x 6oz (175g) skinless boneless
  chicken breasts, cubed
2 tbsp olive oil
zest and juice of 3 lemons
4 pinches of saffron powder, dissolved
  in 1 tbsp boiling water

salt and freshly ground black pepper
2 red onions, finely sliced
1oz (30g) polyunsaturated margarine
basil leaves, to garnish

1 Put the chicken in a large bowl. Whisk together the oil, lemon zest, the juice from 2 lemons and the saffron in its water. Season to taste with salt and pepper. Add the sliced onions and pour over the chicken. Mix, cover, and chill for 2 hours or overnight.

2 When ready to cook, melt the margarine in a small pan with the remaining lemon juice.

3 Preheat the broiler to high. Remove the chicken from the marinade and thread on to skewers. Place under the broiler with the onions and broil for 5–6 minutes. Turn, brush with the lemon-margarine mixture, and broil for another 5–6 minutes or until cooked through. Arrange on a heated plate and serve hot, scattered with basil leaves.

COOK'S TIP
If using wooden skewers, soak them in cold water for 30 minutes before using to prevent them burning.

STATISTICS PER SERVING:

Energy 268cals/1,125kJ

Carbohydrate 2.5g

Sugar 2g

Fiber 0.5g

Fat 10g

Saturated fat 2g

Sodium 0.16g

TURKEY KEBABS

● ○ ○ GI

● ○ ○ CALORIES

● ○ ○ SATURATED FAT

● ● ● SODIUM

MAKES 6   **PREP** 20 MINS   **COOK** 10-12 MINS
PLUS MARINATING

Zingy kebabs served with a refreshing mint yogurt.

2fl oz (60ml) light soy sauce
2 tbsp olive oil
2 garlic cloves, finely chopped
¾ tsp ground ginger
¼ tsp red pepper flakes
1½lb (675g) skinless boneless turkey breasts, cut into 1in (2.5cm) cubes
1 red pepper, seeded and cut into 1in (2.5cm) pieces
1 green pepper, seeded and cut into 1in (2.5cm) pieces
1 large zucchini, cut into 1in (2.5cm) slices
8fl oz (240ml) plain yogurt
2 tbsp mint, chopped
½ tsp ground cumin

1 Combine the soy sauce, oil, garlic, ginger, and red pepper flakes. Add the turkey pieces and toss to coat. Cover, chill, and marinate for at least 1 hour.

2 Thread the turkey, pepper, and zucchini onto skewers and brush with any leftover marinade. Grill for 5–6 minutes on each side, or until cooked through.

3 Mix together the yogurt, mint, and cumin in a small bowl. Arrange the kebabs on a serving platter with the mint yogurt on the side.

COOK'S TIP
If using wooden skewers, soak them in cold water for 30 minutes before using to prevent them burning.

STATISTICS PER SERVING:

Energy 207cals/869kJ

Carbohydrate 7.5g

Sugar 7g

Fiber 1g

Fat 6g

Saturated fat 2g

Sodium 0.8g

⬤◯◯ GI

⬤⬤◯ CALORIES

⬤◯◯ SATURATED FAT

⬤◯◯ SODIUM

CHICKEN AND ARTICHOKE FILO PIE

SERVES 4   **PREP** 15 MINS   **COOK** 25-30 MINS

Filo pastry is quick and easy to use and a healthier alternative to flaky pastry, because it contains considerably less fat.

3 tbsp vegetable oil
1 large onion, finely chopped
4 skinless chicken breasts, cut into bite-sized chunks
1 clove garlic, crushed
4 stalks celery, chopped
7oz (200g) low-fat soft cheese with garlic and herbs

14oz can artichokes, drained and roughly chopped
salt and freshly ground black pepper
6 large sheets of filo pastry
1 tsp sesame seeds

1 Preheat the oven to 375°F (190°C). Heat 2 tablespoons of the oil in a large frying pan and add the onion. Cook, stirring, for 2–3 minutes or until soft. Add the chicken, garlic, and celery and cook for 5 minutes or until the chicken is golden brown all over.

2 Remove from the heat, stir in the soft cheese and artichokes, and season to taste. Transfer the mixture into a shallow ovenproof dish.

3 Lightly brush the sheets of filo pastry with the remaining oil, then scrunch each sheet slightly and place it on top of the chicken mixture. Sprinkle with sesame seeds and bake in the oven for 20–25 minutes or until the pastry is crisp and golden. Serve hot.

STATISTICS PER SERVING:

Energy 327cals/1,370kJ

Carbohydrate 17g

Sugar 4.5g

Fiber 3g

Fat 11g
Saturated fat 1.5g

Sodium 0.16g

CHICKEN PAPRIKASH

GUIDELINES PER SERVING:

● ○ ○ GI
● ○ ○ CALORIES
● ○ ○ SATURATED FAT
● ○ ○ SODIUM

SERVES 4   **PREP** 10 MINS   **COOK** 40-45 MINS   **FREEZE** 1 MONTH

Spicy paprika adds both flavor and color to this hearty stew from Hungary, which gets an extra rush of flavor from cherry tomatoes added at the end.

2 tbsp sunflower oil
2 small red onions, sliced
1 garlic clove, finely chopped
1 tbsp sweet paprika
¼ tsp caraway seeds
8 chicken thighs
9fl oz (250ml) hot chicken stock

1 tbsp red wine vinegar
1 tbsp tomato purée
1 tsp sugar
salt and freshly ground black pepper
9oz (250g) cherry tomatoes
1 tbsp chopped flat-leaf parsley,
  to garnish

1 Heat the oil in a large, flameproof casserole over medium heat. Add the onion, garlic, paprika, and caraway seeds. Fry, stirring, for about 5 minutes, or until the onion softens. Use a slotted spoon to remove the ingredients from the pan and set aside.

2 Add the chicken thighs, skin-side down, to any oil remaining in the pan and fry for 3 minutes. Turn them over and continue frying for a further 2 minutes. Return the onion mixture to the pan.

3 Mix together the stock, vinegar, tomato purée, sugar, and salt and pepper to taste. Pour over the chicken and bring to a boil, then reduce the heat to low. Cover and leave to simmer for 25 minutes, or until the chicken is tender.

4 Add the cherry tomatoes and shake the casserole vigorously to mix them into the sauce. Cover and simmer for a further 5 minutes. Sprinkle with parsley and serve.

STATISTICS PER SERVING:

Energy 324cals/1,356kJ

Carbohydrate 9g

Sugar 7g

Fiber 2g

Fat 14g

Saturated fat 2g

Sodium 0.36g

DEVILLED TURKEY

SERVES 4   **PREP** 10 MINS   **COOK** 15 MINS

Serve these spicy stir-fried turkey strips as a healthy lunch or supper.

2 tbsp wholegrain mustard
2 tbsp mango chutney
2 tbsp Worcestershire sauce
¼ tsp ground paprika
3 tbsp orange juice
1 red chile, chopped
2 tbsp olive oil
1lb (450g) turkey breast escalope, cut into strips

1 onion, peeled and finely chopped
1 red pepper, cored and cut into strips
1 orange pepper, cored and cut into strips
1 garlic clove, crushed

1 Mix the mustard, chutney, Worcestershire sauce, paprika, orange juice, and chile together until well combined.

2 Heat the oil in a frying pan or wok, add the turkey, and cook over high heat until browned. Remove the turkey from the pan and set aside, covered to keep it warm.

3 Add the onion to the pan and fry for 2–3 minutes, or until beginning to color. Add the peppers and garlic and fry, stirring constantly, for 3–4 minutes, or until tender.

4 Stir in the mustard mixture and return the turkey to the pan. Cook for 5 minutes or until piping hot and the turkey is cooked through.

STATISTICS PER SERVING:

Energy   234cals/981kJ

Carbohydrate   13g

Sugar   11g

Fiber   2g

Fat   7.5g

Saturated fat   1g

Sodium   0.36g

CHICKEN JALFREZI

GUIDELINES PER SERVING:

⬤◯◯ GI

⬤◯◯ CALORIES

⬤◯◯ SATURATED FAT

⬤◯◯ SODIUM

SERVES 4   **PREP** 20 MINS   **COOK** 25 MINS   **FREEZE** 3 MONTHS

A spicy dish, with chiles and mustard seeds, for those who like their curries hot.

2 tbsp sunflower oil
2 tbsp ground cumin
2 tsp yellow mustard seeds
1 tsp ground turmeric
2 tbsp masala curry paste
1in (2.5cm) piece fresh root ginger, peeled and finely chopped
3 garlic cloves, crushed
1 onion, sliced
1 red pepper, seeded and sliced

½ green pepper, seeded and sliced
2 green chiles, seeded and finely chopped
1½lb (675g) boneless chicken thighs or breasts, skinned and cut into 1in (2.5cm) pieces
8oz (225g) can chopped tomatoes
3 tbsp chopped cilantro

1 Heat the oil in a large pan over medium heat, add the cumin, mustard seeds, turmeric, and curry paste, and stir-fry for 1–2 minutes.

2 Add the ginger, garlic, and onion and fry, stirring frequently, until the onion starts to soften. Add the red and green peppers and the chiles and fry for 5 minutes.

3 Increase the heat to medium-high, add the chicken, and fry until starting to brown. Add the tomatoes and cilantro, reduce the heat, and simmer for 10 minutes, or until the chicken is cooked through, stirring often. Serve hot.

STATISTICS PER SERVING:

Energy 290cals/1,205kJ

Carbohydrate 9g

Sugar 7g

Fiber 2g

Fat 9g

Saturated fat 1g

Sodium 0.24g

QUICK TURKEY CASSOULET

SERVES 6   **PREP** 15 MINS   **COOK** 35 MINS

A hearty, filling dish that is high in fiber.

3 tbsp olive oil
1 medium red onion, peeled
  and finely chopped
2 cloves of garlic, peeled and crushed
1 red pepper, seeded and diced
2oz (60g) Canadian bacon,
  roughly chopped
2 celery stalks, finely chopped
14oz (400g) can of chopped tomatoes
8fl oz (250ml) chicken stock

2 tsp dark soy sauce
2½oz (75g) wholemeal breadcrumbs
1¾oz (50g) freshly grated Parmesan
  cheese
3 tbsp chopped flat-leaf parsley
2 tsp Dijon mustard
2 x 14oz (400g) cans of mixed beans,
  rinsed and drained
14oz (400g) cooked turkey breast,
  roughly chopped

1 Heat 2 tablespoons of the oil in a large nonstick saucepan, add the onion, and cook over low heat for 5 minutes. Add the garlic, red pepper, bacon, and celery and cook for a further 5 minutes, stirring occasionally.

2 Add the tomatoes, stock, and soy sauce. Bring to a boil, then reduce to a fast simmer and cook for 15 minutes or until the sauce begins to thicken.

3 Meanwhile, mix together the breadcrumbs, Parmesan, and parsley.

4 Add the mustard, beans, and turkey to the saucepan and cook for a further 5 minutes until heated through.

5 Transfer the hot mixture into a shallow ovenproof dish. Sprinkle the breadcrumb mixture evenly over the top and drizzle over the remaining olive oil. Place under a medium-hot broiler for 5 minutes or until the top is golden brown, then serve immediately.

STATISTICS PER SERVING:

Energy 400cals/1,600kJ

Carbohydrate 34g

Sugar 6g

Fiber 9g

Fat 13.5g
Saturated fat 4g

Sodium 0.64g

⬤◯◯ GI

⬤◯◯ CALORIES

⬤◯◯ SATURATED FAT

⬤⬤◯ SODIUM

CHICKEN AND APRICOT TAGINE

SERVES 4   **PREP** 15 MINS   **COOK** 35-45 MINS

The dried fruit and warm spices in this dish are the unmistakable flavors of the Middle East.

2 tbsp sunflower oil
1 onion, finely chopped
1 garlic clove, finely chopped
1 tsp ground ginger
1 tsp ground cumin
1 tsp turmeric
pinch of ground cinnamon
pinch of red pepper flakes
1 tbsp tomato purée

1¼ pint (600ml) chicken stock
4 tbsp fresh orange juice
5½oz (150g) mixed dried fruit, such as apricots and raisins
salt and freshly ground black pepper
1½lb (675g) skinless boneless chicken breasts and thighs, cut into large chunks
2 tbsp chopped cilantro, to garnish

1 Heat the oil in a large flameproof casserole over medium heat. Add the onion, garlic, ground spices, and red pepper flakes and fry, stirring, for 5 minutes, or until the onions have softened. Stir in the tomato purée and stock and bring to a boil, stirring.

2 Add the orange juice, dried fruits, and salt and pepper to taste. Reduce the heat, partially cover the pan, and simmer for 15 minutes, or until the fruits are soft and the juices have reduced slightly.

3 Add the chicken, re-cover the casserole, and continue simmering for 20 minutes, or until the chicken is tender and the juices run clear. Adjust the seasoning, if necessary, then garnish with cilantro and serve hot.

STATISTICS PER SERVING:

Energy 380cals/1,605kJ

Carbohydrate 32g

Sugar 28g

Fiber 1.5g

Fat 9g

Saturated fat 1.5g

Sodium 0.4g

CHICKEN AND CHICKPEA PILAF

SERVES 4   **PREP** 20 MINS   **COOK** 35 MINS

This one-pot rice dish is easy to make and full of flavor.

GUIDELINES PER SERVING:

●○○ GI

●●○ CALORIES

●○○ SATURATED FAT

●●○ SODIUM

pinch of saffron threads
2 tsp vegetable oil
6 skinless boneless chicken thighs,
  cut into small pieces
2 tsp ground coriander
1 tsp ground cumin
1 onion, sliced
1 red pepper, seeded and chopped
2 garlic cloves, peeled and crushed

8oz (225g) long-grain rice
1½ pints (750ml) hot chicken stock
2 bay leaves
14oz (400g) can chickpeas, drained
  and rinsed
2oz (60g) golden raisins
2oz (60g) flaked almonds
  or pine nuts, toasted
3 tbsp chopped flat-leaf parsley

1 Crumble the saffron threads into a small bowl, add 2 tbsp boiling water, and set aside for at least 10 minutes.

2 Meanwhile, heat half the oil in a large saucepan, add the chicken, coriander, and cumin, and fry over medium heat for 3 minutes, stirring frequently. Remove from the pan and set aside. Lower the heat, add the rest of the oil, the onion, red pepper, and garlic, and fry for 5 minutes, or until softened.

3 Stir in the rice, return the chicken to the pan and pour in about three-quarters of the stock. Add the bay leaves and saffron with its soaking water and bring to a boil. Simmer for 15 minutes, or until the rice is almost cooked, adding more stock as needed. Stir in the chickpeas and raisins, and continue cooking until the rice is tender. Transfer to a warm serving platter and serve hot, sprinkled with the toasted nuts and chopped parsley.

STATISTICS PER SERVING:

Energy 621cals/2,604kJ

Carbohydrate 75g

Sugar 15g

Fiber 2.5g

Fat 13g
Saturated fat 1.5g

Sodium 0.44g

CHICKEN BIRYANI

SERVES 4   **PREP** 20 MINS   **COOK** 30 MINS

A subtly spiced, aromatic dish from India.

2 tbsp vegetable oil
1oz (30g) polyunsaturated margarine
1 large onion, thinly sliced
2 garlic cloves, crushed
6 curry leaves
6 cardamom pods
1 cinnamon stick, broken into
  2 or 3 pieces
1 tsp ground turmeric

½ tsp ground cumin
4 skinless boneless chicken breasts,
  cut into 1in (2.5cm) pieces
3 tbsp mild curry paste
10oz (300g) basmati rice
3oz (85g) golden raisins
2 pints (900ml) chicken stock
2 tbsp flaked almonds, toasted

1 Heat the oil and margarine in a large deep saucepan, and gently fry the onion and garlic until softened and starting to turn golden. Add the curry leaves, cardamom pods, and cinnamon stick, and fry for 5 minutes, stirring occasionally.

2 Add the turmeric and cumin, fry for 1 minute, then add the chicken and stir in the curry paste.

3 Add the rice and raisins, stir well, then pour in enough of the stock to cover the rice. Bring to a boil, lower the heat, and cook gently for 10–12 minutes, or until the rice is cooked, adding more stock if the mixture becomes dry.

4 Transfer to a serving dish, fluff up the rice with a fork, and serve with toasted flaked almonds scattered over the top.

STATISTICS PER SERVING:

Energy 723cals/3,026kJ

Carbohydrate 80g

Sugar 17g

Fiber 2g

Fat 22g

Saturated fat 3g

Sodium 0.76g

ARROZ CON POLLO

SERVES 4   **PREP** 20 MINS   **COOK** 45 MINS

This colorful chicken and rice dish from Latin America
is cooked and served in one pot.

GUIDELINES PER SERVING:

● ○ ○ GI

● ● ○ CALORIES

● ○ ○ SATURATED FAT

● ● ○ SODIUM

2 tbsp olive oil
8 chicken thighs
1 Spanish onion, finely sliced
1 green pepper, seeded
  and chopped
1 red pepper, seeded and chopped
2 garlic cloves, finely chopped
1 tsp smoked paprika
1 bay leaf
8oz (230g) can chopped tomatoes

1 tsp thyme leaves
1 tsp dried oregano
6oz (175g) basmati rice
pinch of saffron threads
1½ pints (750ml) chicken stock
2 tbsp tomato purée
juice of ½ lemon
salt and freshly ground black pepper
3½oz (100g) frozen peas

1 Preheat the oven to 350°F (180°C). Heat half the oil in a large flameproof
casserole and fry the chicken thighs over high heat, turning frequently, or
until evenly browned. Remove from the casserole, drain,
and set aside.

2 Add the remaining oil, reduce the heat and fry the onion until softened.
Add the chopped peppers and garlic and fry for 5 minutes, or until they
start to soften. Add the paprika, bay leaf, tomatoes, thyme, and oregano,
and stir in the rice. Fry for 1–2 minutes, stirring constantly.

3 Crumble in the saffron, add the stock, tomato purée, and lemon juice,
and season to taste with salt and pepper.

4 Return the chicken thighs to the casserole, pushing them down into
the rice, cover, and cook in the oven for 15 minutes. Add the peas and
return to the oven for a further 10 minutes, or until the rice is tender and
has absorbed the cooking liquid. Serve hot, straight from the casserole.

STATISTICS PER SERVING:

Energy 476cals/2,000kJ

Carbohydrate 50g

Sugar 10.5g

Fiber 4g

Fat 10g

Saturated fat 2g

Sodium 0.48g

ON THE SIDE

CAJUN-SPICED SWEET POTATO WEDGES

SERVES 4   **PREP** 10 MINS   **COOK** 25-30 MINS

A quick, easy, and healthier alternative to french fries—sweet potatoes are rich in betacarotene, which the body can convert to vitamin A.

3 large sweet potatoes, unpeeled
salt
3 tbsp olive oil
3 tbsp Cajun seasoning mix

1 Preheat the oven to 425°F (220°C). Slice each sweet potato in half lengthwise, then cut each half into 3 fat wedges. Cook the sweet potatoes in a pan of salted boiling water for 5 minutes. Drain well.

2 Mix the oil and seasoning together in a small bowl. Using a pastry brush, brush the mixture over the sweet potatoes.

3 Transfer the sweet potatoes to a non-stick roasting pan and bake for 20–25 minutes, or until crisp and nicely browned.

STATISTICS PER SERVING:

Energy 243cals/1,020kJ

Carbohydrate 34g

Sugar 10g

Fiber 4g

Fat 11g
Saturated fat 3g

Sodium 0.28g

COLESLAW WITH POPPY SEEDS

GUIDELINES PER SERVING:

● ○ ○ GI

● ○ ○ CALORIES

● ○ ○ SATURATED FAT

● ○ ○ SODIUM

SERVES 4   **PREP** 10 MINS

A mayonnaise-free coleslaw that cuts the calorie count of the traditional version but is every bit as delicious.

4 carrots, roughly grated
1 white cabbage, finely shredded
1 red onion, finely sliced
1 orange, segmented and roughly
  chopped
2 apples, halved, cored, and diced
salt and freshly ground black pepper

For the dressing
2–3 tbsp Greek yogurt
1 tbsp poppy seeds
1 tbsp finely chopped flat-leaf parsley

1 Put the carrots, cabbage, onion, orange, and apple in a bowl and stir to combine. Season well with salt and black pepper.

2 Mix the Greek yogurt with the poppy seeds and parsley, then stir into the cabbage mixture.

COOK'S TIP
For ease, you could shred the cabbage and carrots in a food processor fitted with a grater attachment.

STATISTICS PER SERVING:

Energy 117cals/489kJ

Carbohydrate 23g

Sugar 21g

Fiber 6g

Fat 2g
Saturated fat 1g

Sodium 0.08g

◐○○ GI

◐○○ CALORIES

◐◐○ SATURATED FAT

◐◐○ SODIUM

BAKED CHICORY WITH GOLDEN BREADCRUMBS

SERVES 4   **PREP** 10 MINS   **COOK** 30 MINS

Baking the leaves allows you to enjoy the wonderful flavor of chicory without the bitterness that you will sometimes find when it is served raw.

6 heads of chicory
scant 1oz (25g) butter
salt and freshly ground black pepper
3 sage leaves, finely chopped

3 slices of wholemeal bread
scant 1oz (25g) Parmesan, finely
  grated

1 Preheat the oven to 350°F (180°C). Halve the chicory lengthwise then lay the pieces out in an ovenproof baking dish. Dot all over with the butter and season well with salt and pepper, then sprinkle with the sage.

2 Loosely cover with foil and place in the oven to bake for 20–25 minutes or unit the chicory is soft when poked with a sharp knife.

3 Meanwhile, place the bread in a food processor and pulse to crumbs, then spread out on to a baking tray. Place in the oven for about 5 minutes until golden, then put the breadcrumbs back into the food processor, add the Parmesan, and process until fine and well mixed. Remove the chicory from the oven, cover evenly with the breadcrumbs, then return to the oven for a further 5–10 minutes until golden. Serve as a side dish.

STATISTICS PER SERVING:

Energy 140cals/587kJ

Carbohydrate 13.5g

Sugar 1g

Fiber 2g

Fat 5g
Saturated fat 4.5g

Sodium 0.24g

◔◯◯ GI

◔◯◯ CALORIES

◔◯◯ SATURATED FAT

◔◯◯ SODIUM

ROAST ARTICHOKES WITH TOMATO AND GARLIC

SERVES 4   **PREP** 5 MINS   **COOK** 1 HOUR

This is a simple accompaniment, but very colorful and tasty, especially if you use ripe, in-season tomatoes.

14oz (400g) can artichoke hearts, drained and halved
8 small plum tomatoes on the vine
12 garlic cloves, unpeeled
2 tbsp olive oil

2 tsp balsamic vinegar
few sprigs of thyme
salt and freshly ground black pepper

1 Preheat the oven to 275°F (140°C).

2 Place the artichoke hearts in a roasting pan with the tomatoes, keeping them on the vine, and scatter the garlic cloves in the tray. Drizzle with the oil and balsamic vinegar, add the thyme, and season to taste with salt and pepper.

3 Roast for 1 hour, or until the vegetables are cooked, and serve.

STATISTICS PER SERVING:

Energy 78cals/324kJ

Carbohydrate 5g

Sugar 2g

Fiber 2g

Fat 5.5g
Saturated fat 0.8g

Sodium trace

ROAST SQUASH WITH GINGER

SERVES 4   **PREP** 20 MINS   **COOK** 40 MINS

Spicy vegetables make a punchy side dish.

1 butternut squash, peeled
4 tbsp olive oil
½ tsp salt
2 red chiles, seeded and
  finely chopped

2oz (60g) fresh root ginger, peeled
  and grated or finely sliced
freshly ground black pepper
handful of mint leaves, torn
2 limes, cut into wedges, to serve

1 Preheat the oven to 350°F (180°C). Slice the squash into long thick strips and place in a roasting pan. Mix together 2 tbsp warm water, the olive oil, salt, chiles, ginger, and pepper to taste. Drizzle the sauce over the squash, mixing to coat well.

2 Bake the squash for 40 minutes, or until tender, shaking occasionally during cooking to avoid sticking. If the squash dries out, add a little more olive oil.

3 Transfer the warm squash to a large serving dish, and scatter with the torn mint leaves. Serve with lime wedges to squeeze over.

GUIDELINES PER SERVING:

● ● ○ GI
● ○ ○ CALORIES
● ○ ○ SATURATED FAT
● ○ ○ SODIUM

STATISTICS PER SERVING:

Energy 166cals/697kJ

Carbohydrate 16g

Sugar 8g

Fiber 3g

Fat 11g

Saturated fat 1.5g

Sodium 0.2g

ROASTED ONIONS TOPPED WITH PINE NUTS

GUIDELINES PER SERVING:

●○○ GI
●●○ CALORIES
●○○ SATURATED FAT
●○○ SODIUM

SERVES 4   **PREP** 5 MINS   **COOK** 50 MINS

Onions become meltingly soft when baked.

4 red onions, peeled
4 white or brown onions, peeled
1–2 tbsp olive oil
salt and freshly ground black pepper

few stalks thyme
2 slices bread
few sage leaves
2½oz (75g) pine nuts

1 Preheat the oven to 375°F (190°C). Top and tail the onions and sit them in a roasting pan. Drizzle over the oil and use your hands to coat, then sprinkle with salt and pepper, scatter the thyme over, cover with foil, and put in the oven.

2 Add the bread to a food processor and whiz to breadcrumbs, then add the sage leaves, whiz again, and set aside. When the onions have been in the oven for 40–45 minutes and are starting to soften, remove the foil, sprinkle over the breadcrumbs and pine nuts, and return to the oven for 10 minutes or until the pine nuts are golden. Transfer to plates and serve.

COOK'S TIP
You could toast the pine nuts separately then sprinkle them over at end of cooking to make sure they don't burn.

STATISTICS PER SERVING:

Energy 291cals/1,210kJ

Carbohydrate 30g

Sugar 14.5g

Fiber 4g

Fat 16.5g
Saturated fat 1g

Sodium 0.12g

⬤◯◯ GI

⬤◯◯ CALORIES

⬤◯◯ SATURATED FAT

⬤◯◯ SODIUM

RATATOUILLE WITH STAR ANISE

SERVES 6   **PREP** 15-20 MINS   **COOK** 45 MINS

Star anise gives this traditional French dish a delicious Asian twist.

4 tbsp olive oil
2 onions, sliced
4 red peppers, cut into ¾in (2cm) cubes
2 eggplants, cut into ¾in (2cm) cubes
3 zucchini, cut into ¾in (2cm) cubes

1lb (450g) fresh tomatoes, skinned, seeded, and roughly chopped
2 garlic cloves, crushed
2 tbsp tomato purée
1 star anise
salt and freshly ground black pepper

1 Heat the oil in a large saucepan, add the onions and cook over medium heat for 5 minutes or until soft.

2 Add the peppers, eggplant, zucchini, tomatoes, garlic, and tomato purée. Fry for 2–3 minutes.

3 Add the star anise, and salt and black pepper to taste, then cover and simmer for 30 minutes or until the vegetables are tender. Remove the lid and cook for 15 minutes more or until the liquid has evaporated. Adjust the seasoning, remove the star anise and serve hot or cold.

STATISTICS PER SERVING:

Energy 223cals/930kJ

Carbohydrate 23g

Sugar 20g

Fiber 7g

Fat 13g

Saturated fat 2g

Sodium 0.08g

HOMEMADE BAKED BEANS

SERVES 4 **PREP** 12 MINS **COOK** 45 MINS

This homemade version is vastly superior to canned baked beans. Grated apple adds a little sweetness.

1 tbsp olive oil
1 onion, finely diced
2 slices slab bacon, chopped
2 garlic cloves, finely chopped
1 apple, grated
½ tbsp Worcestershire sauce

2 tsp Dijon mustard
8fl oz (250ml) tomato purée
2 x 14oz cans navy beans,
  drained and rinsed
salt and freshly ground black pepper

1 Heat the oil in a shallow, heavy pan, add the onion and cook over low heat until soft. Add the bacon, increase the heat a little and cook until it begins to color.

2 Stir in the garlic, apple, Worcestershire sauce, and mustard. Pour in the tomato purée and bring to a boil. Reduce to a simmer, add the beans, and partially cover the pan. Cook on a gentle heat for 15–20 minutes, topping up with a little hot water as needed. Season to taste.

COOK'S TIP
You could also use dried haricot beans—these need to be soaked overnight and cooked for about 2 hours before they are added to the dish.

STATISTICS PER SERVING:

Energy 243cals/1,029kJ

Carbohydrate 36g

Sugar 5.5g

Fiber 11g

Fat 6g
Saturated fat 1.5g

Sodium 0.24g

CHICKPEAS WITH SPINACH

SERVES 4   **PREP** 15 MINS   **COOK** 10 MINS

Chickpeas are widely used in Spain as a basis for a variety of stews such as this one.

3 tbsp olive oil
1 thick slice of crusty wholemeal
   bread, torn into breadcrumbs
1lb 10oz (750g) spinach leaves
8.5oz can chickpeas, rinsed
   and drained

2 garlic cloves, finely chopped
salt and freshly ground
   black pepper
1 tsp paprika
1 tsp ground cumin
1 tbsp sherry vinegar

1 Heat 1 tablespoon of the oil in a frying pan and fry the bread, stirring, until crisp. Remove from the pan, drain on paper towels, and reserve.

2 Rinse the spinach and shake off any excess water. Place it in a large saucepan and cook over low heat, tossing constantly so it does not stick to the pan. When it has wilted, transfer the spinach to a colander and squeeze out as much water as possible by pressing it with a wooden spoon, then place on a chopping board and chop coarsely.

3 Heat the remaining oil in the frying pan, add the spinach and allow it to warm through before stirring in the chickpeas and garlic. Season to taste with salt and pepper. Add the paprika and cumin, then crumble the reserved fried bread into the mixture.

4 Add the vinegar and 2 tablespoons of water and allow to heat through for several minutes. Divide between 4 small serving dishes or ramekins and serve immediately.

STATISTICS PER SERVING:

Energy 202cals/839kJ

Carbohydrate 15g

Sugar 3g

Fiber 4.5g

Fat 10g
Saturated fat 1.4g

Sodium 0.32g

ROSEMARY-SIMMERED WHITE BEANS

SERVES 4   **PREP** 5 MINS
PLUS SOAKING   **COOK** 2 HOURS

Fragrant and delicate-tasting beans cooked with woody rosemary and orange zest.

12oz (350g) dried cannellini beans, soaked in water overnight
2 garlic cloves, finely chopped
3 rosemary stems
3 tbsp olive oil
2 tbsp white wine vinegar
pared peel of 1 orange
3 pints (1.4 liters) vegetable stock or chicken stock
salt and freshly ground black pepper

1 Drain the soaked beans, then rinse, drain again, and place in a large heavy-based pan. Add the garlic, rosemary, olive oil, vinegar, orange peel, and stock and season with salt and pepper.

2 Bring to a boil then reduce the heat to a low simmer, cover with a lid and cook gently for 2 hours or until the beans are soft. Top up with more stock if needed. Taste and adjust the seasoning, if required. Remove the rosemary and orange peel. This makes a good side for roast lamb dishes.

COOK'S TIP
Using canned cannellini beans will reduce the cooking time by more than a third but they won't be as tasty, so it is well worth the effort to rehydrate and cook dried beans.

STATISTICS PER SERVING:

Energy 377cals/1,589kJ

Carbohydrate 41g

Sugar 3g

Fiber 14g

Fat 12g

Saturated fat 2g

Sodium 0.72g

SPICY PUY LENTILS

SERVES 4   **PREP** 10 MINS   **COOK** 40-45 MINS

One of the benefits of lentils is that, unlike most pulses, they do not require soaking beforehand.

2 tbsp olive oil
1 large onion, finely chopped
4 celery stalks, chopped
1 red pepper, seeded and diced
1 clove garlic, finely chopped
1 red chile, seeded and finely
  chopped

8oz (225g) Puy lentils, rinsed and any
  grit removed
1¼ pint (600ml) chicken or
  vegetable stock
salt and freshly ground black pepper
3 tbsp chopped fresh cilantro

1 Heat the oil in a large, non-stick saucepan. Put in the onion and cook, stirring, for 2–3 minutes. Add the celery, red pepper, garlic, and chile. Cook for a further 3–4 minutes.

2 Add the lentils and stock, bring to a boil, reduce the heat and simmer for 40 minutes, or until the lentils are tender, adding a little extra stock or water if necessary. Season to taste with salt and pepper, stir in the chopped cilantro and serve.

STATISTICS PER SERVING:

Energy 276cals/1,164kJ

Carbohydrate 35g

Sugar 6g

Fiber 7g

Fat 8g
Saturated fat 1.5g

Sodium 0.28g

SPLIT PEA DHAL

SERVES 4   **PREP** 10 MINS   **COOK** 45 MINS

A delicious comfort food to eat simply—enjoy it with wholemeal chapattis.

2 tbsp vegetable oil
2 large onions, finely chopped
salt and freshly ground black pepper
3 garlic cloves, finely chopped
1in (2.5cm) piece of fresh ginger root, finely chopped

1 tsp turmeric
14oz (400g) yellow split peas, rinsed and drained
2 tbsp garam masala
4 lemon wedges, to serve

1 Heat the oil in a heavy pan, add the onions and cook for 5–6 minutes until just beginning to turn golden. Season with salt and black pepper. Add the garlic and ginger and cook for a further 2 minutes.

2 Stir in the turmeric, then the split peas. making sure they are all coated. Pour in 9fl oz (250ml) hot water and bring to a boil. Reduce to a simmer, partially cover the pan and cook over low heat for about 20 minutes, adding more water if and when needed.

3 Stir in the garam masala, season, and partially cover the pan. Cook over low heat for a further 25 minutes, topping up with hot water if needed. Serve with the lemon wedges.

COOK'S TIP
Make this up to a day ahead and refrigerate. Reheat to serve; the taste only gets better.

STATISTICS PER SERVING:

Energy 224cals/948kJ

Carbohydrate 35g

Sugar 3g

Fiber 4g

Fat 4.5g

Saturated fat 0.6g

Sodium 0.12g

DESSERTS

○○● GI

●○○ CALORIES

●○○ SATURATED FAT

●○○ SODIUM

SUMMER PUDDING

SERVES 6   **PREP** 15 MINS   **COOK** 3-4 MINS
PLUS FIRMING

When fresh berries aren't in season, you can make this classic dessert using frozen berries.

2lb (900g) mixed soft fruits,
  e.g. raspberries, strawberries,
  blackberries, pitted cherries,
  or blueberries
1¾oz (50g) fructose (fruit sugar)

8-10 thick slices of day-old
  white bread
½oz (15g) red currants, to decorate
½oz (15g) fresh mint,
  to decorate

1 Place the fruit in a saucepan with the fructose and 3 tablespoons of water. Heat gently and cook for 3–4 minutes or until the juices begin to run from the fruit. Set aside to cool.

2 Remove the crusts from the bread. Cut a circle from one slice of bread to fit the bottom of a 1½ quart (1.5 liter) glass bowl. Arrange the remaining bread, apart from two slices, around the sides of the bowl, overlapping slightly and leaving no gaps. Place the circle of bread over the gap at the bottom of the bowl.

3 Spoon the fruit mixture, together with enough juice to moisten the bread, into the bowl. Reserve the remaining juice. Seal in the fruit with a final layer of the remaining bread, trimming to fit as necessary.

4 Cover the pudding with a saucer or small plate and place a heavy weight on top. Place the pudding in the refrigerator for several hours, preferably overnight.

5 To serve, remove the weight and the saucer, and invert the pudding onto a large serving plate. Hold the two together and shake firmly, then carefully remove the glass bowl. Spoon the reserved juice over the pudding and decorate with the red currants and mint.

STATISTICS PER SERVING:

Energy 149cals/631kJ

Carbohydrate 30g

Sugar 9g

Fiber 4g

Fat 1g
Saturated fat 0.2g

Sodium 0.24g

● ○ ○ GI

● ○ ○ CALORIES

● ○ ○ SATURATED FAT

● ○ ○ SODIUM

CARPACCIO OF ORANGES WITH PISTACHIO NUTS

SERVES 4   **PREP** 10 MINS
PLUS CHILLING

A deliciously refreshing, Moroccan-inspired dessert that is low in calories but full of flavor.

4 oranges
2 pomegranates
generous pinch ground cinnamon
1oz (30g) shelled pistachio nuts,
  roughly chopped

1 Using a sharp knife, remove the skin and pith from the oranges and slice the flesh into rounds. Sprinkle with the cinnamon and chill for 15 minutes.

2 Remove the seeds from the pomegranates, and discard the white membrane.

3 Place the orange slices on a serving dish, and sprinkle with the pomegranate seeds and pistachio nuts.

STATISTICS PER SERVING:

Energy 125cals/525kJ

Carbohydrate 18g

Sugar 18g

Fiber 4g

Fat 4g
Saturated fat 0.5g

Sodium 0.04g

POACHED PEARS WITH TOASTED ALMONDS

SERVES 4   **PREP** 10 MINS   **COOK** 20 MINS

A classic, elegant dessert that can be made with such ease: treat yourself.

juice of 4 oranges
zest of 1 orange
1 cinnamon stick
2 star anise
4 just-ripe pears, halved lengthwise
  and cored

1¾oz (50g) blanched almonds
9oz (250g) reduced-fat Greek yogurt,
  to serve

1 Put the orange juice and zest in a pan along with 7fl oz (200ml) water, the cinnamon stick, and star anise. Bring to a boil.

2 Reduce to a simmer and add the pears. Cover with a lid and cook for 10–15 minutes, or until the pears are soft and tender. Remove with a slotted spoon and put on a serving plate or plates. Bring the juice to a boil and spoon a little over the pears.

3 Meanwhile, put the almonds in a small frying pan and toast them for a few minutes until golden, stirring occasionally so that they don't burn. Serve the pears topped with the almonds and a spoonful of Greek yogurt.

STATISTICS PER SERVING:

Energy 182cals/765kJ

Carbohydrate 24g

Sugar 22.5g

Fiber 4.3g

Fat 8g

Saturated fat 1g

Sodium trace

MANGO, ORANGE, AND PASSION FRUIT FOOL

GUIDELINES PER SERVING:

⬤⬤◯ GI

⬤⬤◯ CALORIES

⬤⬤⬤ SATURATED FAT

⬤◯◯ SODIUM

SERVES 4   **PREP** 10 MINS
PLUS CHILLING

This creamy, golden fruit fool is rich in vitamin C and fiber, and can be whipped up in minutes.

3 large, ripe mangoes, stoned and
  flesh roughly chopped
zest of 1 large orange
4 tbsp orange juice

14oz (400g) Greek yogurt
sugar-free sweetener, to taste
4 passion fruit, seeds extracted

1 Place the mango, and orange zest and juice in a food processor or blender. Process until smooth. Stir in the Greek yogurt and add sweetener to taste.

2 Divide the mixture among 4 glasses or bowls, and chill for at least 30 minutes.

3 Spoon the seeds from the passion fruit on top of the fool and serve.

STATISTICS PER SERVING:

Energy 229cals/962kJ

Carbohydrate 28g

Sugar 26g

Fiber 4.5g

Fat 10g
Saturated fat 7g

Sodium 0.08g

SUGAR-FREE PEACH SORBET

SERVES 4   **PREP** 15 MINS
PLUS FREEZING

A refreshing, melt-in-the-mouth dessert. Make the most of juicy peaches when they're in season with this guilt-free summer indulgence.

2¾lb (1.25kg) ripe peaches,
  pitted and chopped
2oz sucralose sweetener
juice of 1 lemon

1 Put the peaches in a food processor or blender and blend until smooth. Pass through a sieve to make a smooth purée.

2 Put the purée into a clean food processor or blender along with 6fl oz (180ml) water, the sweetener, and the lemon juice. Blend again until smooth.

3 Pour the mixture into a freezerproof container with a lid, and put it in the freezer for 1–2 hours until it has almost set. Remove and stir well with a fork to break up the ice crystals, or put back in the food processor and blend again. Return to the freezer for 4–5 hours until frozen. Serve scoops of sorbet in individual glass dishes.

COOK'S TIP

Choose a shallow container if you can, because the sorbet will freeze more quickly.

STATISTICS PER SERVING:

Energy 83cals/355kJ

Carbohydrate 19g

Sugar 18g

Fiber 4g

Fat 0g

Saturated fat 0g

Sodium trace

CHOCOLATE ESPRESSO POTS

SERVES 4   **PREP** 15 MINS
PLUS CHILLING

These little chocolate pots taste deliciously wicked, but in fact a little chocolate goes a long way and the silky texture comes without any cream being added.

14oz can prunes in fruit juice
5½oz (150g) dark chocolate, broken
 into small pieces

2 eggs, separated
scant 1oz (25g) pistachio nuts,
 finely chopped, to serve

1 Strain the prunes, reserving the juice, then press each prune gently between your fingers to eject the stone. Put the prunes into a food processor or blender with 3½fl oz (100ml) of the juice, and process to a purée.

2 Melt the chocolate in a small heatproof bowl set over a pan of simmering water. Stir in the prune mixture and egg yolks.

3 In a large, clean bowl, whisk the egg whites until they form stiff peaks. Fold the egg whites into the chocolate mixture using a large metal spoon.

4 Spoon the chocolate mixture into 4 espresso cups or individual serving dishes and transfer to the refrigerator to chill for at least 1 hour.

5 Remove from the refrigerator just before serving and scatter with a few chopped pistachio nuts.

GUIDELINES PER SERVING:

● ○ ○ GI
● ● ○ CALORIES
● ● ○ SATURATED FAT
● ○ ○ SODIUM

STATISTICS PER SERVING:

Energy 315cals/1,324kJ

Carbohydrate 38g

Sugar 36g

Fiber 2.5g

Fat 16g
Saturated fat 7g

Sodium 0.06g

⬤⬤◯ GI

⬤⬤◯ CALORIES

⬤⬤⬤ SATURATED FAT

⬤◯◯ SODIUM

DARK CHOCOLATE AND YOGURT ICE CREAM

SERVES 6   **PREP** 25 MINS   **COOK** 2 MINS

Rich in taste but lower in calories than ordinary ice cream.

10fl oz (300ml) milk
7oz (200g) dark chocolate (at least
  70% cocoa solids), broken into
  small pieces

calorie-free sweetener
4 egg yolks
8fl oz (250ml) low-fat natural yogurt

1 Put the milk, chocolate, and calorie-free sweetener to taste in a small pan and heat gently, stirring occasionally, until the chocolate has melted. Bring the mixture just to a boil, then remove from the heat.

2 Whisk the egg yolks together, then slowly pour into the chocolate mixture and whisk until the mixture is smooth.

3 Leave to cool for 15 minutes, then whisk in the yogurt and spoon into a freezerproof container. Cover with a lid and leave to cool completely, then transfer to the freezer to freeze overnight.

COOK'S TIP
You could use an ice cream maker; the result will be smoother and creamier.

STATISTICS PER SERVING:

Energy 266cals/1,116kJ

Carbohydrate 30g

Sugar 27g

Fiber 1g

Fat 14g

Saturated fat 7.5g

Sodium 0.04g

● ○ ○ GI

● ○ ○ CALORIES

● ○ ○ SATURATED FAT

● ○ ○ SODIUM

CRANBERRY AND POMEGRANATE DESSERT

SERVES 4   **PREP** 10 MINS
PLUS SETTING

These tasty little treats are perfect for occasions when you want something sweet, but healthy.

1½ pints (750ml) light cranberry juice
1 tbsp powdered gelatin or
  vegetarian equivalent
2 pomegranates, seeds extracted and
  white membranes removed

1 Place 4fl oz (120ml) of the cranberry juice in a small heatproof bowl, sprinkle in the gelatin and leave to soak for 5 minutes. Place the bowl over a pan of simmering water and stir until the gelatin melts and becomes clear. Stir in the remaining juice.

2 Divide the pomegranate seeds between 4 wine glasses, pour in enough of the liquid to just cover the fruit, and then chill for about 30 minutes or until just set.

3 Pour in the remaining liquid and chill for 3 hours, or until set.

COOK'S TIP
If the remaining cranberry juice mixture sets before you add it in the final step, place it over a pan of gently simmering water until it becomes liquid again.

STATISTICS PER SERVING:

Energy 53cals/221kJ

Carbohydrate 11g

Sugar 11g

Fiber 1g

Fat 0g

Saturated fat 0g

Sodium trace

APRICOT CRUMBLE

SERVES 4   **PREP** 10 MINS   **COOK** 20 MINS

By cooking apricots with a little orange, it helps to bring out their flavor and make this a truly moreish crumble.

GUIDELINES PER SERVING:

GI

CALORIES

SATURATED FAT

SODIUM

1lb 9oz (700g) apricots, pitted and cut into quarters
juice and zest of 1 large orange
2–3 tbsp sucralose sweetener
2oz (60g) all-purpose white flour

2oz (60g) all-purpose wholemeal flour
2oz (60g) jumbo rolled oats
3oz (85g) polyunsaturated margarine
2oz (60g) fructose

1 Preheat the oven to 350°F (180°C). Place the apricots and the orange juice and zest in a saucepan and cook over gentle heat until the apricots are soft. Stir in the sweetener and taste to check the sweetness.

2 To make the crumble, mix together both types of flour and the oats. Rub in the margarine until the mixture resembles coarse breadcrumbs. Stir in the fructose.

3 Spoon the apricots into a shallow heatproof dish, sprinkle the crumble topping over them evenly, and bake for 20 minutes or until the topping is golden brown.

STATISTICS PER SERVING:

Energy   399cals/1,672kJ

Carbohydrate   42g

Sugar   20g

Fiber   6g

Fat   19g

Saturated fat   4g

Sodium   0.12g

APPLE AND WALNUT STRUDEL

SERVES 6   **PREP** 20 MINS   **COOK** 30 MINS

This strudel is made with filo pastry, and is a good choice if you are looking for a heathier alternative to apple pie.

1lb 2oz (500g) cooking apples, peeled, cored, and thickly sliced
zest and juice of 1 lemon
8 large sheets of filo pastry (about 7oz/200g)
1oz (30g) polyunsaturated margarine, melted

1oz (30g) fresh breadcrumbs
3 tbsp fructose (fruit sugar)
2oz (60g) walnuts, roughly chopped
½ tsp ground cinnamon

1 Preheat the oven to 350°F (180°C). Sprinkle the apples with a little lemon juice to prevent them browning.

2 Lay 4 sheets of filo side by side on a clean dish towel, overlapping the long edges by about 2in (5cm). Brush with a little of the melted margarine. Place the 4 remaining sheets of filo on top and brush again. Cover the filo with a clean, damp dish towel to help prevent it from drying out before you are ready to add the filling.

3 Mix together the apples, breadcrumbs, lemon zest, 2 tablespoons fructose, the walnuts, and cinnamon. Spoon the mixture along one long edge of the pastry. Using the dish towel underneath the pastry to help you, roll up the pastry as you would roll up a Swiss roll.

4 Put the strudel on a non-stick baking sheet, seam-side down, curling it slightly if necessary to fit onto the sheet. Brush with the remaining margarine and sprinkle with the remaining fructose.

5 Place in the oven and bake for 15–20 minutes, or until the pastry is golden brown and the apples are soft. Cover with foil halfway through cooking if necessary.

STATISTICS PER SERVING:

Energy 308cals/1,288kJ

Carbohydrate 33g

Sugar 17g

Fiber 3.5g

Fat 17g

Saturated fat 2.5g

Sodium 0.2g

BANANA, CINNAMON, AND PISTACHIO PARCELS

SERVES 4   **PREP** 15 MINS   **COOK** 15 MINS
PLUS COOLING

A quick and easy dessert guaranteed to satisfy even the sweetest tooth.

4 small, ripe bananas, peeled
  and thickly sliced
1oz (30g) pistachio nuts, chopped,
  plus extra to serve
2 tbsp sucralose sweetener
¼ tsp ground cinnamon

zest of 1 lemon
1½oz (45g) polyunsaturated
  margarine
4 sheets of filo pastry, 16 x 11in
  (40 x 28cm)

1 Place the bananas and pistachio nuts in a bowl and sprinkle with the sweetener and cinnamon. Melt half the margarine in a small pan, add the banana mixture, and cook over low heat for 10 minutes. Remove from the heat, stir in the lemon zest, and allow to cool. Chill in the refrigerator.

2 Preheat the oven to 400°F (200°C). Melt the remaining margarine. Lay one sheet of filo pastry on the worksurface, brush lightly with melted margarine, and then fold 3 times, lengthwise, to make a long sausage.

3 Spoon a quarter of the banana mixture onto the pastry about 1½in (4cm) from the end. Fold the left corner of the pastry diagonally to the right side of the dough, to cover the filling. Then fold the right corner diagonally to the left, and continue folding alternate corners in the same way until you reach the end of the sheet, forming a little parcel. Repeat with the remaining sheets of filo pastry.

4 Place the parcels on a lightly greased baking sheet, brush with a little more melted margarine, and bake for 15 minutes or until golden. Sprinkle with a few chopped pistachio nuts before serving.

GUIDELINES PER SERVING:

●●○ GI
●●○ CALORIES
●○○ SATURATED FAT
●○○ SODIUM

STATISTICS PER SERVING:

Energy 252cals/1,055kJ

Carbohydrate 29g

Sugar 21g

Fiber 1g

Fat 13.5g
Saturated fat 2.5g

Sodium 0.12g

CHOCOLATE AND ORANGE PARFAIT

SERVES 4   **PREP** 15 MINS   **COOK** 5 MINS   **FREEZE** 1 MONTH

This rich, creamy, chocolatey dessert has a refreshing tang of orange. It looks sophisticated, yet is easy to make and will be a sure-fire winner when entertaining.

7oz (200g) good-quality
  dark chocolate
2 gelatin leaves, or vegetarian
  equivalent
3 tbsp orange juice or water

3 large oranges
10oz (300g) fat-free fromage frais
5½oz (150g) blueberries, to serve
5½oz (150g) raspberries, to serve

1 Line a 1lb (450g) loaf pan with plastic wrap. Melt the chocolate in a bowl set over a pan of boiling water, making sure that the base of the bowl does not touch the water. Allow the melted chocolate to cool slightly.

2 Meanwhile, soak the gelatin leaves in a bowl of cold water for 3–4 minutes, or until softened. Heat the orange juice or water in a small pan until hot, but not boiling. Squeeze excess water out of the gelatin leaves and put them in the pan, then stir to help the gelatin dissolve. Remove from the heat.

3 Remove the zest from the oranges and stir it into the chocolate along with the dissolved gelatin and the fromage frais. Mix well, then spoon into the prepared pan, place in the refrigerator and leave for 2 hours, or until set.

4 Carefully turn out the chocolate mixture onto a plate and remove the plastic wrap. Using a hot knife, cut the parfait into slices and serve with the blueberries and raspberries. (Alternatively, you could use up the oranges and serve them with the parfait instead of the berries. Remove the pith from the oranges and slice the flesh.)

STATISTICS PER SERVING:

Energy 323cals/1,350kJ

Carbohydrate 39g

Sugar 38g

Fiber 2.5g

Fat 14g
Saturated fat 8.5g

Sodium trace

GUIDELINES PER SERVING:

● ● ○ GI
● ○ ○ CALORIES
● ● ○ SATURATED FAT
● ○ ○ SODIUM

ROASTED FIGS WITH CITRUS CRÈME FRAÎCHE

SERVES 4   **PREP** 5 MINS   **COOK** 20 MINS

A simple dish with "wow factor" flavor. Figs are a good source of iron.

8 fresh figs, stems snipped
juice of 2 oranges
2 tsp sucralose sweetener

pinch of ground cinnamon
5½oz (150g) low-fat crème fraîche
juice and zest of ½ lime

1 Preheat the oven to 400°F (200°C). Make a cross at the top of each fig and gently squeeze the fruit apart a little. Place the figs in an ovenproof dish.

2 Pour in the orange juice, and sprinkle with the sweetener and cinnamon. Put in the oven to cook for about 15 minutes until the figs have softened and are beginning to caramelize.

3 Mix the crème fraîche with the lime juice and zest, and spoon it over the figs in the dish. Serve immediately.

COOK'S TIP
For a special occasion, you could drizzle a tiny amount of cassis over the figs before roasting.

STATISTICS PER SERVING:

Energy 111cals/467kJ

Carbohydrate 13g

Sugar 12g

Fiber 1g

Fat 6g
Saturated fat 4g

Sodium trace

LEMON CHEESECAKE

SERVES 8   **PREP** 10 MINS   **COOK** 50 MINS

This low-fat version of a traditional baked cheesecake is just as full of creamy flavor.

3½oz (100g) sucralose sweetener
juice of 2 lemons and zest of
  3 lemons
4 eggs, separated
5½oz (150g) low-fat cream cheese

7oz (200g) quark cheese
1¾oz (50g) golden raisins
2 tbsp all-purpose flour
butter for greasing

1 Preheat the oven to 340°F (170°C). In a large bowl, dissolve the sweetener in the lemon juice, then add the egg yolks and whisk until pale and thick. Add the cream cheese and quark cheese, and beat until smooth.

2 Add the lemon juice and zest into the cream cheese mixture, then add the golden raisins. Stir to mix. Sprinkle the flour over the mixture and fold it in gently. In a clean bowl, using a clean whisk, whisk the egg whites until stiff, then fold into the cheesecake mixture.

3 Spoon the mixture into a deep, round, 8in (20cm) springform cake pan, greased and lined with wax paper. Bake in the oven for 45–50 minutes or until golden and almost set; it should still wobble slightly in the center. Leave to cool in the oven with the door open (this should prevent it from cracking too much).

4 Once cooled, run a knife around the edge of pan, release the sides and carefully remove the cheesecake.

GUIDELINES PER SERVING:

● ○ ○ GI
● ○ ○ CALORIES
● ○ ○ SATURATED FAT
● ○ ○ SODIUM

STATISTICS PER SERVING:

Energy 121cals/509kJ

Carbohydrate 9g

Sugar 6g

Fiber 0.3g

Fat 5.5g
Saturated fat 2g

Sodium 0.04g

BAKING

BANANA AND THREE-SEED OAT BAKES

MAKES 9   **PREP** 10 MINS   **COOK** 20–30 MINS   **FREEZE** 3 MONTHS

These tasty little bars contain considerably less sugar than most commercial cereal bars, so they'll provide an energy boost without sending your blood sugar levels sky-high.

3½oz (100g) polyunsaturated margarine, plus extra for greasing
3 tbsp maple syrup
5½oz (150g) rolled oats
2 bananas (about 9oz/250g total weight before peeling), roughly diced

3½oz (100g) ready-to-eat dried apricots, roughly chopped
scant 1oz (25g) pumpkin seeds, toasted
scant 1oz (25g) sunflower seeds, toasted
scant 1oz (25g) sesame seeds, toasted

1 Preheat the oven to 350°F (180°C). Lightly grease a 7½ x 7½in (19 x 19cm) baking pan and line the bottom with non-stick baking parchment.

2 Melt the margarine and maple syrup in a heavy saucepan, stirring until dissolved. Remove from the heat and add the oats, bananas, apricots, and seeds. Mix well.

3 Spoon the mixture into the prepared pan, level the surface and bake in the oven for 20–30 minutes, or until golden brown. The mixture will still be very soft in the center.

4 Leave to cool in the pan for 10 minutes, then cut into 9 squares. When cold, transfer the squares to an airtight container. Don't try to remove the bars from the pan while they are still warm or they will break.

COOK'S TIP
You can divide this into more or fewer than 9 pieces if you wish but bear in mind the effect this will have on the calorie count.

STATISTICS PER BAKE:

Energy 250cals/1,040kJ

Carbohydrate 15g

Sugar 12g

Fiber 3g

Fat 15g

Saturated fat 3g

Sodium 0.08g

● ○ ○ GI

◐ ◐ ○ CALORIES

◐ ○ ○ SATURATED FAT

● ○ ○ SODIUM

SEVEN-GRAIN BREAD

MAKES 2 LOAVES (20 SLICES)   **PREP** 20 MINS PLUS RISING   **COOK** 35–40 MINS   **FREEZE** 3 MONTHS

Full of healthy wheat, this bread includes millet, rolled oats, polenta, quinoa, brown rice, rye flakes, and wheat.

3oz (85g) bulgur wheat
1¾oz (50g) polenta
1¾oz (50g) millet
1¾oz (50g) quinoa
1lb (450g) strong white flour
9oz (250g) granary flour or
  strong wholemeal flour
2½oz (75g) rolled oats
2½oz (75g) rye flakes
2 tsp salt

2 x ¼oz (7g) sachets easy-blend
  dried yeast
1¾oz (50g) cooked long-grain
  brown rice
4 tbsp honey, maple syrup,
  or corn syrup, to taste
8fl oz (250ml) milk, warmed
2 tbsp sunflower oil, plus
  extra for brushing

1 Mix the first 4 ingredients in a bowl, stir in 14fl oz (400ml) lukewarm water, cover with a dish towel, and leave to stand for 15 minutes. Mix the next 6 ingredients in a bowl, add the bulgur mixture, and stir in the rice.

2 Heat the honey with the milk until it dissolves and add to the bowl along with the oil. Gradually add up to 7fl oz (200ml) lukewarm water, or until a soft, sticky dough forms. Knead on a lightly floured work surface for 10 minutes or until elastic. Shape into a ball, place in a lightly oiled bowl, then cover the bowl with oiled plastic wrap. Leave to rise in a warm place until doubled in size. Meanwhile, oil and flour 2 x 2lb (900g) loaf pans.

3 Turn the dough out on to a floured surface and knead for 1 minute. (The dough will be sticky again.) Divide into 2 equal-sized balls and, with a floured rolling pin, roll each ball into a rectangle as wide as the pans and twice as long. Fold both ends to the center and pinch the edges to seal. Place in the pans, cover with dish towels, and leave to rise until the dough reaches the tops of the pans. Preheat the oven to 425°F (220°C).

4 Brush the tops with oil and bake for 10 minutes, then reduce the heat to 375°F (190°C) and bake for a further 25–30 minutes, or until the loaves sound hollow when tapped on the base. Leave to cool on a wire rack.

STATISTICS PER SLICE:

Energy 217cals/916kJ

Carbohydrate 43g

Sugar 3.5g

Fiber 2.5g

Fat 3.5g

Saturated fat 0.6g

Sodium 0.16g

RYE BREAD

MAKES 1 LOAF (10 SLICES)   **PREP** 25 MINS PLUS STANDING PLUS RISING   **COOK** 40-45 MINS   **FREEZE** 3 MONTHS

Breads made with rye flour are very popular in central and eastern Europe.

For the starter
5½oz (150g) rye flour
5½oz (150g) pot live natural yogurt
1 tsp fast-action dried yeast
1 tbsp molasses
1 tsp caraway seeds, lightly crushed

For the dough
5½oz (150g) rye flour
7oz (200g) strong white flour,
   plus extra for dusting
2 tsp salt
1 egg, beaten
1 tsp caraway seeds, to decorate

1 Mix all of the starter ingredients together with 8fl oz (250ml) tepid water. Cover and leave overnight, until bubbling.

2 The next day, mix the flours together with the salt, then stir into the starter. Mix to make a dough, adding a little extra water if required.

3 Turn out on to a lightly floured surface and knead the dough for 5–10 minutes, or until smooth and springy. Shape into a ball, put into an oiled bowl and cover loosely with oiled plastic wrap. Leave in a warm place for 1 hour, or until doubled in size.

4 Flour a baking tray. Lightly knead the dough again, then form it into a football shape. Lift onto the tray, re-cover it loosely with the oiled plastic wrap, and leave to rise again for another 30 minutes. Preheat the oven to 425°F (220°C).

5 Brush the dough with the egg, sprinkle with the caraway seeds, and slash the loaf along its length with a sharp knife. Bake for 20 minutes, then reduce the heat to 400°F (200°C) and bake for another 20–30 minutes, or until dark golden with a hard shiny crust. Cool on a wire rack.

COOK'S TIP
The starter must be made the day before you want to make the loaf.

STATISTICS PER SLICE:

Energy 193cals/806kJ

Carbohydrate 40g

Sugar 2.3g

Fiber 4.1g

Fat 2.1g
Saturated fat 0.6g

Sodium 0.32g

●●○ GI

●○○ CALORIES

●○○ SATURATED FAT

●○○ SODIUM

CHAPATTIS

MAKES 8   **PREP** 30 MINS   **COOK** 10 MINS
PLUS RESTING

In India, these flat, unleavened breads would be cooked in a concave pan called a tava. However, a cast-iron frying pan works well.

9oz (250g) chapatti flour or wholemeal all-purpose flour, plus extra for dusting

1 tsp salt
¼oz (10g) ghee or melted butter, for brushing

1 Sift the flour into a bowl and discard any bran left in the sieve. Make a well in the center of the flour, add 3 tablespoons of cold water and mix in. Work in the salt, then mix in another 4 tablespoons of cold water until a dough starts to form.

2 Gradually add another 4 tablespoons of cold water to make a sticky dough. Keep kneading the dough in the bowl until it becomes firm, elastic, and less sticky.

3 Cover with a dish towel and leave to rest for 15 minutes, or until the dough becomes firmer and is no longer sticky.

4 Dust your hands with flour and pull off egg-sized pieces of dough. Shape these into balls, then roll out into rounds 7in (18cm) in diameter.

5 Heat an ungreased frying pan and cook the chapattis for 30 seconds on each side, or until golden and speckled. As you remove each one from the pan, brush with ghee or melted butter, and set aside in a warm place while you cook the rest.

STATISTICS PER SERVING:

Energy 114cals/484kJ

Carbohydrate 25g

Sugar 0.5g

Fiber 1g

Fat 1g
Saturated fat 0.7g

Sodium 0.12g

LOW-FAT GINGER TEA BREAD

GUIDELINES PER SLICE:

MAKES 1 LOAF (12 SLICES)   **PREP** 15 MINS PLUS SOAKING   **COOK** 45-60 MINS   **FREEZE** 3 MONTHS

This low-fat cake is quick and easy to make, and perfect for an afternoon snack that won't pile on the calories.

5½oz (150g) mixed dried fruit
11fl oz (325ml) lemon and ginger tea
  (made with 2 tea bags)
8oz (225g) plain wholemeal flour

2 tsp baking powder
3½oz (100g) fructose
1 egg, beaten

1 Place the dried fruit in a large heatproof bowl, pour the tea over it and leave to stand for at least 2 hours, stirring occasionally.

2 Preheat the oven to 325ºF (160ºC). Grease and line the bottom of a 2lb (900g) loaf pan with non-stick baking parchment.

3 Place the flour, baking powder, fructose, and egg in a food processor or blender and process for a couple of minutes. Add the dried fruit and tea and process again until well mixed.

4 Spoon the mixture into the prepared loaf pan, brush the surface with a little water and bake for 45 minutes–1 hour until the cake looks done and feels springy in the center. You may need to cover it with foil halfway through cooking if it is browning too quickly.

5 Allow the cake to cool in the pan for 5 minutes, then carefully turn out on to a wire cooling rack.

GI

CALORIES

SATURATED FAT

SODIUM

STATISTICS PER SLICE:

Energy 106cals/450kJ

Carbohydrate 23g

Sugar 8g

Fiber 1g

Fat 0.8g

Saturated fat 0.2g

Sodium 0.08g

● ● ○ GI

● ○ ○ CALORIES

● ○ ○ SATURATED FAT

● ○ ○ SODIUM

FRUIT AND SEED SODA BREAD

MAKES 1 LOAF   **PREP** 10 MINS   **COOK** 20-25 MINS   **FREEZE** 3 MONTHS
(10 SLICES)

A tasty loaf that helps you get more fruit into your diet.

sunflower oil, for greasing
1¾oz (50g) mixed dried fruit
6oz (175g) wholemeal flour

1 tbsp baking soda
2oz (60g) sunflower seeds
5¼oz (150g) plain yogurt

1 Preheat the oven to 350°F (180°C). Lightly grease a 1lb (450g) loaf pan. Place the dried fruit in a heatproof bowl, pour over 3½fl oz (100ml) boiling water, and set aside for 10 minutes.

2 Mix the flour, baking soda, and seeds in a large bowl. Stir in the fruit in its water and the yogurt.

3 Pour the mixture into the prepared pan and bake for 20–25 minutes or until firm. Allow to cool for 10 minutes before slicing.

STATISTICS PER SLICE:

Energy 129cals/539kJ

Carbohydrate 9g

Sugar 2g

Fiber 2g

Fat 3g
Saturated fat 0.7g

Sodium 0.12g

● ● ○ GI

● ● ○ CALORIES

● ○ ○ SATURATED FAT

● ○ ○ SODIUM

BANANA AND MUESLI BREAD

MAKES 1 LOAF (12 SLICES)   **PREP** 15 MINS   **COOK** 45–60 MINS   **FREEZE** 3 MONTHS

A slice of this bread makes the perfect treat to pop into a packed lunch.

6oz (175g) wholemeal flour
3oz (85g) sugar-free muesli
4½oz (125g) polyunsaturated margarine
3oz (85g) fructose
2 tsp baking power

¼ tsp ground cinnamon
2 large eggs, beaten
4 ripe bananas, about 12oz (350g), mashed
3oz (85g) pecan nuts, roughly chopped

1 Preheat the oven to 325°F (160°C). Grease and line the bottom of a 2lb (900g) loaf pan with non-stick baking parchment.

2 Place the flour, muesli, margarine, fructose, baking powder, cinnamon, and eggs in a large bowl. Beat together until evenly mixed. Stir in the banana and pecan nuts, taking care not to over-mix.

3 Spoon the mixture into the prepared loaf pan and bake for 45 minutes–1 hour, or until the cake looks done and feels springy in the center. You may need to cover it with foil halfway through cooking if it is browning too quickly. Allow the cake to cool in the pan for 5 minutes, then carefully turn out on to a wire cooling rack.

STATISTICS PER SLICE:

Energy 267cals/1,118kJ

Carbohydrate 34g

Sugar 17g

Fiber 2.6g

Fat 13g

Saturated fat 3g

Sodium 0.2g

BANANA AND PECAN MUFFINS

MAKES 6 **PREP** 10 MINS **COOK** 20-25 MINS **FREEZE** 3 MONTHS

The banana helps sweeten the muffin mixture, reducing the need for sugar in the recipe.

4 tbsp sunflower oil, plus
  extra for greasing
4½oz (125g) wholemeal flour
3 tbsp sugar
2 tsp baking powder
3oz (85g) pecan nuts,
  roughly chopped

generous pinch of ground cinnamon
1 egg, beaten
4 tbsp skim milk
2 ripe bananas (about 8oz/225g),
  roughly mashed

1 Preheat the oven to 400°F (200°C). Grease a six-hole muffin pan; alternatively, line the holes with paper muffin cases. Place the flour, sugar, baking powder, pecan nuts, and ground cinnamon in a bowl. Mix them together and make a well in the center.

2 In a separate bowl, mix together the egg, milk, and oil. Pour the mixture into the dry ingredients and stir until just blended. Stir in the bananas, taking care not to over-mix.

3 Fill the muffin holes or cases two-thirds full, then place the pan in the oven and bake for 20–25 minutes, or until a skewer inserted into the center comes out clean.

4 Transfer the muffins to a wire rack to cool. Store in an airtight container; the muffins will keep for up to three days.

GUIDELINES PER MUFFIN:

GI

CALORIES

SATURATED FAT

SODIUM

STATISTICS PER MUFFIN:

Energy 315cals/1,316kJ

Carbohydrate 32g

Sugar 16g

Fiber 3g

Fat 19g

Saturated fat 2g

Sodium 0.16g

BLUEBERRY AND OAT MUFFINS

MAKES 6   **PREP** 15 MINS   **COOK** 25-30 MINS   **FREEZE** 3 MONTHS

The combination of wholemeal flour and oats helps to reduce the GI of these muffins.

5½oz (150g) wholemeal flour
1½oz (45g) porridge oats
3 tbsp granulated sugar
2 tsp baking powder
1 really ripe banana

5fl oz (150ml) plain yogurt
3 tbsp canola oil
1 egg, beaten
5½oz (150g) fresh blueberries

1 Heat oven to 350°F (180°C). Grease a 6-hole muffin pan well or line with paper muffin cases.

2 Put the flour in a large bowl with scant 1oz (25g) of the porridge oats, the sugar, and the baking powder. In a separate bowl, mash the banana until nearly smooth, then add the yogurt, oil, and egg and stir together until evenly combined.

3 Make a well in the center of the flour, pour the banana and yogurt mixture into the well and stir briskly with a wooden spoon. The mixture will look lumpy, but don't be tempted to over-mix. Tip in the blueberries and give it just one more stir.

4 Divide the mix between the muffin cases, sprinkle the tops with the remaining oats, and bake for 25–30 minutes until risen and golden. Transfer to a wire rack to cool.

COOK'S TIP
These muffins can be kept in an airtight container for up to 3 days.

STATISTICS PER MUFFIN:

Energy 260cals/1,088kJ

Carbohydrate 35g

Sugar 17g

Fiber 3g

Fat 9g
Saturated fat 1g

Sodium 0.2g

⬤⬤⬤ GI

⬤⬤⬤ CALORIES

⬤◯◯ SATURATED FAT

⬤◯◯ SODIUM

CARROT AND OLIVE OIL CAKE

SERVES 12   **PREP** 10 MINS   **COOK** 1 HOUR 40 MINS   **FREEZE** 1 MONTH

This is an incredibly easy cake to make, and it has a wonderfully moist texture.

4½oz (125g) all-purpose flour, sifted
4½oz (125g) wholemeal flour
pinch of cinnamon
1 tsp baking soda
9fl oz (250ml) mild olive oil
3½oz (100g) soft brown sugar
4 eggs

2 tbsp honey
juice and zest of 1 large orange
14oz (400g) carrots, grated
1¾oz (50g) walnuts, roughly chopped

For the topping
juice of 1 orange

1 Preheat the oven to 325°F (160°C). Put both types of flour in a bowl and add the cinnamon and baking soda. Set aside.

2 In another bowl, whisk together the olive oil, sugar, eggs, honey, and orange juice. Pour this mixture into the flour and mix until smooth. Stir in the grated carrots, walnuts, and orange zest.

3 Put the mixture into a greased 9in (23cm) round, loose-bottomed cake pan. Level the surface and put the pan in the oven to bake for 1 hour 30 minutes, or until it is cooked all the way through. To test whether it is cooked, insert a skewer into the center: if it comes out clean, the cake is done.

4 Remove the cake from the oven and while it is still hot, pierce all over with a skewer, and then drizzle with the orange juice. Transfer to a wire cooling rack and leave to cool before turning the cake out of the cake pan.

STATISTICS PER SERVING:

Energy 300cals/1,244kJ

Carbohydrate 28g

Sugar 13g

Fiber 2g

Fat 19g

Saturated fat 3g

Sodium 0.16g

INDEX

ACKNOWLEDGMENTS

Dorling Kindersley would like to thank the following people: editorial consultant Amy Campbell MS, RD, LDN, CDE and contributors Fiona Hunter and Heather Whinney; art director Luis Peral; food stylist Cara Hobday and assistants Georgie Besterman, Ann Reynolds, Emily Jonzen, and Kelly Bowers; prop stylist Victoria Allen; home economists Richard Harris, Emily Shardlow, and Rachel Wood; out-of-house editors Helena Caldon and Fiona Corbridge.

USEFUL WEBSITES
American Diabetes Association
www.diabetes.org

American Heart Association
www.americanheart.org

DASH Diet
www.nhlbi.nih.gov/health/public/heart/hbp/dash/new_dash.pdf

Food Pyramid
www.mypyramid.gov

Glycemic Index
www.glycemicindex.com

Satiety index
www.diabetesnet.com/diabetes_food_diet/satiety_index.php

Weight-control Information Network
http://win.niddk.nih.gov/publications/choosing.htm